WHAT ARE WE WAITING FOR?

Christian Hope and Contemporary Culture

**edited by Russell Rook
and Steve Holmes**

Paternoster:
thinking faith

MILTON KEYNES • COLORADO SPRINGS • HYDERABAD

14 13 12 11 10 09 08   7 6 5 4 3 2 1

First published 2008 by Paternoster
Paternoster is an imprint of Authentic Media
9 Holdom Avenue, Bletchley, Milton Keynes, Bucks, MK1 1QR, UK
1820 Jet Stream Drive, Colorado Springs, CO 80921, USA
OM Authentic Media, Medchal Road, Jeedimetla Village, Secunderabad 500
55, AP, India
www.authenticmedia.co.uk
Authentic Media is a division of IBS-STL U.K., limited by guarantee, with
its Registered Office at Kingstown Broadway, Carlisle, Cumbria CA3 0HA.
Registered in England & Wales No. 1216232. Registered charity 270162

British Library Cataloguing in Publication Data
A catalogue record for this book is available from the British Library.

ISBN-13: 978-1-84227-602-0

Design by James Kessell for Scratch the Sky Ltd (www.scratchthesky.com)
Print management by Adare
Printed and bound in the UK by CPI Mackays, Chatham ME5 8TD

Contents

1 Introduction: The dangers of being Left Behind   1
Stephen R. Holmes

Hopeful Word

2 Eschatology in the Old Testament   13
Lena-Sofia Tiemeyer

3 Eschatology in Isaiah   24
John Goldingay

4 Eschatology at the Heart of New Testament Theology   35
I. Howard Marshall

5 Eschatology in the Book of Revelation   48
Richard Bauckham

Hopeful Church

6 Eschatology in the Church Fathers   63
Thomas A. Noble

7 Eschatology in Evangelical History   75
David Bebbington

8 Eschatology and Mission   87
Tim Chester

9 Hell   98
Robin Parry

10 Heaven   112
Justin Thacker

NB what happens when we die

Hopeful Culture

11 Eschatology and Imagination   127
    Trevor Hart

12 In God's Good Time   138
    Russell Rook

13 Eschatology and Pop Culture   149
    Krish Kandiah

14 Eschatology and Politics   161
    Luke Bretherton

15 Eschatology Goes to Work   175
    Darrell Cosden

Hopeful World

16 Living for the Future   189
    John Colwell

17 Eschatology and the Environment   200
    Ruth Valerio

18 We are but Shadows of our Future Selves   211
    Ann and Douglas Holt

    Glossary   223
    Endnotes   227
    Selected Further Reading   240

1

Introduction

The dangers of being Left Behind

Stephen R. Holmes

I knew I was going to regret it as soon as I heard myself say it.

I was preaching on a text in Revelation, and I was in the middle of making a point about how Revelation reverses all our expectations of what it is for Jesus (and, incidentally, his saints) to conquer and reign. My notes had a carefully measured comment about the Left Behind series of books, suggesting in guarded language that maybe they were less than adequately biblical on this particular point. But, as preachers sometimes do when they warm to their theme, I'd left my notes some way behind in that particular sermon. What actually came out of my mouth was: 'The Left Behind series – astonishingly popular; astonishingly badly written; astonishingly wrong . . .' I knew I was going to regret it, as soon as I heard myself say it.

In one sense I did, as I fended off hordes of irate church members with a microphone stand after the service (OK, that's a slight exaggeration; we use radio mikes). In another sense, however, I was glad to have said what I did. It is what I believe, and I said it clearly enough to be heard. My original notes had been much more mealy mouthed. My day-job, you see, is as an academic theologian. Eschatology, the biblical truth about the last things, interests me – it interests most theologians these days. Christian theology has been fascinated by the uses of eschatology for a couple of generations now, and there are lots of profound insights, useful explanations, and serious disagreements out there. In our churches, though, the choice seems to be Tim LaHaye or an embarrassed silence. (Most evangelical churches in Britain, displaying good sense, and an instinctive understanding of the gospel, have tended to opt for the embarrassed silence.)

I first met Russell Rook when his previous Ph.D. supervisor, my friend and colleague Colin Gunton, died very suddenly, and I seemed to be the best replacement they could find. As Russ and I got to know each other through talking about his doctoral work, and other things, we discovered a shared passion for the mainstream evangelical churches of this nation, and a shared desire to take the good things that academic theology has to offer (and it has some less good things, of course) into the lives of those churches. When Russ told me that he had been asked to oversee the study material for Spring Harvest 2008, and that the theme was eschatology, we both had the same visions. A nightmare world, where the rightness or wrongness of book twenty-three of the Left Behind series was the only topic of conversation, and debates raged as to whether Saddam Hussein was the Antichrist (one of the lessons of church history is that the letters of anyone's name can add up to 666 if you try hard enough . . .). And an awareness of all the good stuff that was out there, of how a proper eschatological vision could speak powerfully and pastorally to broken and hurting people, could answer the pressing questions that our non-Christian friends put to us about the presence of suffering in the world and so on, could, very simply, help the people who come to Spring Harvest.

We talked. Somewhere along the way (I have a feeling it was in the Seafood Restaurant in St Andrews, as I discovered that I find the idea of oysters much more attractive than the reality, but I could be wrong) we hit upon a plan. A book. Chapters on Scripture, the church, the world, by some of our best scholars, who could also write accessibly, entertainingly. A chance to open up the riches that we both knew, and offer at least some of them to others. We came up with the idea about nine months after the last date we could possibly make it work, and we need to thank our writers and our publishers for closing that gap. Robin Parry from Paternoster shortened deadlines with a nonchalance that I know belied the effort he would have to put in, and time after time the people we went to, some of them the best in the world in their fields, promised cheerfully to write a chapter in, really, just a few days. And here, remarkably, it is.

And what is it? It is a series of brief discussions of what in academic circles gets called 'eschatology'. *Eschaton* in Greek means 'the end'; *eschata* means the 'things of the end'. Once, 'the things of the End' were listed as 'death, judgement, heaven and hell,' and eschatology was the study of these things. It was neat and boring, a list of things to be believed if you wanted to be an orthodox Christian. Not so long ago, something changed, at least among academic theologians. Suddenly the subject wasn't neat anymore – and it emphatically wasn't boring.

Two names perhaps stand out in causing the change. One is Albert Schweitzer, one of the most astonishing men of the early twentieth century. Schweitzer was amongst the best organists of his generation, and published on Bach; he was also an impressively able surgeon; and a theologian. He wrote a book about the New Testament that is so significant it is still read a hundred years later. In the book he surveyed a hundred years of scholarship, which had been devoted to trying to find the 'real' Jesus behind the 'myths' of the gospels. Schweitzer proclaimed the quest impossible: the real Jesus could never be found by civilised Europeans. Jesus had believed that he was bringing history to an end, that God was about to do something astonishing to transform the world. Schweitzer said that Jesus was wrong, and died for his delusion. Then he turned his back on a glittering musical career, on offers from the best universities in Europe, and on a comfortable and prosperous medical practice to become a missionary doctor, preaching this Jesus in the most inhospitable corners of the African continent. He received the Nobel Peace Prize for his work in 1953.

Schweitzer's book was brilliantly argued, and beautifully written (add 'novelist' to the list of careers he turned down . . .). For Jesus, he claimed, the 'things of the End' were not remote and abstract things to be believed, but pressing, decisive realities, things more real, closer, than daily work and food. Schweitzer believed Jesus was tragically, if heroically, wrong in this belief, but left no room for doubt that this was what Jesus believed. Jesus' message was not a comforting confirmation of the benefits and insights of European civilisation; it was something so strange, so startling, so radically other, that it made no sense within the comfortable certainties of civilised Europe.

Schweitzer published his book in 1906; eight years later, 'civilised' Europe began perhaps the most callously brutal conflict ever fought. As poison gas rolled across the fields of Flanders, theologians on all sides queued up to offer their support for the war effort. In Switzerland, a youngish pastor, schooled in the liberal theology of Germany, was dismayed to see his former teachers accepting the actions of the Kaiser; if theology could not point out the immorality of the war policy of Prince Wilhelm II (or indeed of H.H. Asquith), then a better theology was needed. Casting about for an answer with an old friend, pastor in the next village, he finally (to his self-confessed astonishment) found his way back to the Bible. His name was Karl Barth, and his commentary on Romans was so electrifying that one writer described it as 'a bomb in the theologians' playground'. In it, on page after page after page, he hammered home one simple message: God is utterly, radically, incomprehensibly above and beyond and before anything we human beings can even dream of. Theologians and churches had been satisfied with imagining a god they could grasp and understand, but this was just an idol; the one true God was forever infinitely beyond our grasp, beyond our understanding.

Unlike Schweitzer, Barth accepted a university job where, as he recalls entertainingly, he was faced with a problem: his sudden fame was based on the thoroughness with which he had torn down all that had passed for theology in his youth; if he was to teach, he needed to find something to put in its place.

Barth found his answer in Jesus Christ. He never deviated for a second from the conviction that God was utterly beyond any human attempt to understand, but realised that we did not have to reach God: God had graciously given himself to us in Jesus. The unthought-of, the unthinkable, the awesome otherness that is the God of Scripture, had – astonishingly – chosen to link himself with his people in Israel and in the church through Jesus. This gift was revealed in the Bible. The task of theology was to give itself to understanding the witness of Scripture to what God has done in Jesus, and what that meant. And Barth gave himself to it. Over ten million words flowed from his pen. As Europe descended into war again, Barth wrote the documents that became the theological basis for those churches who refused to compromise with Hitler's regime. After the war he refused to agree with those who saw God on the side of the West against communism, insisting still that no human programme, no human nation or government, could be unambiguously identified with God's truth. ('Are you with us, or with our enemies?' asked Joshua of a strange figure he met as he obeyed God's command to conquer; 'Neither – I am the commander of the army of the LORD,' came the answer [Josh. 5:13–14]).

After Schweitzer and Barth, then, theology has been fascinated with the thought that in Jesus, a wholly new and different reality is breaking into this world. This increasingly has been understood in terms of eschatology. The coming reality is the kingdom of God, which begins to break in through the ministry, and particularly the resurrection, of Jesus, and will be completely inaugurated at the second coming. In the meantime, Christians are called to live as citizens of the coming kingdom, to live out its values and to believe its promises in the face of a passing world.

Amongst academic theologians, ideas like this are now second nature. We simply assume that this is the right way to think about the world. The coming promised end is not something obscure or confusing; it is the shining reality that transforms our thoughts and our lives in this present darkness. Ask almost any Christian theologian today how to deal with the problem of evil, or what he or she thinks about a Christian approach to politics, or how to negotiate an ethical issue concerning reproductive technology, and the response will probably assume, and be shaped by, an eschatological vision. The existence of evil in the world can only be made sense of in the light of God's future action; politics must be understood in terms of what God will do in the future; we do not know what a human being is until we realise the destiny that God has created us for; and so on. I certainly don't think that there is any duty or need for Christian people to be interested in everything that theologians argue about, but when there is a set of ideas that are well-founded biblically and profoundly useful for Christian thinking and living, we need them. And generally good and useful ideas do find their way from the university through the pulpit or bookstore into the lives of Christian believers.

Somehow, though, these eschatological perspectives – helpful, useful, perspectives that can guide our thinking and acting about live issues – haven't made the journey from universities and colleges to local churches, particularly not local evangelical churches. They have been the common currency in academia for a couple of generations, but have not been broadly received outside that world. And paradoxically, it is our faithful, orthodox, Bible-believing congregations that are most in danger of being 'Left Behind' just now, left behind as others move on into gifts of understanding and truth that are profoundly helpful.

The reason for this is, I think, simple enough. In our churches, particularly our evangelical churches, we think we know what any discussion of eschatology will look like. Various obscure texts of Scripture will be placed on the table, ripped cruelly from their literary and canonical context; there will be a claim that these point to a series of events that will usher in the end of time and the final judgement; and a heated argument will develop about the precise ordering of these events. We think eschatology is about making sense of a few obscure passages in the New Testament that are regarded as somehow prophecies of the End, and we are, to be honest, not very interested. We hear people angrily throw around terms like 'postmillennial' or 'pre-tribulational', and we would rather not know what they mean, if we're honest. Evangelical eschatology is wrapped up in sterile debates over such things, and as a result most evangelicals, in Britain at least, simply ignore it.

The problem is not whether a particular account ('pre-tribulation rapture,' or whatever) is right or wrong, so much as the sense that they do not matter very much. Perhaps I could be convinced that the Scripture clearly teaches not just that at some point in the future, possibly imminently, the Lord Jesus Christ will return, but also that a particular series of events, including a miraculous removal of Christians from earth ('rapture') followed by a seven-year period of horrendous suffering ('tribulation'), will precede that event. I cannot, however, see that believing this would make very much difference to the way I try to live in faithfulness to the gospel.

I suspect that this connects with the sense that such questions are more the stuff of American evangelicalism than British evangelicalism. The two movements tend to express their fundamental orientation to Scripture differently: most British statements insist that the Bible is trustworthy and authoritative; the term, 'inerrancy', ubiquitous in the USA, is almost never used. We should not make too much of this difference (I suspect that a 'trustworthy' Bible is necessarily inerrant, if one thinks about the meaning of the words), but it does suggest a difference in tone: British evangelicals see the Bible primarily as a 'rule of life' to be followed; our American sisters and brothers see it firstly as a 'deposit of truth' to be believed. (The differing popularity of creationism either side of the Atlantic might result from the same difference in emphasis.)

As a result, when American evangelical Christians get very excited about whether the rapture will precede or follow the tribulation, in Britain we tend to simply turn off. Such arguments are divisive and irrelevant, as far as we can see. Even the basic division between those who believe the return of Christ will usher in a thousand-year period of perfection on earth ('premillennialism') and those who believe that the thousand years of perfection will occur before the return of Christ ('postmillennialism') is largely uninteresting to us. Our evangelical missionary societies, after all, were largely founded by postmillennialists, who passed the baton after a couple of generations to premillennialists. They are now run by people who tend towards amillennialism (believing that the thousand years mentioned in Rev. 20:1–6 should not be interpreted as a literal prophecy of a future event at all); the work of spreading the gospel and of seeking justice in human societies has been gloriously unaffected by these changes.

(I should note that Tim LaHaye would disagree with my estimation here. On his website, I find the following:

> Dr. LaHaye and PTRC ['Pre-Trib Research Centre'] stresses three practical implications that flow from the rapture teaching. The first implication of pretribulationism is that it leads to godly living in an unholy age. Next, this New Testament teaching promotes a strong emphasis upon evangelism of the lost. Finally, when believers come to understand this eternal perspective, it leads to a zeal for worldwide missions.[1]

All I can say is that these three things seem to me, both logically, and in observing the lives of Christian churches, to flow from any serious belief in the return of Christ and the final judgement, not from pre-tribulationism per se. If these are the things that Dr LaHaye stresses in his ministry, then I am glad; I hope he also has the honesty to acknowledge that a convinced postmillennialist such as Jonathan Edwards was also not unconcerned about godly living or the evangelism of the lost.)

In British evangelical churches, then, we have learnt to ignore discussion of eschatology, seeing it as merely divisive and irrelevant. This, however, is a very particular, and to my mind very unhelpful, take on what 'eschatology' means. If we could get hold of something akin to the eschatological vision of Schweitzer and Barth, that might be different. Imagine if we were seized by the realisation that the kingdom of God is a present reality. Think what it means to believe that Jesus' resurrection has decisively changed the nature of human history. Consider the implications of the fact that the Holy Spirit is even now rushing us towards the promised end when Jesus shall return and bring in his kingdom of justice and joy. This is eschatology. This is what is explored in this book.

What difference does it make? Well, read on through the book. But let me close with a bit more personal testimony. I preach fairly regularly, several times each month. In all my preaching career, it happens that I have never yet preached on Revelation 21, but I think it is the text I have quoted more than any other. Wrestling, as a Christian preacher must, with the radical evil in the world, facing up to this place of half-truths and ethics painted in shades of grey, I find myself repeatedly closing sermons by asking my people to raise their eyes for a moment and to look beyond, to the day when:

> the dwelling of God is with men, and he will live with them. They will be his people, and God himself will be with them and be their God. He will wipe every tear from their eyes. There will be no more death or mourning or crying or pain, for the old order of things has passed away. (Rev. 21:3–4, NIV)

Note: Popular Evangelical Eschatology

After everything in this introduction, it is perhaps useful nonetheless to give some guide to the sort of eschatology I am hoping this book might replace. This eschatology has two basic premises: a belief that the Bible prophesies certain climatic events which will, in a certain order, bring about the ending of the present order and the coming of the new heaven and new earth; and a conviction that the time for these events is drawing near, based on certain prophecies or indicators in the Scripture.

An example of the level to which devout Christian foolishness can aspire on the latter point is 'the Rapture Index' (http://www.raptureready.com/rap2.html), which assigns numerical values to no less than forty-five supposed indicators of the coming end. (Even granting the – rather bizarre – assumption that there is some sort of biblical defence for regarding bad unemployment, high interest rates, or whatever, as adequate predictors of the return of Christ, it is surely merely comical to privilege the American economy over the rest of the world as a way of measuring such things . . .) The idea that we can trace the approaching end in world events need not be so ridiculous, however: claims that, for example, the return of the Jewish people to their ancestral homeland indicates the nearness of the End are extraordinarily common.

The end-time events that tend to be of most interest to popular evangelical eschatology include the 'rapture', the 'millennium', and the 'great tribulation'. The idea of the rapture comes from 1 Thessalonians 4:16–17, where Paul suggests that at the return of Christ the dead will be raised, and then believers who are alive will be caught up to meet the coming Lord 'in the air'. (Lk. 17:30–35 is also cited.) The 'millennium' refers to the thousand year period referred to repeatedly in Revelation 20:1–6. This is sometimes read as a literal thousand-year reign of Christ and the saints on earth. The phrase 'great tribulation' comes from the KJV translation of Matthew 24:21; it is a time of unimaginable suffering preceding the return of Christ. Hal Lindsey linked this idea to the last of the seventy weeks of Daniel 9:24–27, and so suggested it would last seven years.

The arguments over evangelical eschatology turn on the precise ordering of these events in relation to the return of Christ. In its origin the evangelical movement was generally 'postmillennialist', believing that world history would grow towards perfection, and a thousand years of glory, after which Christ would return. More recently (see David Bebbington's chapter in this book for the history) premillennialism has become popular in some circles. The idea here is that Christ's second coming is before his thousand-year reign. A refinement of this sees a seven-year great tribulation immediately before the return of Christ, itself preceded by the departure of all Christians with Christ ('pre-tribulational rapture'). This is the pattern assumed in the 'Left Behind' books, which describe the horrors of the tribulation after the saints have been 'raptured'.

Of course, there are other ways of reading the texts. Almost no-one in the history of the church read 1 Thessalonians 4:17 as referring to a 'rapture' until J.N. Darby at the beginning of modern evangelical eschatology. Matthew 24:21 is generally regarded by modern biblical scholars as referring to the destruction of Jerusalem in AD 70, and Luther and Calvin, amongst many others, read it that way also. Given the highly symbolic and pictorial language of Revelation, it is not surprising that it has been similarly common to read Revelation 20:1–6 as not referring to any literal thousand-year period at all ('amillennialism').

Hopeful Word

2

Eschatology in the Old Testament*

Lena-Sofia Tiemeyer

Introduction

As Christians, many, if not most of us, think of eschatology in terms of the 'doctrine of the end'. When speaking about eschatology in the Old Testament, however, this traditional definition must be slightly modified, as the Old Testament speaks very seldom about the end times, as in the final days before the world will come to an end. Instead, the Old Testament envisions the 'end' as taking place *within history* and within the framework of earthly Israel and its religion. Thus, the present chapter describes how ancient Israel envisioned a future that was fundamentally *different* from and *better* than the present. It was improved beyond what could be expected from human progress, but was nevertheless still of this, albeit transformed, world. In a sense, eschatology in the Old Testament portrays the *ideal* future from the point of view of the ancient Israelites, brought about by God.

In this chapter, we shall look at the eschatological references primarily against their Old Testament background, and focus on how a given prediction can be understood within its immediate

---

* D.E. Gowan, *Eschatology in the Old Testament* (T&T Clark, Edinburgh, 1986). The present chapter owns much to this study, in particular in terms of lay-out.

Old Testament context, rather than within the wider context of the Christian Bible. We shall discuss four themes that feature in many, if not most of the eschatological writings of the Old Testament:

- The transformation of the land of Israel and of the city of Jerusalem.
- The transformation of human society.
- The transformation of the human being.
- The transformation of nature.

As a result, some of the key features of eschatology that we are familiar with from the New Testament, such as the resurrection of the dead and the coming of the Messiah/the Eschaton, will not be discussed at any great length as they play merely a marginal role in the Old Testament.

The Transformation of the Land of Israel and of the City of Jerusalem

It is fitting to begin our discussion on Old Testament eschatology with Jerusalem, given its primary theological significance within the Old Testament, taken together with the sheer abundance of references to it.

While, as David's new capital (2 Sam. 5:6–16), Jerusalem is a relative newcomer to the Old Testament stage, it quickly reached both political and theological prominence. As well as serving as the military and administrative capital over the united northern and southern tribes of Israel, the building of the temple during the reign of Solomon gave rise to the theological idea of Jerusalem as God's earthly dwelling place and thus as the palpable symbol of his presence.

Both Jerusalem's political and theological status took a near fatal blow by its destruction by the Babylonian army in 586 BC. As a result of the destruction and the subsequent Babylonian conquest of Judah, the top layers of the Judahite society were exiled to Babylon. This in turn caused the inhabitants to be divided: some continued to live in the partly ruined Judah and some were forcibly removed to live in exile in Babylon. From this time and onwards, much prophetic writing therefore focuses on the restoration of Jerusalem/Zion.

The question then arises as to the nature and the character of this writing: how much of it can rightly be understood as eschatological, i.e. in a transformed world, and how much should be understood as referring to God's acts within the regular course of history? In other words, what did the Old Testament authors think would happen after the restoration; a changed world or the continuation of the world as they knew it but with a rebuilt Jerusalem?

The answer is not easy. The book of Haggai is a case in point. Throughout most of the book, the prophet speaks about the combined human and divine endeavour to rebuild the temple, under the tutelage of the earthly and already living governor Zerubbabel. Then in Haggai 2:20–23 the tone of the book suddenly changes. The prophet writes about a day of divinely originated cosmic upheaval when God will overturn the political and military might of the nations and choose Zerubbabel as his signet ring. Through this, the reader is catapulted into the eschatological future where God will turn everything right on behalf of his people.

Zechariah 1–8 is another example where the hope of the imminent rebuilding of Jerusalem interacts with Israel's eschatological hopes and expectations. While Zechariah 1:14–17 seems to envision the rebuilding of the cities of Judah to come to pass shortly, the following oracles in Zechariah 2:6–13 are less clear: did the author foresee the joining of the Gentiles with the people of Israel as happening in the near future or in a more distant and different one (cf. Zech. 8:22–23)? It is therefore justifiable to ask whether the prophets themselves had a clear idea when future things were going to take place. It may, in fact, be argued that they did not clearly distinguish between the end times, and the more immediate future. In the present context, we shall deem descriptions of Jerusalem to be eschatological if the descriptions go beyond what can reasonably be expected from the existing, earthly city.

We can discern several key features in the texts that represent Jerusalem as an 'ideal' city.

1. God will dwell anew in Jerusalem. In fact, the new conditions will far supersede those of the past. God will live in
   her permanently: his glory will be visible in Jerusalem, as
   her eternal light and her secure walls, and his glory will be
   forever manifest in the temple (e.g. Isa. 4:5–6; 60:1–2; 19–20;
   Ezek. 43:7–9; 48:35; Zech. 2:8–9).
2. In part as a result of her being God's earthly dwelling place,
   Jerusalem will take her rightful place at the centre of the
   universe. Isa. 65:17–18 aptly parallels the creation of a new
   heaven and a new earth with the re-creation of Jerusalem.
   People from the surrounding nations will arrive in
   Jerusalem, sometimes voluntarily to worship the God of
   Israel (e.g. Isa. 2:2–4; Mic. 4:1–4; Isa. 56:3–8; 60:3; 66:18–21;
   Zech. 2:1; 8:22–23), and sometimes less voluntarily to serve
   the people of Israel (e.g. Isa. 60:10–14), and their wealth will
   be for the benefit of Jerusalem (e.g. Isa. 60:4–16; Zech. 14:14).
3. God will actively work on Jerusalem's behalf. She will be
   God's own special partner (e.g. Isa. 49:14–16), and a safe haven
   (e.g. Isa. 33:20; Zech. 14:13). God will fight on her behalf
   against the nations that attack her (Zech. 12:1–9; 14:1–3), and
   God will bring her people home from exile, creating a popu-
   lated city once more (e.g. Isa. 27:12–13; Zech. 8:7–8).

Transformation of the Human Society

This brings us to the wider promise of the return to Jerusalem
and to Israel and Judah in general of all the people of Israel
who are presently living outside its borders. This restoration
from exile is often described in eschatological language. Most
prominently, Ezekiel 37 and the vision of the dry bones depict
how Israel will be brought to life again, and restored to her
land (vv. 12, 14).

This return of all the exiles to the land of Judah (e.g. Isa.
11:12–16; 43:5–7; 49:12; 51:11; Jer. 16:14; 30:3; Zeph. 3:20; Zech.
8:7–8; 10:6), together with the restoration of Jerusalem, is in
many Old Testament texts understood to be the *prerequisite* for
the fulfilment of the rest of the eschatological hope. Thus, the
ingathering of the people of Jerusalem and the re-establishing

of Jerusalem and Judah as nations again are the first, necessary step without which nothing else will come to pass.

The establishment in Judah/Jerusalem of a divinely appointed leader is another eschatological motif in the Old Testament. On the one hand, this motif does not necessarily correspond to what in New Testament terms can be labelled Messianic prophecies. Most of the prophecies that are traditionally labelled by the New Testament as Messianic can be best understood, in their Old Testament context, as speaking about a contemporary human king (e.g. Isa. 9:2–7; Ps. 2:2). Zechariah 9:9–10 may be an exception, describing 'the king of Jerusalem', a humble person riding into Jerusalem on a donkey. Again, however, it is impossible in its present context to determine whether the author had anything else but a *human* king in mind. Likewise, it is unclear whether the references to a shepherd in Ezekiel 34:23–24 (God's 'servant David') and in Jeremiah 23:1–6 (a righteous shoot to David) in their respective contexts refer to an earthly king of the Davidic line or to something more exalted.

On the other hand, there are elements in Old Testament eschatology relating to future leaders that are not emphasised in the New Testament. Notably, Jeremiah 33:14–26 speaks about the perpetuation of the Davidic line and of the Levitical priesthood. While the former is picked up in the New Testament, the latter is not. Furthermore, Ezekiel 45:7–46:18 speaks of a future prince that, although not divine, will have an elevated, although not particularly influential, position in the eschatological Jerusalem. Finally, Haggai 2:23, one of the most explicit references to a coming, eschatological ruler, identifies him with the *human* governor Zerubbabel, a contemporary of the prophet.

The nations, i.e. the peoples apart from the people of Israel, are also mentioned in the Old Testament eschatological text, but they are mostly treated in relation to Israel rather than in their own right. Most eschatological texts see them as Israel's enemies, and accordingly envision their destruction, while a few texts predict more peaceful interaction between them and God.

The nations are often labelled as those who have caused suffering to the people of Israel. At the same time, they are also frequently described as acting in accordance with God's will: God used them as tools in order to punish Israel. The matter that needs rectifying, as the prophetic texts describe it, is that they overdid it, carrying out God's commands too harshly (e.g. Zech. 1:15; cf. Jer. 30:11–17; Ezek. 25; Zech. 6:7–8). As a just punishment of the nations, God is then described as fighting the nations. Most of these battle scenes are not fully fledged eschatology but are rather assumed to take place within normal history. Nonetheless, there are exceptions. Isaiah 11:11–16, for example, speaks about God's final ingathering of the people of Israel from all corners of the earth, followed by his destruction of Israel's neighbouring states, and of Egypt and Mesopotamia.

The Old Testament contains further the idea of a *final battle* between God and the nations (e.g. Zech. 12; 14). In particular, Ezekiel 38–39 depicts God's battle against Gog. This passage stands out in many ways. First, it is not immediately related to the ingathering of the people of Israel but instead envisions a time when Israel already is dwelling securely in the land. Secondly, Israel is not the immediate focal point of the text; instead God's actions against Gog serve to display his power among the nations (e.g. 38:16; Ezek. 39:21). Thirdly, rather than speaking about a known country, one of Israel's traditional enemies, the text speaks about a remote country with the up till now unheard name of Magog.

Along similar lines, other texts depict an eschatological *judgement scene* where the nations will be held accountable for their actions against Israel. In particular, Joel 3:1–3 envisions that, at the time of God turning the fates of Judah and Jerusalem (for the better), God will gather the nations in the valley of Jehoshaphat and make them answer for the evil acts against the people of Israel.

In contrast to these violent images, other eschatological passages envision more peaceful times. A few texts depict people from other nations as coming to Jerusalem to join with the people of Israel. As we noted above, Isaiah 56:3–8; 60:3; 66:18–21; Zechariah 2:11 and 8:20–23 speak of non-Israelites who will travel voluntarily to Jerusalem, seeking to join with the people of Israel and to worship their God.

Standing somewhere in between the destruction of the nations and their worship of the God of Israel, Ezekiel 29:13–14 tells of God's dispersion of the people of Egypt but also how he will gather them together again. True, Egypt will never again reach its former glory, but it will not be totally destroyed. Isaiah 19:18–25, an even more unusual text, speaks of Egypt turning to the God of Israel and how the Egyptians, together with the people of Assyria, will sacrifice to him. Israel will be equal to these two ancient superpowers, and they will all three be called God's peoples.

Lastly, Isaiah 25:6–8 speak in truly eschatological terms of a banquet for all nations on 'this mountain', presumably Mount Zion in Jerusalem. The immediate context, however, is not unequivocally friendly to the nations, as the following verse 10 predicts the destruction of Moab, and 26:21 predicts God punishing the peoples of the earth for their sins.

Transformation of the Human Person

Together with the restoration of Israel, as a land and as a society, several eschatological texts in the Old Testament also speak of a transformation of the *human person*. Although less well attested than those discussed previously, this theme is nevertheless a significant aspect of the changes that are expected by Israel in the eschatological future. This transformation is focused on sin: how to deal with the Israelites' already existing sins and how to enable them never to sin again.

The idea of expiation, i.e. the forgiveness of sins, exists throughout the Old Testament in various forms, most of which are connected with the cult: if a person committed a sin, repentance and/or confession, followed by sacrifices, would bring forgiveness to the offender. Nonetheless, it would not inoculate the offender from sinning again. Rather, there was a continuous need for repentance and for atoning sacrifices. Furthermore, the repercussions of the sin, although forgiven, would still exist in the world. Many of the eschatological texts therefore deal with these two problems of continuous sinning and the repercussions of committed sins.

Would there ever be a time when these things would be different?

Much of the Old Testament's eschatology stems from texts relating to, and influenced by, the destruction of Jerusalem in 587 BC. Thus this literature explains the destruction and subsequent exile as the result of, indeed as God's punishment for, the sins of the people of Judah. It further presupposes that the people could have influenced the outcome: had they merely behaved differently and repented in time, the destruction could have been averted. In contrast, parts of the books of Jeremiah and Ezekiel, probably composed at the time immediately prior to the destruction, doubt the people's *ability* to refrain from sinning, asking instead whether they are not prone to sin by their very nature (Jer. 8:5; 13:23; Ezek. 3:7). Along similar lines, they envision that Israel's repentance will *post-date* her punishment: only after she has been punished and only after God has forgiven her will she be able to realise her sins and to repent (Isa. 44:22; Jer. 4:4–7; Ezek. 16:59–63). At present, Israel appears to be unable to obey God.

The same prophets also envision a solution to this inability: the creation of a new type of human being that would only be able to do good. This change would be God's initiative rather than the result of human endeavour: God himself would transform the people of Israel from the inside by giving them a new heart and a new spirit that would act solely in accordance with his will (Jer. 24:7; 32:39; Ezek. 18:31; 36:24–32; 37:23). Thus, God would restore them to what they were meant to be – a people with a heart of flesh instead of with a heart that had turned to stone – and Israel would be able to freely obey God again.

Part of this inner transformation of Israel is expressed through the idea of a *new covenant* between God and the people of Israel (Jer. 31:31–34): God will begin his relationship with his people afresh. Through their persistent sinning, the people of Israel had broken the earlier, conditional covenant between God and Israel, a covenant that was characterised by human obligations towards God (Exod. 19–24; 32–34). As a result, God had punished them in the form of the destruction of Jerusalem in 586 BC. Now, however, God will place his law within the people so that Israel will know intuitively to obey God, and he will forgive them all their past sins.

Joel 2:28–29 (cf. Ezek. 39:28–29) attests to another vision of restored communication between God and Israel. In the last days, direct access to God will no longer be restricted to some select few but be shared by all the people of Israel, servants and masters, young and old, men and women, alike. Thus, the prophet envisioned that in the end times, the barriers between God and Israel would fall as sin would be removed. God would communicate directly to the people, and they, having internalised the law, would gladly respond to him. As a result of the forgiveness of sins and the restored direct communication with God, the eschatological texts of the Old Testament envisioned changes to humanity, in particular with regard to health, longevity and 'the good life'.

Significant parts of the Old Testament explain much of the suffering of everyday human life, including physical illness, as caused by human disobedience against God (e.g. Gen. 3:16–19). Accordingly, in the final days when the sins are forgiven and the very ability to sin no longer exists, illness and premature death will disappear (Isa. 33:24; 65:20, 22–23) and God will bring healing and health (Jer. 33:6). Moreover, the people of Israel will then be living a good and happy life, both in material and in more abstract ways. Zechariah 3:9, for example, envisions that after God has expiated the people's sin, the people will enjoy life, feasting together under vines and fig trees. The people of Jerusalem will in fact be *perfectly happy*, filled with joy and full of food (Jer. 31:12–14)! The people will prosper, as the New Jerusalem will be built of precious stones, and as her inhabitants, being raised by God himself, will live in peace, security and prosperity (Isa. 54:11–14). In addition, there will be a palpable sense of security in their relationship with God. God will never again abandon them, for, as long as day and night exist, he will remain steadfast to the people of Israel (Jer. 33:25).

There is also evidence, although rare and only attested in very late texts, of the hope for the resurrection of the dead (25:6–8; 26:19 and Dan. 12:1). Isaiah 25:6–8 declares that God will abolish death and mourning forever. Presumably, the abolition of death implies the resurrection of the dead. In more clear language, Isaiah 26:19 declares that the dead and buried will receive life again. Finally, Daniel 12:2 remains as the only Old Testament text that not only speaks of the resurrection of the dead but also distinguishes between those who receive eternal life and those who are condemned to eternal shame and reproach.

Transformation of Nature

Lastly, many of the eschatological texts of the Old Testament envision significant changes in nature, what we may call the redemption of the natural world. As we shall see, many of these changes have humankind as its focal point in that they benefit the human population (of Israel).

First, nature was going to be rendered harmless to humans. Nature was often viewed by the ancient Israelites and their Mesopotamian contemporaries as threatening, and the ideal, in many ways, was an organised, settled and domesticated natural world. In contrast, human habitations left deserted, except for roaming wild animals, are presented as a worst case scenario (e.g. Isa. 13:21–22; Jer. 50:39). Therefore, one significant aspect of Old Testament eschatology is the disappearance of wild animals that are potentially harmful for humans. Ezekiel 34:25–30 speak of a time where God will make wild animals extinct, and, as a result, the people will be able to dwell securely, not fearing to be devoured by wild animals anymore. Alternatively, other texts speak of peace within the animal kingdom itself and with the human world. Most famously, Isaiah 11:6–9 and the corresponding Isa. 65:25 speak of how, in the end times, the wolf, the leopard and the lion will dwell peacefully together with the lamb, the kid and the calf, and how they shall be led by a small child.

Secondly, nature was going to be rendered useful to humans. An important aspect of nature was to serve as food provider for humans. Therefore, eschatological texts often envision a time of plentiful food (e.g. Hos. 2:21–23; Ezek. 34:29; 36:29), and focus on increased, indeed miraculous, fertility.

Ezekiel 47:12 is a case in point, envisioning fruit trees that would give fruit twelve times annually, and the preceding 47:1–11 speaks of a stream running through the wilderness, rendering the Dead Sea into sweet and life-giving water abundant with fish for human consumption. Never losing sight of the human interest, however, the prophet declares that a small portion of the Dead Sea will be left as it is, to serve as a supply of salt! Likewise, Isaiah 35:1–2, 6–7 speak of the blossoming of the wilderness and how the formerly dry and infertile land, the home of wild animals only, will be water-filled enough to support papyrus plantations. At the same time, there are some texts that envision rather impractical changes that are probably best understood symbolically. Isaiah 60:20, for example, predicts the cessation of day and night, as does Zechariah 14:6–7.

Conclusion

As we have seen, the eschatology of the Old Testament is unequivocally tied to Israel, the land and Israel, the people. The prophetic hope for the final days can be summarised as political freedom, moral perfection and earthly (material) happiness for the people of Israel, finally gathered together again in its own land. Christians, who for the most part are of Gentile origin and thus part of 'the nations', may find this focus on Israel and on the Jews, together with God's final killing of the nations around Israel, disconcerting.

Paul, speaking about the grafting of the Christians into the olive tree of God's people (Rom. 11:17–24), makes clear, however, that as Christians, we can count ourselves as part of the people of God. This, however, does not mean that Christians *replace* the people of Israel (Rom. 11:28–29). Rather, it is preferable to see the birth of Christianity as part of the realised eschatology of passages such as Isaiah 56:3–8; 60:3; 66:18–21; Zechariah 2:11 and 8:20–23 that speak of people from all the nations worshipping the God of Israel.

3

Eschatology in Isaiah

John Goldingay

I tell students that whenever they use the word eschatology they should wash their mouth out with soap, because it sounds like a technical term with a defined meaning, but actually means different things to different people. I am inclined simply to use the word 'End', which has the advantage of not sounding like a technical term. It is also a word that the prophets use to refer to God's decisive act in Israel's history (e.g. Amos 8:2), though ironically it does not come with this meaning in Isaiah.

Jerusalem's Destiny at Last Realised

The Greek word *eschatos*, 'last', from which we derive the word eschatology, does sometimes appear in the Greek translations of Isaiah. It first comes in 2:2–4 in introducing something that will happen 'in the last days' (NIV). (The prophecy also appears as Micah 4:1–3. We do not know whether it originally came from Isaiah or Micah or some other prophet. It is an indication that Isaiah, like other prophetic books, is not simply the words of Isaiah but a kind of anthology of prophecies, all in some way linked to Isaiah – for instance, coming from prophets who were expounding the later implications of his prophecies – but many not uttered by him. The prophecies that come from Isaiah himself appear only within chapters 1–23 and 28–39.)

This vision offers a contrast with the story of sin and punishment in the book's first chapter. God will do something extraordinary and miraculous to turn Zion into a place to which nations will stream. The unimpressive hill of Zion will become a towering peak that will draw the nations with the desire to learn from Israel how to walk in God's ways. Presumably that is a figure of speech rather than a declaration about a geophysical change in the mountain ranges in the Middle East; there is no reason why such a geophysical change should appeal to the nations in that way. Through their streaming to Zion, they will find themselves submitting to God's authority instead of fighting to impose their will on one another. God will make the decisions between nations that usually go to war with one another. They will therefore be able to recycle their weapons instead of spending a huge proportion of their GNP on war.

From the Beginning in Genesis 12:1–3, God's purpose in choosing Abraham was to draw the world to seek the blessing God promised to him. Isaiah 2:2–4 restates that intention. Fairly consistently, what God intends to do at the End is formulated in light of the purpose God formulated at the Beginning, and of the way things are in the present.

The chapters that follow first describe Judah's waywardness and God's intentions about that (Isa. 1–12) and then broaden the picture to portray God's intentions with the individual nations around (Isa. 13–23) before chapters 24–27 extend the horizon much further, indeed extend it as far as it will go, geographically and temporally. They suggest an end-times scenario overlapping with that in 2:2–4 but with a number of further features.

Judgment and Devastation, then a Great Celebration

Isaiah 24 begins by speaking of 'the earth' laid waste. It does not anchor its picture in a time or place, but neither does it imply that this devastation will not come for two or three thousand years; it describes this disaster as if it is already happening. The devastation affects the earth itself as well as its peoples. But it comes about because earth's peoples 'have transgressed teachings, violated statute, broken the ancient [or eternal] covenant' (24:5). The whole world is in covenant relationship with God, knows the covenant's terms, and has ignored them.

The vision's far-reaching nature is extended in 24:21–26. Parallel to earthly forces working against God's purpose are heavenly ones, parallel to earthly armies are heavenly armies, and parallel to conflicts on earth are conflicts in the heavens. The frustrating of God's purpose on earth reflects the self-assertion of powers in the heavens (and vice versa?). Earthly events show that the sovereign God does not always assert sovereignty but lets things happen that conflict with the divine will. But 'that day' will see an assertion of God's sovereignty over heavenly and earthly powers.

On that day, God will kill Leviathan (27:1), a monstrous embodiment of opposition to God, an Old Testament way of speaking of what the New Testament refers to as Satan. In the Old Testament, usually the battle in which God put Leviathan, the serpent, or the dragon in its place happened in the past, before creation or in an event such as God's victory at the Red Sea. Isaiah 27 is distinctive for seeing this victory happening at the end. It again starts from the fact that God's purpose is not realised in the world; powers of resistance to God often have their way. Whatever victory God won in the past was not the final one. But God will win that final victory.

God's putting down opposition and tyranny will mean a great celebration, a festive banquet on Mount Zion such as happens at Sukkot when people bring their harvest offerings and also celebrate God's bringing them out of Egypt (25:6–8). One can imagine a king being the host at such a meal; here God, the divine King, is the host. Alongside the feasting is God's enabling people to forget their griefs and losses. God will swallow death and bring mourning to an end. There will be no more battling of one people against another, with the grief as the bodies come home (or don't), no more warring on God's part, no more judgment, no more wrath, for Israel or for other peoples.

The vision says nothing about the resuscitation of dead people, and need not imply that the people at the banquet will themselves not die. (Paul quotes v. 8 in connection with the resurrection of believers in 1 Cor. 15:54, but as is common, this involves an inspired reuse of the text that does not correspond to its own meaning). In general the Old Testament does not worry too much about death in itself; while the Psalms are full of protest at death when it comes before its time, people accept that at the end of a full life one dies and goes to be with one's family.

What is the relationship between the picture of world judgment and the picture of world celebration? The tension between Isaiah 24 and Isaiah 25 reappears through Isaiah 40–66. The focus on judgment often emphasises powerful people (nations or groups within the nation); conversely, the beneficiaries of the judgment are the weak (peoples subordinate to a superpower or weak groups within a nation). So it is the powerful who fall, the weak who celebrate. But 25:3–4 raises another possible implication of that tension. It speaks of nations honouring and fearing or revering God; perhaps they choose whether to honour and revere God voluntarily, and thereby escape destruction, or to honour and fear God under compulsion. The two attitudes to the nations in Isaiah offer them alternative scenarios. They cannot come to the banquet as oppressors. But if they choose to shape up, they can come.

Israel's Restoration

Alongside the nations' partaking in that feast and consolation is the promise that the shame of Israel's subordination to other peoples is taken away (25:8). And after the banquet, true life will continue forever. 'On that day' Judah will be able to sing of its city that God has made permanently strong (26:1–4). It will know it can 'rely on Yahweh for ever', because in Yahweh it has 'an everlasting crag', 'a crag of ages'. It will know that peace will last forever.

In the past, the people have seen God act against their overlords, who have behaved as if they were gods. They are dead now, mere ghosts, and they will never rise from the dead (26:13–14). The trouble is that God's people themselves are uncomfortably like that – as good as dead, like the community in the exile that sees itself as resembling the bones of a corpse left to be picked bare by vultures, totally cut off, hopeless (Ezek. 37:11). Ezekiel envisioned God turning these bones into corpses and the corpses back into a living army, and Isaiah 26:19 envisages a similar resuscitation. The lines are obscure in detail, and they could be reinterpreted in relation to the resurrection of individuals, but in the context they refer to the resuscitation of the nation. (It is not surprising that the Old Testament makes no reference to the resurrection of individuals. Theologically it is only after Christ's resurrection that such a resurrection is possible. The Old Testament is correct that until that event, human beings are just bound for Sheol. After that, they are still asleep, in Sheol, until resurrection day, but being in Sheol can be reframed as being with Christ, because while we sleep through those years, Christ protects us and keeps us safe for that final day when we will awake and be raised.)

In that day, people will sing about the 'lovely vineyard' and God will enjoy protecting it and watering it (27:2–6). The picture offers a marked contrast with the original vineyard song, which threatened that God might totally abandon the vineyard (5:1–6). That day is one of restoration beyond chastisement when the pathetic things in which Israel now glories will be replaced by God as one who is a real embodiment of glory, and when there will be proper exercise of authority and successful defence against attackers (28:5–6). And in that day, God will bring about an absolutely complete gathering of people exiled in Mesopotamia and Egypt (27:12–13).

The reference to further attacks is a surprise. But as the Old Testament's looking back to the Beginning does not see it as the unequivocal bliss that Christian tradition attaches to it (there was a violent world to subdue, and a strange temptation to face, before Adam and Eve went in for their disobedience), so at the End, even after the consummation of God's purpose, there is still resistance to God, opposition to God's people, and the reality of death.

After Isaiah 24–27, anything that looks like talk of final judgment and renewal largely disappears from Isaiah until the last two chapters, which thus complete a bracket round the book as a whole with the opening chapter or so. They again combine talk of the world's desolation, the nations' sharing in Israel's relationship with God, and the restoration of Jerusalem.

Isaiah 65:17–25 begins with God 'creating new heavens and a new earth', but it soon segues into God 'creating Jerusalem a joy' where there will be no more weeping or people dying before their time. In light of the way the New Testament adapts the imagery, it is easy to over-interpret the opening mention of new heavens and a new earth. The prophet refers to them only very briefly on the way into speaking of the matter that really counts, the renewal of Jerusalem, where people will live long lives, build houses and live in them, plant vineyards and eat their fruit, and enjoy close relationship with God. The new heavens and earth are thought of more as the context for social and political transformation and therefore are not the focus of attention in themselves, as is the case in apocalyptic writings from the Greco-Roman period.'¹ It is striking that Isaiah 65 closes with a reprise of the vision in Isaiah 11 of the animal kingdom transformed, in fulfilment of the original creation commission to humanity ('subdue the earth'), yet with the serpent still knowing its place.

Isaiah 66:22–24 adds another reference to new heavens and new earth, again as backcloth to something else: Israel's seed and name will be as permanent as these. Alongside the security of the Israelites' future is the regular week by week, month by month worship of all flesh; the previous verses have described all the nations joining in pilgrimage to Jerusalem, some of them serving as ministers in the temple (66:18–21). Yet neither Israelites nor Gentiles can take their position for granted; they will need to keep reminding themselves of what happens to rebels. In reading this chapter in worship, the Jewish community repeats the penultimate verse so that the reading does not end on the sombre note of the last verse. Christian readers react with similar distaste; there is some irony about that, given Jesus' taking up phrases from it to say something more frightful, not just about death but about Hell.

The Day of the Lord, Then and Now

At the beginning and end of Isaiah, then, and in that block of chapters near the middle, the book speaks of how things will be when God brings his purpose to a consummation. But the book has another way of raising questions that we might call eschatological, one that makes it possible to suggest connections between the ultimate fulfilment of God's purpose and what happens now. Following on that opening exposition in 1:2–2:5, Isaiah introduces the idea of 'the day of the Lord', the time when God's purpose for Israel and for the world will be fulfilled. The chapters we have already considered would encourage Israel to assume that this would be a day of great blessing and celebration. Prophets such as Isaiah (and Amos: see Amos 5:18–20) turn it into a day of calamity and grief. God intends to put Judah down for its preoccupation with weaponry and wealth and its serving of and relying on other deities: and then 'Yahweh alone will be high up on that day.' Because the Lord 'has a day against all that is high and lofty' (2:11–12), against lofty trees, high mountains, tall ships, and impressive people (cf. 2:17, 20; 31:7).

God intends to use Assyria to put Israel in its place, and subsequently will also use Babylon to do that. The day of the Lord is thus not merely one occasion at the End, after which there is no more history. It can refer to a day when God's ultimate purpose is fulfilled, or a day within Israel's expected or actual experience when something of that purpose is realised. Thus it can keep happening. Jerusalem's fall in 587 BC is 'the day of Yahweh's wrath' (Lam. 2:1, 21). A cliché of Christian talk speaks of the 'now' and the 'not yet'. This way of thinking goes back at least to Isaiah's time.

But the day of the Lord *is* designed to be a day of great blessing. When God's people is felled like a tree, this will not be the end of the story. God's branch will grow and produce beautiful fruit. God will cleanse the city of the stain of its bloodshed and protect it from sun and storm in the future (4:2–6; cf. 10:20). Isaiah 12 is a song to sing 'on that day', a day of confessing what God has done for Jerusalem when comfort and deliverance have replaced anger, which will deserve making known in the entire world.

The other side of the coin is that the day of Israel's restoration also has to be the day the superpowers are put down. A 'pronouncement regarding Babylon' declares that the day of the Lord is near for Babylon, as the Lord stirs up the Medes against them (13:1–22). The declaration relates to the time two centuries after Isaiah's day when Babylon is about to fall. By then, the Lord's day has come on Judah, in the way Lamentations describes; now it is coming on Babylon, to make Judah's restoration possible. God had a similar 'plan' for Assyria, without using the expression 'day of the Lord' (14:24–27). The Old Testament does not speak of God having a long-term detailed plan for the whole of world history or for the End, but God does from time to time formulate plans for particular peoples, and then implements them. Superpowers make plans; events prove that God is a superior planner. God likewise has a 'day of redress' (English translations have 'day of vengeance', but this gives a misleading impression), a 'year of recompense', for Zion in relation to Edom (34:8). 'Edom has replaced Assyria and Babylonia as the personified embodiment of the evil empire.'[2] Like Babylon's downfall, this redress makes it possible for the feeble and fearful to be delivered and the people God ransoms and restores to return to Zion singing (35:1–10).

The Day of the Lord for the Nations: Bad News and Good News

Putting down the nations and restoring Zion are thus interwoven, as they must be. In 61:1–2 the prophet speaks of being anointed to proclaim release to captives, to proclaim 'Yahweh's year of favour, our God's day of redress.' Proclaiming release is a term associated with the freeing of people in servitude for debt in the seventh year (Jer. 34:17), and it is presumably this that is 'Yahweh's year of favour'. God is declaring the intention to free people in servitude to foreign overlords (cf. Ezra 9:9). That will involve this 'year of favour' also being a 'day of redress', a moment when God puts down these foreign overlords. The day of redress, then, is again not one that belongs solely to some final day that might be far off; it is the day God is bringing now. (When Jesus looks at his own ministry in light of Isaiah 61, he similarly associates the year of favour with his ministry, and the days of redress with the destruction of Jerusalem; see Lk. 4:19; 21:22). It is the prophet's job to announce this day or year. When the political powers fail to bring about justice in the world, God accepts the responsibility to bring it about: 'the day of redress has been in my mind, my year of restoration has come' (Isa. 63:4).

The phrase 'that day' is used most spectacularly in 19:16–25, where six times it denotes a day when Egypt will come to acknowledge God. On that day, Egypt will quake in fear before the Lord and before Judah, though that fear will turn out to imply a positive breakthrough in its attitudes. On that day five Egyptian cities will swear loyalty to the Lord. On that day there will be an altar for the Lord in Egypt and a pillar for the Lord at its border, places to remind Egypt to cry out to the Lord against its oppressors. On that day Egypt will serve the Lord with sacrifices and offerings. Indeed, on that day Egypt and Assyria will serve the Lord together on the basis of the convenient location of Israel between them. On that day the Lord will declare blessing on Egypt as 'my people' and on Assyria as 'my handiwork' as well as on Israel as 'my possession'.

We noted that Isaiah 13 speaks of the earth being made a desolation, but anchors this event in a particular historical context. It is also suggestive that Isaiah 24:21–23 envisages the putting down of supernatural foes happening in two stages. Heavenly and earthly powers will first be imprisoned, then in due course be 'attended to'. The prophecy thus sows a seed that will come to fruition in the idea of the millennium. This two stage process corresponds again to the conviction that the ultimate Day of the Lord can be realised in a way that is interim and not complete. Babylon's defeat, like Egypt's defeat at the Red Sea, constitutes the defeat of earthly and heavenly forces of resistance to God, something like their imprisonment. But the day still lies in the future when God will finally attend to them. As Babylon falls, God begins to reign, in returning to Jerusalem and making it possible for the exiles to do so

(52:7–12). Yet this did not amount to the ultimate assertion of God's sovereignty, and 24:23 sees God finally sovereign.

So . . .

I draw the following conclusions.

First, the main features of Isaian eschatology are these. God intends to lay waste to the earth and to individual peoples, superpowers and others, because of their waywardness and as a means of liberating Israel. God also intends to put down supernatural forces of opposition to God. Indeed, God intends to put down Israel for its waywardness. But God's purpose for Israel will be fulfilled. It will be cleansed, beautified, and brought back to life, it will embody faithfulness and divine blessing, and instead of being humiliated will draw the nations to its God. This will issue in harmony among the nations, who will join in a celebration at God's thus swallowing up death, and join in God's ongoing worship. The worship specifically includes archetypal enemies and superpowers such as Egypt and Assyria. Yet all this does not mean that for Israel life 'in that day' is without pressures or temptations; it does mean these need not overwhelm God's people. Conversely, neither Israel nor the nations wait for the End to experience the End. They know the negative and the positive aspects to the End in their historical experience.

Second, the appropriate responses are these: to walk in Yahweh's light (2:5), living in light of what God intends to do; to exult in but also to be horrified at God's judgment and/or the treachery that warrants it (24:14–16); to urge God to fulfil these promises (26:13–19); and in light of God's coming punishment of the world for its bloodshed, to hide (26:20–21). Isaiah does not indicate that the people of God do anything to bring about the fulfilment of the divine purpose, as Jesus says nothing about us furthering or extending or working for God's kingdom. Their job is to be faithful and let God take care of the rest.

Third, from these prophecies we could not draw up a schedule of what must happen before the End, or at the End. There are several reasons for this. One is that much of the prophecy is in images; one cannot systematise images. Another is that God's plans are worked out in dialogue with human responses. God will not go back on the purposes embodied in these prophecies, but the way they work out is subject to continuous renegotiation.

Fourth, what we do with this Isaian eschatology reflects how we see the relationship of Isaiah to what God did in Christ and to the New Testament. The usual Christian practice is to reinterpret Isaiah in light of (our understanding of) the New Testament and thus to emasculate it. This dishonours the fact that the Holy Spirit was involved in the inspiration of Isaiah. We need rather to accept the Isaian eschatology as the book expounds it, and ask after its implications. It means, for instance, that God's purpose for the Jewish people will be fulfilled (as Paul argues in Rom. 9–11). (It does not follow that one supports the policies of the state of Israel.) That includes drawing the nations, coming to govern them and draw them into harmony, and giving them reason to celebrate. But Isaiah also emphasises judgment on the peoples of the world, superpowers and others, and emphasises that as a reality of the End that we also experience now.

Fifth, insofar as the church is a body that has come to share in Israel's relationship with God (not to replace Israel), it shares in the warnings and the promises of the Isaian eschatology. The church is characterised by similar waywardness to that described in Isaiah 1, and by similar reversals. Its experience is thus that the End is the moment when judgment begins with the household of God (1 Pet. 4:17). We have to ask whether we see that judgment embodied in events such as the demise of the church in Europe and the progressive demise of the church in the USA.

4

Eschatology at the Heart of New Testament Theology

I. Howard Marshall

'Slippery Words' was the title of a series of articles carried by a theological journal back in 1977–78 : they included such terms as 'apocalyptic' and 'myth', and also, as the one assigned to myself, 'eschatology'.[1] It would certainly have seemed impossible at that time to do theology without these slippery terms, as the frequency of their use in books and articles on the Bible amply testified, but they were definitely slippery, usually because they were hard to define or carried multiple possibilities of meaning. Subsequently Robert P. Carroll said that 'In the study of the Hebrew Bible eschatology has been one of the most systematically misleading concepts used by interpreters of the text.'[2] Not an encouraging prelude to an article which is presumably intended by the editors who chose this title to rehabilitate eschatology in the New Testament!

Ignoring the Issue

For much of Christian history the 'last days' were taken to be in the dim and distant future, so that, although it was recognised that the imminent death of every person fast-tracks them into the presence of God at the last judgment, people were not greatly concerned about the details of what was to happen. Consequently, there was a good deal of biblical teaching that people tended to pass over somewhat unconsciously as if it had no relevance to them. This was particularly the case with those surprisingly long accounts of the teaching of Jesus that are found in Matthew 24–25; Mark 13; and Luke 17:20–37; 21, where Jesus appears to give a fairly detailed account of what is going to happen in the future. The very extent of this teaching should perhaps have made people realise that it was important and could not be lightly passed over, but nevertheless it is doubtless still the case that for many people these chapters (and similar material elsewhere) are on the margin of their canon of Scripture and play next to no part in their Christian faith and practice. 'Eschatology', understood to mean 'the biblical teaching about what will happen at the end of the world' or 'the study of what will happen at the end of the world', tends to be ignored.

Forecasting the Future Course of Events

There were two major exceptions to this attitude of neglect. First, defenders of a literalistic understanding of the Bible who took all its teaching seriously had to come to terms with these passages, and there developed a great interest in the literal fulfilment of the prophecies concerning the future. It had two main features. On the one side, there was the problem of making sense of the apparently inconsistent teaching found in the predictive passages in the Old Testament, especially in Daniel, and in the New Testament, including especially Revelation, and numerous schemes were invented to harmonise the different strands of teaching, including the various varieties of dispensationalism. On the other side, it was recognised that the coming of the end was described as 'soon' in various passages, and, since nearly two thousand years had passed since the composition of the prophecies, there was much attempting to recognise 'signs of the times' in contemporary phenomena that could be identified as belonging to the events described in Scripture as harbingers of the end. Despite the clear teaching of Jesus that no person knows the day or the hour (Mk. 13:32), attempts were made to work out a future chronology; my father had a book which showed clearly that the second coming of Christ would take place in the then future year of 1934 (actually the year of my own arrival on the scene, but also of many other folk!), and the Jehovah's Witnesses used to believe that Christ really did return in 1914 (but secretly to heaven, so that there is no way of testing their claim). Aside from the Witnesses this kind of approach has tended to fade away.

Jesus Got it Wrong

Second, there was a major shift by theologians at the end of the nineteenth century. Up till then many were inclined to under-stand the 'kingdom of God' in the teaching of Jesus as either a way of describing the inner, spiritual experience of salvation (so John Calvin) or as the human establishment of a society on earth governed by Christian moral principles (so Albrecht Ritschl or the philosopher Immanuel Kant). Then came Johannes Weiss and Albert Schweitzer, who demonstrated beyond all cavil (a) that the kingdom of God was the central theme in the message of Jesus, and (b) that for him the kingdom of God was not the activity of human beings trying to live in ethical harmony nor some inward experience. Rather it was the cataclysmic interven-tion of God in human history, bringing it to an end and setting up his rule. Moreover, Jesus expected this to happen in the immi-nent future, at the latest 'within this generation' (e.g. Mt. 10:23; Mk. 13:30). For Schweitzer, Jesus failed to see the fulfilment of his hopes and died in disappointment that God had not intervened; for Weiss, Jesus was simply wrong, and we must reluctantly set this piece of his teaching aside and retreat to something like the liberal and moralistic understanding of Christianity for today.

Scholarly Stalemate

The lasting result of the Weiss-Schweitzer movement was to make scholars recognise that *the kingdom of God, understood in this way as God's imminent action, was absolutely central to the mission of Jesus.* Put jargonistically, the centre of Jesus' message was 'escha-tology'. What was not so clear was whether their interpretation of his teaching was correct. At this point an English scholar, C.H. Dodd, entered the debate and demonstrated that there were a number of places in the teaching of Jesus where he spoke and acted as if the kingdom of God had already come rather than being something about to happen in the future. When Jesus says 'the kingdom of God has come near' (Mk. 1:15; Lk. 10:9, 11) or 'If I drive out demons by the finger of God, then the kingdom of God has come upon you' (Lk. 11:20) or 'the kingdom of God is in your midst' (Lk. 17:21), he appears to be speaking about the kingdom as something that is already happening. It is perhaps impossible to separate rigidly between the kingdom of God as the sovereign rule of God and as the community or territory over which he rules, but sayings where the former translation is more appropriate help us to recognise that God can be powerfully at work even though a kingdom in the conventional sense of the term is hard to discern.

Dodd's interpretation was not universally accepted. Its obvious weakness was that it could not account satisfactorily for those sayings of Jesus that referred to the kingdom of God and accompanying events in the future tense (e.g. Mk. 9:1), and Dodd's attempt to reinterpret them as timeless utterances ('accommodations of language') was not persuasive. Advocates of the Weiss-Schweitzer line also questioned his interpretations of the present sayings of Jesus and argued that they too referred to the future. But their own reinterpretations of these sayings were also not convincing.

So there were these two positions. The Weiss-Schweitzer one came to be named 'thorough-going eschatology', meaning that *all* of the teaching of Jesus about the kingdom referred consistently to its manifestation in the (near) future. The Dodd line was then dubbed 'realised eschatology', meaning that the coming of the kingdom had already being 'realised' (i.e. was taking place) in the here and now.

Getting the Balance Right

Stalemate? Not quite. Another German scholar, W.G. Kümmel, wrote a decisive technical monograph in which he demonstrated pretty convincingly that both sides were right in what they affirmed and wrong in what they denied. Jesus could and did speak about the kingdom both as already present and as yet to come. Put like this, it sounds paradoxical, and indeed it is difficult to avoid some element of paradox in it. But other significant scholars, including G.R. Beasley-Murray, G.E. Ladd and R. Schnackenburg, have all upheld Kümmel's broad conclusions and sought for ways of explaining how Jesus could speak in this paradoxical manner. In essence, they agree that what God was doing in the mission of Jesus was establishing his kingdom here in this world, so that Jesus could speak of it as already present and active in and through his own work as God's agent. At the same time, the kingdom has not yet come in its fulness, and Jesus looked forward to God bringing this about in the future.

Victory already achieved

Various ways of expressing this 'already . . . not yet . . .' have been suggested. The most helpful is perhaps that developed by O. Cullmann who drew an analogy with the decisive event on the western front in the Second World War. In 1944 the American and British forces landed in Normandy and began the push that led to the capitulation of the Nazi invaders of France the following year. The day of the landing was code-named 'D-Day' ('Deliverance Day'); the day of the surrender was celebrated as 'VE-Day' ('Victory in Europe Day'). The war was not finally won until the latter day, but in reality the decisive action that led inexorably to inevitable defeat of the enemy was the successful landing in France. One could say that the war was as good as won in Normandy, and all that remained to do was mopping up the enemy and awaiting their recognition that they were defeated. So too the mission of Jesus, culminating in his death and resurrection, was the decisive event in the establishment of the kingdom of God, and from then onwards the process of consolidating that victory continues until the end when Christ will come again and the power of evil will be totally overcome.

A new kind of king and kingdom

The action of God in the mission of Jesus was not what people expected at the time. Popular ideas of how God should act were generally military in character, involving the forcible deliverance of the Jewish people from their Roman conquerors (the Herod dynasty was a puppet of the Romans and Pontius Pilate was one of a line of direct Roman rulers). Jesus, however, went about 'doing good and healing all who were under the power of the devil' (Acts 10:38), and consequently did not look in any way like a conventional king. Certainly the language of kingship and messiahship (a term for the future king who would establish God's rule) was in the air and people wondered whether Jesus fitted the bill, and indeed he said and did things that suggested that he saw himself as the Messiah, so that when he was put to death, it was as 'The king of the Jews'; nevertheless, he was very much a king incognito. It would be fair to say that he radically altered the popular understanding of such terms as 'Messiah' and 'kingdom' by his performance of the role. Hence, one of the main difficulties in recognising that the kingdom had come in the mission of Jesus is met by the realisation that Jesus was radically redefining what it meant.

How long, O Lord?

The teaching of Jesus and of his followers after him contains the hope of the full coming of the end of history as we know it, with the winding up of history, the last judgment and the transformation of the universe. This hope is envisaged as being fulfilled in the near future, although it is fair to say that a precise period within which it must happen is never delineated. The idea that world history would go on for at least another couple of millennia was outside the horizon of the early Christians. We therefore face in an even more massive way the objection of the people who appear in 2 Peter, asking 'Where is this "coming" he promised? Ever since our ancestors died, everything goes on as it has since the beginning of creation' (2 Pet. 3:4). Has there been such a long passage of time with nothing happening that the hope should be abandoned as false? Does it make sense for God to start something that has still not come to completion? Should we say of him, 'This person began to build and wasn't able to finish'? (Lk. 14:30). Does the long lapse of time signify that what we thought was the arrival of the kingdom of God in the mission of Jesus has been wrongly interpreted, and Jesus was nothing more than a good teacher who was deluded (like his followers) into thinking that he was God's agent to change the world?

This is perhaps one of the two most powerful objections to the truth of Christianity (the other, of course, being the problem of evil, which is perhaps ultimately the same problem – why doesn't God act more quickly to bring an end to suffering and death?) Peter answers it by pointing out that God's timescale may be different from ours ('a thousand ages in thy sight are like an evening gone') and that he graciously delays the final end 'not wanting anyone to perish, but everyone to come to repentance' (2 Pet. 3:9).

God's ongoing action

These points show that the concept of a kingdom that is both come and still to come is a defensible one. Another German scholar came up with the phrase 'self-realising eschatology' to characterise the interpretation that has been expounded here: an eschatology that is in process of becoming reality.[3] What this amounts to is that there is an ongoing process that is prophesied in the Old Testament, fulfilled in the mission of Jesus, and still to be consummated in the future, through which the dominion of evil over the world is overthrown, its captives set free, and God's new world of love, justice and peace fully and finally established.

Eschatology and Ourselves

On the assumption that this is the correct interpretation of the biblical teaching, we can now develop some aspects of it further.

The last days have already begun

'Eschatology' properly means teaching about the last things (or study of them). But in phrases like 'self-realising eschatology' it has come to mean (by a natural extension of language) the last things themselves rather than teaching about them. Consequently, what we are talking about in this essay, and this book, are the events that make up the end of human history with all its evils as well as all its positive achievements, and the crucial point that is being made is that these events are already taking place. This is a point made clearly in the New Testament where, for example, on the Day of Pentecost Peter sees what is happening as fulfilment of the prophecy by Joel which says: 'In the last days, God says, I will pour out my Spirit on all people' (Acts 2:17). If you look up Joel you will find that he actually says, 'And afterward I will pour out my Spirit on all people' (Joel 2:28). In common with other early Christians Peter reworded his citation of Scripture to bring out more clearly what he took to be the intended meaning. Here his consciousness that what is happening is part of the last events is unambiguously expressed. Similarly the Letter to the Hebrews begins by contrasting how 'God spoke to our ancestors through the prophets' with the way in which 'in these last days he has spoken to us by his Son' (Heb. 1:1–2). The end-time has begun. History can be broken up into two, the period of promise (BC) and the period of fulfilment (AD). Admittedly it has been suggested that early Christians, disappointed that the End showed little sign of coming near, divided time into three periods, the period of promise (from creation to John the Baptist), the middle of time (the mission of Jesus), and the ongoing period of the church (from Jesus on into a distant and unknown future), but this scheme does not do justice to the references to living in the last days and to the lively hope of the second coming (or parousia) of Christ that persists throughout the New Testament.

The essential point, then, is that the coming of Jesus marks the beginning of the last days.

God's action – and ours

A second vital point is that to talk of 'eschatology' is to talk about what God is doing. It is the establishment of God's kingdom by his action. There is something of a paradox here in that the stress throughout the New Testament is on what God does, whether as Father, Son or Holy Spirit. He plans, takes the initiative, and acts. We pray 'Your kingdom come', which is a prayer for God to do something. Nevertheless, the fact remains that God normally works through his people, and therefore it has been said that the Lord's Prayer really implies 'Your kingdom come in and through me [and the rest of your people]'. There is a tension between:

> Rise up, O men of God,
> Have done with lesser things;
> Give heart and soul and mind and strength,
> To serve the King of kings.
>
> *(W.P. Merrill)*

and

> Sit down, O men of God,
> His kingdom he will bring,
> Whenever it may please his will:
> You cannot do a thing.
>
> *(Anon.)*

Future blessings now

Perhaps the main point that emerges is that realised or self-realising eschatology means that we can experience now the blessings of the world to come because God has already started to bring his kingdom in. We are in the position of those who live 'between the times'. The new world has begun, but the old world still continues, and therefore our experience of the world to come is limited by our situation in this world of flesh, corruption and temptation. Our life is shaped by the cross and resurrection of Jesus, this means that we do know the power of his resurrection but at the same time need always to be conformed to his sufferings. There is a technical/jargonistic name for this, and it is 'eschatological tension'. It means that we truly experience the powers of the new age here and now, but we do not experience them to the full; we are truly redeemed from sin, but we have not fully escaped from it. It is the kind of experience depicted by Paul in the opening chapters of 2 Corinthians with their remarkable expression of the tensions of the Christian life. What is going on is that the new life is already at work within us, but it is within our frail, corruptible bodies that this work of renewal is secretly going on. We are always bearing in the body the dying of Jesus that the life of Jesus may also be visible in our corruptible bodies.

Consequently we are to avoid the defeatism which sees only the decay and powerlessness that we experience, but equally we are to avoid the triumphalism and unreality which thinks that we already enjoy full perfection and deliverance. These dangers can be seen in the early church where some of the Corinthian Christians thought that they were already reigning with Christ and Paul had to say, 'How I wish that you really had begun to reign so that we also might reign with you!' (1 Cor. 4:8) and remind them that the lot of the apostles was rather different.

Jesus and the future

Why, then, do the Gospels record Jesus as spending so much time talking about the future? The forty years after his death were a period of increasing insecurity and conflict in Judaea, culminating in the horrendous siege and destruction of Jerusalem by the Roman armies in AD 70. This and other crises were in danger of being seen as the last manifestations of evil before the final intervention of God in world history, and it was necessary to warn people against this natural assumption that the end of the world was at hand and to prepare them for an uncertain, possibly lengthy time ahead during which their faithfulness to God and their trust in his promises would be tried to the limit. They were instructed not to be misled by false hopes – such as the appearances of people claiming to be the Messiah that still happen today – and to hold fast to their faith in God. There would be many discouragements, including persecution and betrayal, and they would need to be prayerful and watchful at all times (cf. Lk. 21:3–36). The end is always near and yet it may not come as soon as we would like. When you walk along a path on the edge of a cliff, you may have to walk a long way before you fall off the edge, but that danger is present at every step of the way; so too the second coming of Christ and the end of history are near in that they are genuine possibilities at any time, but God may lengthen the period of waiting beyond what we expect.

A securely based hope

A quotation that I have found helpful is:

> Our religion survived the disappointment [of the failure of Christ to return as quickly as people hoped] because it was primarily a possession and only secondarily a hope.[4]

The writer is making the point that, when hope seems in vain because time goes on and nothing seems to change, we do not give up believing and hoping because our religion is founded upon something that has already happened and something that we already possess, namely our salvation in Christ, and our hope depends upon the assurance that the God 'who began a good work in us will carry it on to completion until the day of Christ Jesus' (Phil. 1:6). Contrast this with the kind of hope for something to happen in the future which is more like the expression of a wish without a basis. '"Cheer up", they said, "Things could be worse"; so I cheered up, and, sure enough, things did get worse.' Ordinary hope is often nothing more than the expression of a longing without any reason to suppose that it will be satisfied; Christian hope is rooted in two things, what God has done for us and the fact of his faithfulness. So it is right to say that our religion is primarily based on what has already happened.

But once we have established that priority, there is a significant place for the future. Indeed, one of the various definitions of 'eschatological' (I said that it was slippery) is that it refers to the kind of existence that is determined by the future. Contrast two attitudes to life, that of the person who is still suffering from the effects of an accident and each day is constrained by the ongoing problems that it causes and that of the young woman who is counting down the days until her wedding and whose daily life is constrained by what is going to happen and the need to prepare for it. On this definition of the term, our present life should be shaped and encouraged by what lies ahead, by the fulfilment of the purposes of God for his people and his world and for us within that company. It is the attitude of Paul who describes the one thing that he does: 'Forgetting what is behind and straining toward what is ahead, I press on toward the goal to win the prize for which God has called me heavenward in Christ Jesus' (Phil. 3:13–14). The prize is, of course, to know Jesus Christ fully, to see him face to face, and the race is like the caucus race defined in *Alice in Wonderland* as one in which all the runners win and therefore all receive prizes, by contrast with the competitive 'I'm going to get more than you' attitude of the sinful, selfish world.

Conclusion

Eschatology at the heart of New Testament theology? Well, yes, provided that we recognise that it is there as the indispensable partner to what God has already done in Christ and what he has already given to his people. Or (which is another way of putting it) provided we recognise that we are talking about 'self-realising eschatology' and the decisive eschatological event, on which everything depends, took place nearly two thousand years ago on a hill called Golgotha and in a nearby tomb. Throughout this essay I have tended to write in terms of the 'kingdom of God', which is how Jesus expressed the matter. But the kingdom is bound up integrally with the person of the King, and therefore in fact we are talking about the Jesus Christ who came to earth to establish God's rule, who even now is our living and active King and Lord (even though we cannot see him and even though the world is not fully under his control), and who will come again gloriously to bring about the full establishment of God's rule in peace and justice. Reduced to its simplest terms eschatology tells us that the Jesus Christ who will come again has already come as our Saviour and is present with us: the last things have begun and will not be left uncompleted, the 'last Adam' (1 Cor. 15:45) has already come to reclaim God's world, and he will come again 'to bring unity to all things in heaven and on earth' (Eph. 1:10).

The Christ who has come will come! 'Amen. Come, Lord Jesus.'[5]
(Rev. 22:20).

5

Eschatology in the Book of Revelation

Richard Bauckham

Readings of Revelation

Unfortunately, the book of Revelation is probably best known as a happy hunting-ground for millenarian enthusiasts who find the events of their own time plotted in marvellous detail in its prophecies and can thereby predict the precise course of future events up to and including the rapture, the second coming, and the millennium. In the United States, in particular, this kind of interpretation is as popular as it ever was, perhaps more so. But similar kinds of interpretation – identifying current events as specific fulfilments of Revelation's prophecies and thereby concluding that the final events of history are soon to come – have flourished in most periods and places of Christian history. The sheer variety of such readings down the centuries should make one cautious of supposing that now, at last, we can get it right. Is this kind of prediction really what the book is for?

People sceptical of this kind of approach, often those who have imbibed it from their own church contexts but have become disillusioned with it, often give up on the book of Revelation altogether. However, literalistic prediction is not by any means the only way that the book has been read by Christians of the past. Revelation is a book that in all centuries has inspired the martyrs, nourished the imagination of visionaries, artists and hymn-writers, resourced prophetic critiques of oppression and corruption in state and church, sustained hope and resistance in the most hopeless situations. Both the Christian mainstream and the prophetic minorities who have often reminded the church of its forgotten vocation owe a great deal to Revelation.

So we should not be put off too quickly. Reading Revelation with profit can be demanding but it is also richly rewarding. We have to learn how to read it. The reason it is opaque or forbidding to many modern readers is that it is unlike anything else they are used to reading. Readers of the New Testament become familiar with gospels and apostolic letters, but Revelation is like nothing else in the New Testament. An important first step is therefore to ask what sort of literature it is.

We approach different types of literature with different expectations and different mindsets that enable us to read them appropriately. We do this unthinkingly with genres we're familiar with: novels, biographies, travel writing, textbooks and so forth. With unfamiliar genres, like some of those in the Bible, we have to do some deliberate thinking about how such a kind of literature works and requires to be read. We have to learn its conventions. What sort of literature is the book of Revelation? There are three good answers to this question, and all three can help us know how to read it. Revelation is a *prophecy*, an *apocalypse* and a *circular letter*.

The Climax of Prophecy

Revelation situates itself in the tradition of biblical prophecy, in continuity with the prophetic books of the Old Testament. In fact it presents itself as the culmination of the whole biblical prophetic tradition (see especially 10:7). It stands appropriately at the end of the whole Bible, summing up the way the whole of Scripture points prophetically to the eschatological future.

For this reason its text is a closely woven fabric of allusions to the Old Testament, and is largely unintelligible without awareness of this essentially inter-textual character. This is one

major clue to understanding the book: we must acquaint ourselves at least to some extent with Revelation's Old Testament
sources and observe the way in which they are taken up into
the book's own message. The author, the prophet John, sees
the unity of Old Testament prophecy in its hope for the coming of God's universal kingdom on earth, and so he gathers up
all those strands of Old Testament expectation which point to
the eschatological future, focusing them in a fresh vision of the
way they are to be fulfilled. (Note, as just one example, the
way the oracle against Babylon in chapters 18 – 19 echoes
every one of the Old Testament's prophecies against that city,
as well as its two main oracles against Tyre.) As a Christian
prophet, he reads Old Testament prophecy in the light of the
beginning of its fulfilment in the life, death and resurrection of
Jesus, but he also interprets Jesus and his church by means of
Old Testament prophecy. It is through Jesus' way of cross and
resurrection that God's kingdom will come.

However, Revelation does not just gather up previous
prophecy; it offers a new prophetic revelation as to the way in
which God's kingdom is to come (1:1–2; 10:1–11; 22:6). This is
that the Christian churches are called to participate in Jesus'
victory over evil by following his path of witness even to the
point of death. This will be the great conflict between God's
kingdom and the worldly powers that oppose God. The conflict is for the allegiance of the nations, and John's new revelation is full of hope that by this means of victory over evil,
witness to the truth in the face of the illusions and delusions of
idolatry and even at the price of life, the nations may be converted to the worship of the true God.

Biblical prophecy has three main elements. First, it begins
with discernment. The Spirit enables the prophet to perceive
the real truth of the present situation, exposing deceit and misleading appearances, revealing how things really stand in the
sight of God. Language of truth and deceit is prominent in
Revelation, which is centrally concerned with the issue of truth
in the public world and the way the fabric of lies can be dispersed so that people may see the truth. Secondly, prophecy
includes prediction. Revelation reads and contributes to the
whole biblical prophetic tradition as prophecy of the coming

of God's kingdom in all the world. Readers learn how the kingdom will come, with an emphasis on the sort of happenings that will lead to the kingdom, rather than necessarily a literal sequence of particular events.

Thirdly and importantly, prophecy includes a demand for response. Biblical prophecy is not deterministic or fatalistic. It does not predict a future for which we can only passively wait, but a future that engages our response and contribution now. Doom-laden oracles are warnings, utopian visions are invitations (see, e.g., 9:20–21; 13:9–10; 14:12; 18:4; 19:9; 21:6–8; 22:17).

The Apocalypse of Jesus Christ

Here we must forget the way the word 'apocalypse' has come to mean something like a coming catastrophe. The Greek word *apokalypsis* (used in 1:1), of which the book's usual English title 'Revelation' is simply a translation, means 'unveiling' or 'revelation'. It refers to a type of literature, to which Revelation belongs, in which a prophet or visionary receives from heaven a revelation of hidden mysteries. In the case of Revelation the disclosure is about the course of history and its outcome, and so there is no difficulty in thinking of this book as an apocalypse in close continuity with Old Testament prophecy. With regard to literary forms (such as visions and oracles) it draws on the latter as well as the conventions of the apocalyptic literature.

Revelation shares important features with many of the apocalypses, such as a concern with the contradiction between God's rule over his creation and the apparently unchecked dominance of evil in the world, the hope of an impending final resolution of history in which God will bring eternal good out of all the evils of this world and renew his creation, the use of symbolic visions and more or less fantastic imagery to fund alternative perceptions of the world, its history and future.

The apocalypses are a literature which deploys the theological imagination to draw its readers into different ways of seeing things, and the most important sense in which Revelation resembles them is in its aim to 'reveal' or 'unveil' the truth of things as seen from God's heavenly perspective. It speaks to a world whose imaginative view of the world is controlled by the power and propaganda of the dominant political and economic system. John in vision is taken up to heaven so that he can envision the same world from the perspective of God's kingdom, which means both from the perspective of heaven, as God sees it, and from the perspective of the final future, as God's purposes intend, the final coming of God's kingdom in all creation, which John foresees.

In this way Revelation liberates its readers from the dominant worldview. It exposes the idolatry that from top to bottom infuses and inspires the political, economic and social realities in which its readers live, and calls them to uncompromising Christian witness to the true God who despite earthly appearances is sovereign. By seeing the world differently, readers are enabled to live and to die differently, as followers of Jesus' way of faithful witness to God even to the point of death. They are empowered to live their allegiance to a different way of being the world, the kingdom of God, and to live in hope of the coming of God's kingdom as the ultimate truth of the world which must prevail over all that presently opposes God's rule. Revelation's purpose is to enable its readers to continue to pray and to live Jesus' prayer: 'Your kingdom come.'

An important element here is the powerful visual imagery of the book. It composes a symbolic world into which the readers are invited to enter imaginatively. It has the effect of purging their imagination of ways of seeing their world derived from the dominant ideology, and reshaping their perception of the world by means of alternative images. By re-visioning the world from the heavenly perspective, they are enabled to resist the dominant vision of the world, and to live for God and his kingdom rather than for the beast and his kingdom. The clash of perspectives – heavenly and earthly, God's and the beast's – on reality is signalled in Revelation by constant reference to truth and deceit. The visions enable God's people to see the truth of God, to see through the lies of the beast and so to witness to God in the world.

A Letter to the Seven Churches

Among prophecies and apocalypses, Revelation is distinctive in that it is also a circular letter written to seven specific churches in the Roman province of Asia (1:4, 11). The seven messages to the churches in chapters 2 and 3 are not really, as they are often called, 'letters,' but prophetic oracles addressed to each church. It is the whole book of Revelation that is a circular letter, addressed to all seven churches, and the seven messages in chapters 2 and 3 comprise each church's introduction to the rest of the book. This means that we must take the first-century historical context of its first readers seriously in reading the whole book, just as we do when reading, for example, Paul's letters to specific churches. The whole book was an urgent and relevant message to them, not a coded prediction decipherable only by later generations. Of course, like much biblical prophecy, the book also transcends that immediate context and speaks also to us, but not in a way that bypasses its first readers altogether.

The seven messages graphically sketch for us the various contexts of the book's first readers, as seen with John's prophetic insight. We are shown Christian communities living in various degrees of conflict and compromise with Roman power and the Roman political religion, the business and social life of the cities with its inextricable associations with idolatrous religion, and the local Jewish synagogues. We find that the readers are by no means all poor, oppressed and persecuted; many are complacent, compromising and close to apostasy, when judged by the demands of faithful witness to God's kingdom as Revelation understands these. To these diverse readers in their various contexts, Revelation points the way of faithful witness. To each group of readers is given the call 'to conquer,' that is, to engage through suffering witness in the great conflict with the idolatrous world system that is described in the central portion of the book, and thereby to inherit the promises of God in the new world to which God's purposes are assuredly leading.

While the seven messages speak directly to carefully characterised circumstances, the fact that they are seven (the number

of completeness) also means that these churches stand repre-
sentatively for all churches. Readers in other churches (then or
now) may take the diversity as representative of the different
kinds of situations to which the prophecy may speak. The messages may be alternative introductions to the rest of the book for
us too. But we should not, as is sometimes done in preaching,
detach the seven messages, as though they were not integrally
part of the whole book. They are not free-standing, but keys to
reading the rest of Revelation.

That Revelation is a letter to its first readers highlights a feature essential to appropriate reading of the book today.
Although this prophecy concerns the final victory of God's
rule over all evil and the final completion of God's purpose in
the new creation of all things, it portrays the coming of God's
kingdom in direct relation to the situation of its first readers.
The eschatological future is envisaged in terms of its impact on
the present, so that the first readers might see how to live in
their own situation in the light of the coming kingdom. This
means that we cannot ignore the situation of the first readers if
we are to perceive correctly the continuing relevance of
Revelation to later readers. We need to bear in mind throughout both the original context to which it first spoke and the
way it continues to illuminate the truth of new situations in the
light of God's kingdom and to point the way to the eschatological future for us later readers too.

Reading the Imagery

I have already mentioned the way the profusion of visionary
imagery in Revelation creates a symbolic world that engages
its readers' imagination. It is far from being just a code to be
deciphered so as to yield a matter-of-fact sequence of future
events. We need to read the images for the meaning they
evoke, and often this entails both reference to their Old
Testament sources and some appreciation of the resonances
they would have had for the first readers.

Take, for example, the descriptions of the plagues of the
seven trumpets (8:6–9:21) and the seven bowls (16:1–21). We

should note at once that these form a highly schematised literary pattern that points the meaning of the kinds of events that form one aspect of the coming of God's kingdom. The content of the judgments suggest, among many other things, the plagues of Egypt that accompanied the Exodus, the fall of Jericho to seven trumpet blasts from Joshua's army, the army of locusts depicted in Joel's prophecy, the revelation of God at mount Sinai, as well as the fear of invasion from the Parthian empire to the east that was very real in the Roman empire of John's time, the earthquakes to which the cities of Asia Minor, including those of the seven churches, were often subject, and very possibly the eruption of Vesuvius that had recently terrified the Mediterranean world.

Once we begin to feel these rich resonances of the imagery we find that to look here for predictions of nuclear warfare, for example, is simply beside the point. The point is to explore the meaning of the divine judgment that is impending on the sinful world. Part of that point is that judgments in themselves do not produce repentance and conversion to the true God (9:20–21; 16:9, 11, 20); what is needed for that purpose is the prophetic witness the church must bear, even to the point of death (11:3–13; 15:2–4).

The last of the seven bowls results in the fall of the great city of Babylon in an earthquake of unprecedented proportions (16:17–21). If we took this as literal prediction, we should soon find it contradicted by later images of the downfall of Babylon. In 17:16, Babylon, now portrayed as a harlot, is stripped, devoured and burned by the beast and the ten kings. The traditional punishment of a harlot is here superimposed on the image of a city sacked and razed to the ground by an army. Chapter 18 extends the image of a city besieged and burned to the ground (see especially 18:8), but we are also told both that the site of the city becomes the haunt of desert creatures (18:2) and that the smoke from her burning continues to ascend forever (19:3).

On the literal level these images are inconsistent with each other, but on the level of theological meaning, conveyed by the allusions to the Old Testament and to first-century myth, they offer complementary perspectives on the meaning of the fall of the metropolis of the world system. The earthquake (16:17–21) is that which accompanies the theophany of the holy God coming to judgment. The sacking of Babylon by the beast and his allies alludes to the late first-century myth of the return of the emperor Nero from the east to destroy Rome. It is an image of the self-destructive nature of evil, which on the level of theological meaning is not inconsistent with the idea of the destruction of evil by divine judgment but presents it under another aspect. The fire of 17:16 becomes in chapter 18 the fire of divine judgment, of which the paradigmatic example in the Old Testament was the destruction of Sodom and Gomorrah. Like an apocalyptic Sodom sunk in the eternal lake of fire and sulphur, Babylon's smoke ascends forever (cf. Gen. 19:28; Rev. 14:10–11; 19:20). The desolation of Babylon as a haunt of desert creatures evokes Old Testament pictures of the fate of both Edom and Babylon, the two great enemies of the people of God in much biblical prophecy. All this – and more – makes up a wonderfully varied but coherent evocation of the biblical and theological meaning of the divine judgment John's prophecy pronounces on Rome, but if we try to read it as literal prediction of how that judgment will occur we turn it in a confused muddle and miss the real point.

The Story

Revelation is a complex narrative, but we should notice that the sequence is that of John's reception and recounting of his visions, not of the events in past and future that the visions depict. There is a sequence implied in the way the kingdom of God will come, but it is not necessarily the order in which John's visions proceed.

We have no space here for a full account of how the story of the revelation unfolds, but a very simplified sketch may assist readers approaching the book for the first time. After a prologue (1:1–8), John recounts a vision of Christ among the lampstands, which signify the churches, and relays a prophetic message from him to each of the seven churches (1:9–2:29). The messages are designed to fit these communities for 'conquering', that is, to take part in the metaphorical holy war through which the kingdom of God is to come. The seven promises to the conquerors at the ends of the messages correspond to a similar promise in 21:7, given by God at the beginning of the book's concluding vision of the new creation. Promises to those who 'conquer' thus frame the book, and pose the question: how does God's purpose get from the situations of the churches in chapters 2 – 3 to the coming of the new creation in chapter 21?

In chapter 4 John is taken up to God's throne-room in heaven, from which God rules the cosmos. Here God's rule is uncontested, but very soon, in chapter 5, we face the issue: how will God's kingdom come on earth, as it already is in heaven? The answer Revelation gives is twofold. The first part of the answer is given immediately: the Lamb has conquered. He has won the victory in the Messianic battle against evil, but he has done so by faithful witness to the truth of God even to the point of sacrificial death. Nevertheless the full outworking of this victory remains future, and how it is to be achieved is the content of the newly revelatory feature of John's prophecy, symbolised by the scroll with seven seals.

The content of the scroll is not revealed until it has been opened (8:1) and received by John who ingests it so that it may become the subject of his own prophetic message from Jesus Christ for the world (10:1–11). Meantime the intervening chapters (6 – 9) depict the kinds of judgments that biblical prophecy has expected, showing that these judgments achieve only destruction, not repentance and conversion. They are not themselves the second part of the answer to the question how God's kingdom will come, but this answer is already suggested by the interlude that interrupt the sequence of the seal-openings (chapter 7) and expounded more clearly in the interlude that separates the seventh from the sixth trumpet-blasts (10:1–11:13). It is the content of the scroll and is given a preliminary exposition in chapter 11. The answer is that, just as the Lamb's victory was won by faithful witness to the truth of God even to the point of death, so it must be continued by the followers of the Lamb in the same way.

Unlike warning judgments, this suffering witness of the church will result in the conversion of the nations (11:3–13).

But it would be better to say that John's prophecy actually leaves the outcome open. It juxtaposes, without reconciling, a vision of the nations turning to God, as the Old Testament prophets had foreseen (15:2–4; cf. 21:3, 24), and the expectation of final judgment on unrepentant humanity (chapter 16; cf. 21:8, 27). The stark alternatives with which the church's witness to truth presents the nations are simply posed.

The image of holy war continues through chapters 12 – 14, in which the content of the scroll is further described. It is the war between the three monsters and the followers of the Lamb, and the question here posed is: whose is the real victory? Two quite different perspectives on the same event – the death of the martyrs – are presented. The brute force of the beast, aided by a deceitful ideology, seems irresistible and secures the worship of the whole world. But the true victors are the martyrs, who win victory not by force but by faithful witness carried to the point of death. This is a victory, not by the standards of the world, but from the heavenly perspective that John's prophecy brings to bear. The witness of the martyrs can be the point of illumination where God's truth breaks through the lies of the beast.

In chapters 17:1–22:5 John's visions shift to presenting the outcome of the war. Here the emphasis is on the transition from the dominance of evil to the coming of God's kingdom. It is a story of judgment not for its own sake but as the necessary precondition for renewal. The corrupt city of Babylon must be replaced by the New Jerusalem, God's city (17:1–19:9; 21:2). Here we see most clearly how the prophecy brings the final future – the triumph over evil that must, in God's purpose, be the outcome of history – into immediate confrontation with the current realities of John's contemporaries in the Roman empire. The coming new creation (21:1–4) is the fulfilment of all God's promises for his whole creation. It is a vision of the world transformed by the immediate presence of God. It is an overturning of all the negative features of this present world (21:4, 27; 22:3) and the fulfilment of all the positive features (21:24–26). This new world depicted in the closing chapters of the last book of the Bible is in part a return to the paradise lost in Genesis 3 (Rev. 22:2), but it is also much more: the assumption of all the true glory of human life into the eternal glory of God (21:22–26; 22:3–5).

To some degree we could recognise fulfilment of John's prophecy in the witness of the martyrs in the early centuries, the growth of the church as a result especially of their witness to the point of death, and the fall of pagan Rome. But, of course, like all historical fulfilments of the church's prayer for the coming of God's kingdom, this had its limitations and its ambiguities. As in the case of the Old Testament prophecies taken up into Revelation's visions, the prophecy of Revelation itself retains a surplus of expectation beyond every partial fulfilment. It continues to point us to the still future coming of the kingdom. It can bring that final outcome of God's purposes also into confrontation with our own present and summon the churches of our time to 'conquer' through continuing the faithful witness to the truth of God that Jesus himself bore. One factor of special relevance to our time may be Revelation's transmutation of the violent language of holy war into the meaning of steadfast non-violent witness.

The epilogue to the book (22:6–21) leaves us with a promise and a prayer to appropriate for ourselves. The promise is Jesus' promise to come (22:7, 12, 20) and the prayer is for his coming (21:20). Since the coming of Jesus at the end is the focus of all God's promises for the redemption and completion of his whole creation, we could call it the promise of everything, while the prayer for Jesus' coming is the prayer for everything. It is the one prayer that includes all other prayers we could offer. The church's continued praying of that prayer keeps it aligned in hope and witness to the coming of God's kingdom in the whole of creation.

Hopeful Church

6

Eschatology in the Church Fathers

T.A. Noble

Eschatology, the hope of the End of 'this present evil age', arose in Judaism. In the earliest Christian church, still seen as a sect of Judaism, it took a paradoxical form, that the age to come had in some sense *already* come in Jesus, and yet this was still a form of the Jewish hope. But the Christian Fathers who inherited this eschatology, the bishops and teachers of the church in the first five centuries, were Greeks and Romans. How was Christian eschatology changed by that cultural transition from Judaism to the Hellenism of the Graeco-Roman world?

It is already evident in the New Testament that the preaching of the gospel was adapted in the mission to the gentiles. When Peter preached on the day of Pentecost, he addressed himself (according to Acts 2) to Jewish people drawn from the Dispersion, Greek-speaking Jews from every part of the known world. Peter could assume the common heritage of Jewish eschatology, and quoted Joel's vision of 'the last days' when the Spirit would be poured out. He linked this directly to the resurrection of Jesus of Nazareth. David, no less, had prophesied that his descendant, the Messiah, would be raised from the dead. The expectation of general resurrection at the end of the age was part of the mental furniture of most Jews, but Peter's proclamation was that *already* 'this Jesus whom you crucified' had been raised from the dead, and exalted to the place of authority at the right hand of God. This gospel was eschatological through and through.

But once Paul and Barnabas had been set apart for the mission to the gentiles (Acts 13), the gospel had to be re-expressed. The eschatology of Jewish apocalyptic was not part of the Hellenistic framework of thought, and the restoration of the kingdom to Israel would mean nothing to Greeks. The gospel had to be preached in a culture where ancient Greek and Roman mythology jostled with mystery and fertility religions from the east, deeply ingrained superstition and occult practices, magic, sooth-saying, and cults of various kinds, including the worship of the emperor as 'lord' and 'saviour'. This Graeco-Roman society was characterised by a lack of hope. Through all its many cults and religions there ran a deep-seated pessimism and fatalism, a consciousness of being bound by fate and death, and what we may call a deep 'spiritualism'. The mainstream philosophical tradition was at one with popular religions in devaluing the physical life of the body. It was the human soul or spirit which was in some sense 'divine' or 'immortal', and salvation from pain and from the death of the physical body was thought to be found in some kind of 'spiritual' experience. This could give the only possible hope – escape from the life of the body and this material world.

Already then, in the gentile mission of New Testament times, the preaching of the gospel brought the Christian adaptation of Jewish eschatology into a completely different cultural context. Instead of the cyclic worldview of the pagan world, the gospel proclaimed the Eschaton, that is, the End of the present evil age. The Son of God, identified with the Logos (a familiar term in Hellenistic thought), had become incarnate in human flesh, had been crucified for our sins, and had been raised from the dead in order to be the One by whom God would judge the world. The Christian hope was still the coming of the kingdom, but this was now more clearly seen in cosmic terms as the coming of a new heaven and a new earth in which the resurrected saints would live. This would all be inaugurated by the *parousia* or 'coming', the second advent of the Lord Jesus for which the church looked expectantly.

The continuing struggle to keep true to the eschatological expectations of the New Testament church, and yet to articulate this in ways which made sense in Hellenistic culture, continued to characterise the teaching of the bishops and theologians of the church over the next five centuries. Their understanding of eschatology was never presented in any comprehensive and systematic form, but it will help to keep track of the developing doctrine to see a tension between two tendencies running through their writings. On the one hand, there were those whose starting point was the gospel and the Scriptures and who generally tended to emphasise an understanding of the Christian hope which was both spiritual and physical. On the other hand, there were those who were equally passionate in their loyalty to the church and the Scriptures, but who were prepared nonetheless to deny what appeared to be crudely literal ideas and to move toward a more 'spiritual' interpretation in order to commend the gospel to the culture.

The Apostolic Fathers

The 'apostolic fathers', the generation of Christian teachers immediately after the apostolic age, give us significant clues about the eschatological beliefs in the first half of the second Christian century. Four moments may be distinguished in their expectation: the *parousia* or coming of the Lord, the general resurrection, the judgment, and the end of the present world order.

The Didache, an anonymous manual of church order, finishes with the warning of false prophets to come, culminating in a world deceiver and a fiery trial in which many will fall away from the faith. Eventually the general resurrection will come (apparently only of Christians), and the Lord will return.[1] Clement, the bishop of Rome, in writing to the Corinthians, refers to the coming of the Lord and the general resurrection. He gives as illustrations the annual sprouting of the grain and the rising of the phoenix from its ashes.[2] Ignatius, bishop of Antioch, the church which had sent out Paul and Barnabas some sixty or seventy years earlier, wrote several letters to different churches while on his way to martyrdom in Rome, and while eschatology is not a major theme, he clearly expected the Lord to return in the same body in which he ascended. Otherwise, 'how shall those "see him that pierced him", and when they recognize him, "mourn for themselves"?'[3] He did not wish to be rescued from martyrdom, so strong is his belief that death will bring him to be with Christ. Polycarp, bishop of Smyrna, who was later martyred at the age of eighty-six, linked the physical body of Christ with the coming resurrection:

> For whoever does not confess that Jesus Christ has come in the flesh, is antichrist: and whoever . . . says that there is neither a resurrection nor a judgment, he is the first-born of Satan.[4]

The link between the incarnation and the resurrection emphasised the physicality of both, an emphasis which was probably in intentional opposition to Docetist and Gnostic teachings. Gnosticism valued the intellectual or spiritual (i.e. the soul), and despised the physical, especially the body, and was seriously infiltrating the Christian church. Salvation was redefined as the soul's deliverance from the body and this led to the heresy of Docetism, that Christ was a divine spirit, but only appeared (*dokein*) to have a physical human body.

The Epistle of Barnabas, an anonymous work, developed the theory that the six days of creation in Genesis 1 represent the six thousand years of the world's existence, since (referring to Ps. 90:4) 'a day is with him a thousand years'. The seventh day, when the Lord would return to 'sanctify' the Sabbath, was about to begin:

> This meaneth: when His Son, coming [again], shall destroy the time of the wicked man, and judge the ungodly, and change the sun, and the moon, and the stars, then shall he truly rest on the seventh day.[5]

The writer seems to imply that the Sabbath will also last a thousand years – a millennium.

Justin, Irenaeus and Tertullian

In the middle and late second century, some major figures appear, and with them a more developed teaching about the expected millennium. Justin was the most prominent of a number of philosophers who were converted to the Christian faith and who are known as the Apologists. In his 'Dialogue with Trypho, a Jew', Justin rejects the idea of some philosophers that the soul, as a spiritual substance, is naturally immortal. He believes that at death the souls of the righteous go to a better place, while those of the wicked go to a worse place until the time of judgment. He admits that some Christians have spiritualised the truth, denying the coming resurrection and teaching that their souls will be taken straight to heaven:

> But I and others, who are right-minded Christians on all points, are assured that there will be a resurrection of the dead, and a thousand years in Jerusalem which will then be built, adorned, and enlarged, as the prophets Ezekiel and Isaiah and others declare.[6]

He quotes Isaiah 65 to his Jewish conversation partner, Trypho, but he has to turn to the book of Revelation to find explicit mention of the millennium:

> And further, there was a certain man with us, whose name was John, one of the apostles of Christ, who prophesied by a revelation that was made to him, that those who believed in our Christ would dwell a thousand years in Jerusalem; and that thereafter the general, and, in short, the eternal resurrection and judgment of all men would likewise take place.[7]

Justin declares that those before Christ who lived their lives by the law of Moses and those who did that which is universally, naturally and eternally good, shall be saved through Christ at the resurrection. But Christ had become incarnate:

> in order that . . . the serpent that sinned from the beginning, and the angels like him, may be destroyed, and that death may be condemned and for ever quit at the second coming of Christ himself, those who believe in him and live acceptably, and be no more: when some are sent to be punished unceasingly into

judgment and condemnation of fire; but others shall exist in freedom from suffering, from corruption, and from grief, and in immortality.[8]

Irenaeus, missionary bishop of Lyons in Gaul, similarly rejected a merely spiritual survival of death. The fruit of the wine and the grain of wheat become for us the Eucharist, which is the body and blood of Christ, so that 'our bodies, nourished by it, and deposited in the earth, and suffering decomposition there, shall rise at the appointed time, the Word of God granting them resurrection to the glory of God, even the Father'.[9] He also rejects any endeavour to allegorise the prophecies of an earthly prosperity centred in Jerusalem after the resurrection.[10]

Tertullian, the first major Latin Father, devotes a whole work, 'On the Resurrection of the Flesh', to refute the spiritualizing tendency. The flesh was created by God, Christ himself participated in flesh, and the power of God would bring about the resurrection of the flesh. The future judgment will take account of the works of the body no less than of the soul, and the flesh will share with the soul the future rewards or punishment.[11] In the meantime the souls of the righteous wait in Paradise.[12] After the resurrection the redeemed will enjoy the earthly millennium, followed by the destruction of the world at the judgment and the transformation of the righteous into their eternal nature to be removed to heaven.[13]

In later life Tertullian became an adherent of Montanism, a Christian sect following the prophet Montanus and two prophetesses, Priscilla and Maximilla. Speaking in tongues, they claimed to be mouthpieces of the Holy Spirit, proclaimed that the New Jerusalem would be in Phrygia (their homeland) and was expected so soon that absolute chastity was to be practised by all Christians and persecution and martyrdom was to be welcomed.

Origen

Origen became head of the catechetical school in Alexandria at the beginning of the third Christian century, and with him

comes a new slant on eschatology. As one of the greatest intel-
lects of the age, he was fiercely loyal to the church, but he
moved further into speculative thinking which went beyond
church doctrine. These speculations were presented as his personal opinions, but, shaped by his Hellenistic culture, they
became immensely influential.

In loyalty to the church, Origen rejected the spiritualism of
the Gnostics, who assumed a cosmic dualism between 'spirit',
which was essentially divine, and physical, material reality
(including the body) which was debased and evil. But while the
human soul was not divine, Origen was sufficiently Platonist to
speculate that it was immortal, meaning that individual souls
had always existed and always would. He differentiated
between the 'form' (*eidos*) of the body and its material substra-
tum which was always in flux. In the resurrection therefore the
body would have the same 'form', but the matter of the body
would be completely different so that it was a 'spiritual' body.[14]
In the intermediate period between death and resurrection,
righteous human souls would be provisionally separated from
the unrighteous,[15] but at the last judgment that division would
become definitive.[16]

But when he comes to the *parousia*, the millennium, the nature
of the last judgment and the eternal fate of the damned, Origen
strikes out in even more original directions to present less physical and more 'spiritual' interpretations. The second advent of
Christ would not occur in one specific place as the symbolic language of the gospels suggested, but rather all would be aware
of it everywhere. He rejected the idea of a millennium in an
earthly Jerusalem with physical pleasures.[17] To speak of the last
judgment simply meant that each human being would become
aware of their status before God. The suffering of the damned
would not be in literal, physical flames in hell, but would simply
be the anguish of their separation from God.[18]

But more startling that any of these 'spiritual' reinterpretations of physical language is Origen's belief that the punishment
of the damned had a deterrent and reformative purpose and
would one day come to an end. He expected that every 'rat-
ional nature' would eventually participate in the *apokatastasis*,
the final universal restoration of all things[19]

The Reaction to Origen

After Origen died in 253 AD, his thinking remained influential. It was particularly defended by Dionysius, bishop of Alexandria in the late third century, who rejected the idea of a literal millennium, together with the book of Revelation on which the belief was based.[20] But at the end of the third century, Origen's views were attacked by Methodius of Olympus. Methodius rejected Origen's distinction between the form and matter of the body together with the idea that only the form will be raised at the resurrection.[21] He also rejected the separation of soul and body and insisted that since it was the flesh which had become corruptible, it must be the flesh which put on incorruption in the resurrection.[22]

In the course of the fourth century, the anti-Origenist arguments of Methodius were taken up by Eustathius of Antioch, a leading bishop at the Council of Nicea in 325, and later by Epiphanius of Salamis, who conducted a sustained offensive against Origenism till he died in 403 AD. One of Epiphanius's converts in 394 was Jerome, the polyglot translator from the Latin west who had settled in Bethlehem, and who then conducted a virulent campaign in opposition to his own bishop, John of Jerusalem. In opposition to Origen's thought, he strongly emphasised the physical nature of the resurrection body.[23]

The Emerging Consensus: Advent, Resurrection, Judgment and Eternity

By the end of the patristic period a consensus had been reached on the four main aspects of eschatology: the second coming, the general resurrection, the last judgment, and heaven and hell.

The *parousia* or second advent remained basic to the eschatology of the later fathers, and in contrast to Origen, few tried to spiritualize this expected cosmic event. The resurrection of the body also remained part of the consensus despite the increasing influence of Platonism. While Epiphanius and

Jerome campaigned against Origenist spiritualization, bishops in the mainstream cautiously incorporated some of Origen's ideas.

Cyril, bishop of Jerusalem in the mid-fourth century, expected that God in his omnipotence would reunite the particles of corpses, even those which had decayed or been scattered to the elements. But the resurrection body would not be the same as the old body. With reference to Paul (1 Cor. 15:44), he taught that it would be a 'spiritual' body: 'For this body shall be raised, not remaining weak as now; but raised the very same body, though by putting on incorruption it shall be fashioned anew.'[24] The western bishops, Ambrose of Milan and Hilary of Poitiers, took a similar stance.[25]

Gregory of Nyssa took a line slightly closer to Origen, holding that the 'form' (*eidos*) of the body, which was distinguishable from the matter, would draw all the material of the body to itself in the resurrection, and that the resurrection body would be free from the consequences of the fall such as illness, age or death.[26]

But significantly, the reaction against Origen's 'spiritualizing' of the eschatological hope did not revert to the belief in a literal millennium which had been so much part of the doctrine from the Apostolic Fathers up to Tertullian.[27] Based on one text in a book filled with apocalyptic imagery, Millenarianism lacked a secure biblical basis, and while it was to attract some popular support in the modern era, it never again became part of the theological thinking of the church, either in the medieval era, or in the theology of the leading Reformers. Augustine particularly attacked the idea of carnal rather than spiritual joys which the Chiliasts or Millenarians expected in an earthly New Jerusalem, and interpreted the thousand years of Revelation 20 as referring either to the last thousand years before the judgment or as the age of the church.[28]

All agreed on the coming judgment, arguing that since all wrongs are not righted in this age, the justice of God demands that they be righted in the next. John Chrysostom proclaimed:

> If God is such as indeed He is, it follows that He also be just, for if He is not just He cannot be God. But if He is just, He requites

each man as He deserves. But we see that people do not all receive their deserts here. We must therefore look for another requital, so that each may duly received what he merits and God's justice may stand revealed.[29]

But while the last judgment is usually referred to as a literal, physical future event, it is out of one's own conscience that one is judged. 'The terrible countenance of the Judge will force you to speak the truth,' Cyril of Jerusalem warns his catechumens, using the parable of the sheep and the goats to admonish them to good works.[30] Some western fathers speculated that the wicked will be already judged while the righteous will need no judgment, leaving Christians who have been inconstant to be judged. Hilary of Poitiers takes Psalm 1 to imply that the wicked will not be resurrected nor annihilated, but judged in their state as 'dust'.[31]

Augustine insists, however, that all will appear at the last judgment. God's judgment is active throughout human history, but the 'day' of judgment refers to a coming time 'when Christ shall come from heaven to judge the quick and the dead'.

> For that day is properly called the day of judgment, because in it there shall be no room left for the ignorant questioning why this wicked person is happy and that righteous man is unhappy. In that day true and full happiness shall be the lot of none but the good, while deserved and supreme misery shall be the portion of the wicked, and of them only.[32]

The fathers generally envisage an intermediate state between the individual's death and the resurrection and last judgment, and in fact the rewards and punishments may well begin even then. Augustine states his view:

> But in this intermediate period between the putting off and the taking again of the body, the souls are either tormented or they are in repose, according to those things which they have done during the period of bodily life.[33]

Eternal punishment awaits the wicked. Chrysostom is quite sure that this will be eternal fire and that the wicked have been made immortal in order to endure it eternally:

> For when you hear of fire, do not suppose the fire in [that] world to be like this: for fire in this world burns up . . . but that fire is continually burning those who have once been seized by it, and never ceases: therefore it is called unquenchable.[34]

Gregory of Nazianzus refers to some who wondered whether eternal punishment was worthy of God.[35] And his friend, Gregory of Nyssa, explicitly shares in Origen's hope of *apokatastasis*, universal restoration after long periods of punishment and correction, so that even 'the inventor of evil' will eventually be saved.[36] But Augustine dismisses any idea that punishment is anything other than everlasting.[37]

By contrast, eternal blessedness awaits the redeemed. Those who are 'in this holy catholic church, receiving instruction and behaving ourselves virtuously', as Cyril of Jerusalem puts it, 'shall attain the kingdom of heaven and inherit eternal life'.[38] He understands this in a Trinitarian way:

> The real and true life then is the Father, who through the Son in the Holy Spirit pours forth as from a fountain His heavenly gifts to all.

Gregory of Nazianzus ends his panegyric on his old friend, Basil, with the prayer that when he too is translated:

> As we dwell together, and gaze more clearly and more perfectly upon the holy and blessed Trinity, of which we have now in some degree received the image, our longing may at last be satisfied.[39]

The eastern fathers used the language of 'deification', meaning that our human nature would be so transformed with divine qualities – incorruptibility, life, honour, grace, glory, and power, and every kind of perfection, attributes of God, so that it will truly be in his image.[40] The western fathers were attracted by

the idea of meeting and conversing with those who had gone
before, 'the communion of the saints', but for them too, especially Augustine, God was our *summum bonum*, our highest
good, and therefore our final happiness would be in knowing
and loving the Holy Trinity in the beatific vision.[41]

A Different Eschatology?

How then was Christian eschatology changed by passing out
of Jewish into Graeco-Roman culture? It is evident that the
expectation of the second advent of the Lord, the general resurrection, the last judgment and eternal rewards and punishments remained part of the eschatology of the fathers. What
had changed was the loss of the idea that in some sense the age
to come had already begun, although it is true that in the lit-
urgy of the church the sacraments (or 'mysteries') continued to
point to that. What had also changed was the modification of
the expectation of coming of the kingdom to earth to become
more exclusively the expectation of eternal life in heaven.

7

Eschatology in Evangelical History

David W. Bebbington

Evangelical Christians have held diverse views over questions relating to events at the end of the age. The chief bone of contention has been the relation of the second coming of Jesus to the millennium, a period of one thousand years of blessing expected on the basis of Revelation 20. The convictions of evangelicals have normally fallen into one of three categories: postmillennial, premillenial and amillennial. Postmillennialists have believed that the second coming would take place after ('post') the millennium; premillennialists, who have been subdivided into many groups, have nevertheless been united in the expectation that Jesus would return before ('pre') the millennium; and amillennialists have argued that, since Revelation 20 should be interpreted as referring to a past era or else figuratively, the millennium is not to be looked for in the future at all. The interplay between these different opinions has been a marked theme of evangelical history in the British Isles, America and in many other parts of the world.

In the Reformation, to which many evangelicals looked back for sanction for their doctrinal positions, there was little support for millennial expectations. Anabaptists, it was true, often entertained high hopes for an immediate future when the structures of the church and the world would be overturned in favour of true believers. Their endorsement of millennial beliefs, however, was an inducement for the magisterial reformers to steer clear of views which they associated with social subversion. Lutherans and Calvinists alike repudiated millenarianism on the ground that it was a Jewish opinion that had been superseded by New Testament teaching. Luther held that the millennium, a period within Christian history, was already over, and Calvin, who avoided the exegesis of Revelation, branded millenarians as ignorant fanatics. The commonest view among early English-speaking Protestants sprang from John Bale, the writer of the first commentary on Revelation in the English language, *The Image of Both Churches* (1545). Bale's opinions were incorporated in the notes of the Geneva Bible (1560), which until the appearance of the Authorised Version in 1611 was the chief edition of the Bible circulating in England and which until the eighteenth century was the preferred version in Scotland. Although, like Luther and Calvin, Bale had no doubt that the pope was to be identified as the Antichrist, again he held that the millennium was past. Apart from among the Anabaptists, there was therefore a general amillennial consensus during the century of the Reformation. That widespread agreement left a legacy of lingering suspicions that any form of millennialism was mistaken and dangerous. The Westminster Confession of 1643, though professing belief in the immortality of the soul, the resurrection of the dead and the last judgement, was silent on questions relating to the millennium.

Already, however, a number of intellectuals were inaugurating a millennial revival. Thomas Brightman, a Puritan Fellow of Queens' College, Cambridge, composed a treatise on the apocalypse before his death in 1607 contending that a second millennial period was rising to its completion. Joseph Mede, a Fellow of Christ's College, Cambridge, contended in his *Clavis Apocalyptica* (1627) that Revelation must be interpreted strictly, applying its successive images to historical events in their order. Because Revelation 19 described the second coming before the chapter on the thousand-year binding of Satan, the return of Jesus was to be expected before the millennium. From these two writers sprang the postmillennial and premillennial schools of interpretation, though during the seventeenth century the distinction was not rigidly drawn. The British civil wars of the middle of the century were a propitious period for apocalyptic speculation, and so the ideas of the intellectuals were rapidly popularised. Mede's writings, originally confined to a scholarly audience by being written in Latin, were translated into English in 1641–43. Puritans in general became advocates of millennial expectations. Teaching about a millennium of some kind became normal among theologians of the later seventeenth century and many thinkers in other fields shared their hopes. The scientist Sir Isaac Newton, for example, revered Mede. In 1684–90 Thomas Burnet, Master of the Charterhouse, published his enormously influential *Sacred Theory of the Earth*, arguing that humanity was advancing steadily in knowledge towards the millennium. Some form of millennialism was widely credited by the opening of the eighteenth century.

The early evangelicals, emerging from the 1730s onwards, were often marked by the enthusiasm for millennialism that in recent years had been shared by Puritans and thinkers of broader theological views. Although some evangelicals were aware of the reserve of the reformers and so rejected any notion of a millennium, most embraced expectations that the preaching of the gospel would lead on to an age of blessedness on earth. Jonathan Edwards, the American Congregational divine who participated in the revivals of the 1730s and 1740s in New England, supposed that they might well lead on towards a time when the earth would be full of the knowledge of the Lord. He was confident that over the next 250 years the truth of God would extend to more and more nations until, around the year 2000, the whole earth might enter 'the happy state of the millennium'.[1] His hope was a Christian version of the idea of progress, the widespread belief of the era of Enlightenment that humanity was advancing in wisdom, morality and control of the environment. Both ideals expected gradual improvement over time until something like human perfection was attained. Secular writers such as the French *philosophe* Condorcet might assume that human ingenuity would be the motor of change while evangelicals looked to providential guidance to achieve the desirable goal, but both were expressing the characteristic optimism of the age.

Evangelicals were fired by their vision of a future in which the gospel would steadily permeate the world. A few such as

Charles Wesley were premillennialists, but far more, like his brother John, upheld postmillennial teaching. By the end of the century the French Revolution, with its assault on the Roman Catholic Church, seemed to inaugurate the fulfilment of prophecies of the fall of Antichrist. It seemed a favourable time for the launching of new efforts to spread the gospel to heathen lands. William Carey, the founder of the Baptist Missionary Society (1792), believed that no prophecy awaited fulfilment before the ingathering of the Gentiles that would precede the millennium. The whole foreign missionary movement that captured the imagination of Anglo-American evangelicals in the early years of the nineteenth century was inspired by fervent expectation that gospel work across the world would usher in the universal reign of Christ. John Venn, Rector of Clapham and the first chairman of the Church Missionary Society, declared in 1802 that it is 'clear in Scripture that there is yet to be a long period of peace and glory in the Church, such as has never yet been known'.[2] The belief that prophecy assured the triumph of the church was a powerful motor of evangelical expansion.

Postmillennial teaching was normal in nineteenth-century evangelicalism. In Scotland it was a mainspring of the thinking of Thomas Chalmers, the leader first of the evangelicals in the national church and then of the Free Church; in America it animated the revivalist Charles Finney, who in the 1830s believed that his new measures would help bring in the millennium. 'Taking the Scriptures as our guide', declared an English General Baptist in 1854, 'by the millennium we understand the spiritual and triumphant reign of Christ for a thousand years over all nations, and the consequent diffusion of the ten thousand blessings flowing from his righteous and gentle government.' Hence there would be an end to war, famine, heavy taxes, crime, drunkenness, lewdness, slavery, government oppression, scandal or loose talk, false teachers and 'the damnable superstitions of popery and paganism'.[3] This was a very this-worldly species of eschatology, but its grand vista of the future animated evangelicals in much of their social and political commitment. The Peace Society, for example, which aimed to establish perpetual harmony between all nations,

was founded on this teaching. The expectation of the millennium proved a powerful spur to reform.

From the 1820s, however, there were stirrings of an entirely
different formulation of eschatology. The Romantic temper
that produced the poetry of Wordsworth and Coleridge began
to impinge on the assumptions of evangelicals. It was becoming more fashionable to look for the strange, the awesome and
the dramatic. The literati of the age began to stress the sudden
and supernatural rather than the gradual and natural. So
instead of the notion that the gospel would steadily bring
about a millennium that would be distinguishable only in
degree from the present state of things, the idea was broached
that the current age would soon end in a cataclysm associated
with divine judgements on the world. It was Edward Irving, a
minister of the Church of Scotland serving at Regent Square
Church in London, who transposed evangelical thinking into
the new Romantic key. A close friendship with Coleridge
induced him to read the New Testament with fresh eyes and so
to generate a string of novel teachings that included the need
of missionaries to rely on the Almighty alone for their support,
the restoration of the gift of tongues to the church and the
assumption of potentially sinful human flesh by the incarnate
Son of God. Perhaps his most striking innovation was the
assertion of Christ's 'own personal appearance in flaming
fire'.[4] There was a strong insistence that the second coming
would be not merely metaphorical but a physical return of the
Saviour. At a series of conferences at Albury Park in Surrey,
held in successive years from 1826, a group including Irving
elaborated the implications of the new form of adventist belief.
They concluded that the millennium could be located only
after the second coming. The type of evangelical eschatology
associated with Romantic taste was thereafter normally premillennial.

Because postmillennial convictions were so widespread, the
new views spread only slowly. In Scotland the hymn-writer
Horatius Bonar took up the cause; in England Lord
Shaftesbury was the most eminent champion of premillennial
teaching. In America William Miller, a Baptist minister, predicted that the second coming would take place in 1843–44,

and, after it did not, many of his followers consolidated themselves in a number of enduring bodies including the Seventh-
Day Adventists. The classic statement of the premillennial case
appeared in the writings of Henry Grattan Guinness, the
founder of the Regions Beyond Missionary Union, especially
in *The Approaching End of the Age* (1878). Guinness, like most
premillennial advocates of the nineteenth century, was a historicist in his approach to the exposition of Revelation. In the
manner of Joseph Mede before him, he matched events of the
Christian centuries to the events predicted in the biblical book.
Students of prophecy eagerly scanned the newspapers for
signs of the times indicating that the second advent was near.
The historicists almost always adopted the traditional
Protestant view that the papacy was Antichrist and so their
gaze was frequently turned critically towards the Vatican.
Many of them, including Shaftesbury, put effort into resisting
Romanising developments in the Church of England and the
nation at large. They were also characteristically pessimistic.
By the end of the century the clergy of the evangelical party in
the Church of England were generally premillennialists and, to
the despair of a Methodist postmillennialist who mingled with
them, shared a gloomy perspective. 'Looking for our Lord's
speedy coming', the Methodist remarked, 'they expect things
to go from bad to worse, and frankly tell me they have no hope
of amelioration.'[5] Historicist premillennialism fostered a distinctive worldview, stoutly Protestant and resigned to the
deterioration of the world.

The nineteenth century, however, also witnessed the emergence of a different brand of premillennialism. Because its
adherents placed all the events of the book of Revelation in the
future, they are usually labelled futurists. The founder of this
school of interpretation was John Nelson Darby, an Irish graduate of Trinity College, Dublin, who, like Irving, fell under the rising Romantic influence of the age. Drawing on Catholic sources,
he formulated a distinctive approach to biblical teaching about
the end times. Adopting the hermeneutic principle that the
whole Bible is to be understood as conveying literal truth,
Darby taught from the 1830s that Old Testament prophecies
should be applied not to the church, as had been customary, but

to Israel. Hence there was to be a glorious future not for the Christian community, as the postmillennialists supposed, but for the Jewish people. No prophecy about the church remained to be fulfilled, and so the second coming that would terminate the Christian epoch could be expected at any time. True believers would be removed from the earth when, as they were secretly caught up into the air at the rapture, their Lord came for his saints. Next the world would fall into the chaos of the 'Great Tribulation', and only afterwards would Christ come with his saints to reign. The second coming was therefore divided into two stages and human history into a set of distinct periods, such as the Jewish and the Christian eras, which were called dispensations. For that reason Darby's eschatological scheme is usually known as dispensationalism. It was to exert enormous influence over subsequent generations.

Darby became one of the leading figures in the Brethren movement that developed from the 1830s. His beliefs about prophecy, together with their implication that politics was to be shunned as a worldly diversion from spiritual matters, were warmly received within the tight-knit circles of that intensely evangelical body. Soon, however, his views were contested by Benjamin Wills Newton, a leader in the Plymouth assembly of the Brethren. Newton posited less of a break between the prophecies relating to Israel and those relating to the church. He contended that the rapture of the church would take place after the tribulation, not before, so breaking with dispensationalism but not with the futurist variety of premillennialism. Darby's followers, who turned into the Exclusive Brethren, divided over other issues from those associated with Newton, but the opinions of the two men coexisted uneasily within the Open section of the movement during subsequent years. Futurist premillennialism, partly because it seemed to be the esoteric possession of a suspect sect, made relatively little headway outside Brethren until, between 1859 and 1874, Darby undertook several transatlantic trips, injecting his teaching into North America. Through the annual Niagara Bible Conferences from 1883 to 1900, the futurist scheme attracted growing numbers of adherents, though they were still riven by disputes over the timing of the rapture. With the publication of the Scofield Bible in 1909, however, Darby's viewpoint gained a huge advantage. The notes by C.I. Scofield, once the pastor of the evangelist D.L. Moody, expounded dispensationalism as the authoritative explanation of the biblical text. Dispensational teaching rapidly turned into the standard orthodoxy of American Fundamentalism.

Meanwhile postmillennialism remained the most widely held eschatology among the Methodists, Presbyterians, Congregationalists and Baptists on both sides of the Atlantic. Nonconformists in England, believing that the gospel could transform the whole of human life, saw the scriptural promises of a renewed world order as a reason for demanding social reforms through the Liberal Party. Many evangelicals in North America took up similar causes, and especially the campaign for temperance, for the same reason. In all the English-speaking countries the expectation of steady improvement in the human lot under providential guidance was a foundation of the social gospel. Gradually, however, during the later nineteenth century the biblical hope became secularised, merging imperceptibly with the widely diffused idea of progress. Hugh Price Hughes, a leading Wesleyan Methodist exponent of the social gospel, declared that the biblical vision of the New Jerusalem was not to be relegated to the future in heaven. Rather it was to be realised here and now at Charing Cross.[6] Such achievements were to be the result of human effort rather than of divine agency. In this perspective the second coming of Christ faded from view. The result was a liberal evangelical position that minimised the supernatural dimension of eschatology almost to the point of extinction.

The result of the rise of dispensationalism and the broadening of postmillennialism was a polarisation of evangelical expectations of the future in the inter-war period. 'The testimony of the coming again of the Lord Jesus Christ', according to the *Advent Witness*, 'is practically dividing Christendom.'[7] On the conservative side were those who insisted that the second coming would be personal, premillennial and imminent; on the liberal side were the champions of progress into an improved future as the kingdom of God was gradually realised on earth. In America the two positions were characteristic respectively of fundamentalists and modernists. In Britain the separation into two camps was less sharp, yet this eschatological disagreement formed one of the dividing lines between those who supported the university Christian Unions of the Inter-Varsity Fellowship (IVF) and those who backed the more inclusive Student Christian Movement. The IVF did not insist that the second coming would be premillennial, but it did hold that it would be personal; and most Christian Union members were in practice premillennialists.

The more conservative stance was attracting fresh recruits in the inter-war years. Brethren were growing and the new Pentecostal denominations upheld premillennial teaching. In 1917 F.B. Meyer, a venerable Baptist minister, established the Advent Testimony and Preparation Movement. Its members, already fired by the apocalyptic atmosphere of wartime, were further encouraged by the surrender of Jerusalem to General Allenby and the Balfour Declaration of British support for a Jewish homeland in Palestine. These events seemed to fulfil biblical predictions and to show that the end of 'the times of the Gentiles' was at hand, a sure portent of the return of Christ. Christabel Pankhurst, the former Suffragette leader who was now a fervent evangelical, wrote a sequence of popular works beginning with *"The Lord Cometh": The World Crisis Explained* (1923). Premillennial opinion in Britain, however, was far from giving unanimous endorsement to Darby's dispensationalism. The Advent Testimony Movement maintained an uneasy internal truce between historicists and futurists; the parallel Sovereign Grace Advent Testimony, a Calvinist body, reasserted B.W. Newton's belief in a post-tribulation rapture; and the Brethren Bible teacher G.H. Lang urged that only watchful believers would be raptured. The consequence of divided counsels was that the premillennialists as a collective body could not be as dogmatic as their American counterparts. Dispensationalism became much less entrenched in Britain than in America.

In the post-war era the heirs of American Fundamentalism were commonly insistent on all the details of Darby's scheme of the future – including rapture, great tribulation and Armageddon. The establishment of the state of Israel in 1948

gave encouragement to their hopes, and thereafter Israeli interests were promoted by premillennially minded Christians.
Publications abounded on the theme of the end times. Hal
Lindsey's *Late Great Planet Earth* (1970) proved the best-selling
non-fiction work of the decade; the Left Behind series of novels
by Tim LaHaye and Jerry Jenkins achieved sales of more than
63 million copies by 2006; and the associated PC game *Left
Behind: Eternal Forces* was advertised as allowing players to join
'the ultimate fight of good versus evil, commanding Tribulation
Forces or the Global Community Peacekeepers'.[8] More academic restatements of dispensationalist teaching were issued
by scholars from Dallas Theological Seminary such as John F.
Walvoord, its president from 1952 to 1986. It was commonly,
but mistakenly, supposed by many secular observers that the
whole evangelical community of the United States upheld a
dispensationalist scheme of eschatology.

In reality there was far more variety. In 1977 Inter-Varsity
Press issued *The Meaning of the Millennium: Four Views* in which
there were parallel evangelical expositions of amillennialism,
postmillennialism and historicist premillennialism as well as
dispensationalism. Many in Reformed traditions preferred the
amillennial stance of Augustine and Calvin. There were also
reassertions of the postmillennial view among Christian recon-
structionists led by Rousas J. Rushdoony, who argued that as
the Old Testament law is implemented, so the millennial age
will gather force. In Britain the roots of postmillennialism were
pointed out in Iain Murray's *The Puritan Hope* (1971) and for a
while some radical charismatics, buoyed by their rapid
advance, toyed in the journal *Restoration* with postmillennial
expectations of the triumph of the church. At the same time
British premillennialism of all varieties fell into disfavour,
even among more progressive Brethren. Its decay, associated
with the resurgence of social engagement in the 1960s and
1970s, led to a more or less unconscious acceptance of amillennial views in many quarters. In Britain a tentative approach to
eschatological questions generally came to contrast with the
outspoken boldness of many American preachers.

Two conclusions follow from this analysis. One is that
expectations of the last days among evangelicals have been

shaped to a large extent by their settings. In this respect the
doctrine that they have professed has been substantially
moulded by their cultural context. Although the postmillennial position originated among the Puritans of the seventeenth
century, it became closely associated with the Enlightenment
of the eighteenth century. The early evangelicals, for the most
part deeply immersed in the atmosphere of the Enlightenment,
upheld a Christian view of progress that paralleled its secular
equivalent. As the nineteenth century wore on, the two
became identified so that the hope of a renewed world order
came to rest on human potential rather than divine promise.
The rise of premillennial teaching in general, and of dispensational thought as part of it, was equally clearly bound up with
the growth of Romantic feeling. Premillennial doctrine had
particular appeal in Britain as Romantic styles of thinking
became more widely diffused and fell away again in Britain as
Romantic taste evaporated in the late twentieth century. By
then, however, dispensationalist beliefs had become firmly
lodged in American popular culture and remained embedded
there even though Romantic sensibility withered in higher culture. Consequently it is evident that eschatology is an aspect of
the gospel that has been deeply affected by changing cultural
assumptions. In expounding the Scriptures, evangelicals were
usually far more coloured by the contemporary intellectual
mood than they supposed.

There has been, in the second place, a converse impact of the
eschatology professed by evangelicals on their cultures. The
different viewpoints on questions of prophecy have exerted
contrasting influences over evangelical attitudes to broader
questions. Postmillennialists were almost always optimistic,
believing that Christian teaching will gradually spread over
the globe and so transform society for the better. Premillennialists tended to be pessimistic, expecting the return of Christ
to be imminent and so not seeing the world as worth reforming. Nevertheless they usually held that, because time was
short, evangelism was an urgent priority. Amillennialists were
likely (at least in their own eyes) to be realistic, not having the
prospect of a millennium to excite them or a sense that a world
without its rightful king was in a state of degeneration.

Postmillennialism has usually spurred socio-political effort while premillenialism has often discouraged it. Premillennialists have tended to be quietists, deliberately shunning public affairs, or else actively resistant to change, believing that it would operate in the wrong direction. Consequently the evangelical impulse to promote reforms has usually operated much more powerfully when undergirded by postmillennial hopes. Because eschatological convictions have a powerful effect in moulding worldviews, these doctrines have exercised a remarkably strong sway over the role of evangelicals in society at large. That is one of the reasons why beliefs about the future God has in store have been of such major moment in evangelical history.

8

Eschatology and Mission

The Kingdom of God is at hand

Tim Chester

I was involved in organising a mission conference a few years ago. During the planning process I was told, 'People in missionary societies are not interested in eschatology.' It was no use making eschatology the conference theme: people would not come. I could not quite decide whether I should be appalled or perplexed. Eschatology is central to any understanding of mission. Consider the classic text of world mission, the Great Commission of Matthew 28:18–20:

> Then Jesus came to them and said, "All authority in heaven and on earth has been given to me. Therefore go and make disciples of all nations, baptising them in the name of the Father and of the Son and of the Holy Spirit, and teaching them to obey everything I have commanded you. And surely I am with you always, to the very end of the age."

The statement not only oozes eschatology but only makes sense in an eschatological framework.

The Message of Mission: The Risen King

Why do we go and make disciples of all nations? The answer of Matthew 28 is because all authority has been given to the

Risen Christ. In raising Jesus from the dead, 'God has made this Jesus, whom you crucified, both Lord and Christ' (Acts 2:36). His resurrection is his enthronement. The trial on earth which declared him to be blasphemer and traitor has been overturned by the heavenly court of appeal. Jesus is about to ascend, as promised in Daniel 7, to receive from the Ancient of Days 'an everlasting dominion that will not pass away and his kingdom is one that will never be destroyed'. 'He was given authority, glory and sovereign power,' Daniel says, 'all people, nations and men of every language worshipped him' (Dan. 7:14).

Because Jesus has been given authority over the nations, he sends his disciples out to call on the nations to submit to that authority. He exercises his rule on earth through the proclamation of his word – just as God has always reigned through his word. We are ambassadors of Christ bringing an authoritative pronouncement from the king. When we proclaim the gospel we are heralds of a coming king. It is as if we go to the citizens of a country and say that a king is coming who rightly claims their allegiance. Those who currently rule them are usurpers and tyrants. But the true king is coming and he will be king; he will reign. (This is the story Jesus tells in Mk. 12:1–11.)

The gospel is an eschatological message. In evangelism we declare that Jesus is king and that Jesus will be king. The earliest encapsulation of the Christian message was 'Jesus is Lord' – confessed at a time when the rest of the world was declaring Caesar to be Lord (Rom. 10:9). Jesus has been given all authority by the Father and one day every knee will bow before him. If people acknowledge his lordship now, they will experience his coming rule as blessing, life and salvation. If they reject him, they will experience his coming rule as conquest, death and judgment.

We live in a culture where choice is everything and value judgments are relative; I alone decide what is right for me. The declaration of Christ's kingship cuts right across this. We do not invite people to make Jesus their king; we tell people that Jesus *is* their king. We do not invite people to meet Jesus; we warn people that they will meet Jesus as their conquering king. We do not offer people a gospel invitation; we command people to repent and submit to the coming king. Of course, we do this graciously and gently (1 Pet. 3:16). We cannot force or manipulate repentance. But one day everyone will bow the knee before Jesus one way or another (Phil. 2:9–11).

Matthew 28 may be the classic text of mission, but, as Chris Wright emphasises, the whole Bible is a missionary text. It is a missionary text[1] because it tells this story – the story of God reasserting his rule over the world through the kingship of Jesus. It is all there in Psalm 2, one of the Old Testament passages most often quoted in the New Testament. The Psalm begins with humanity, in the form of the kings of the earth, rejecting the rule of God and his anointed. 'Let us break their chains', they say, 'and throw off their fetters.' (Ps. 2:3) In Acts 4 the early church identified the cross as the climax of this rebellion against God (Acts 4:25–28). When we get the chance we kill our Creator.

Notice, too, that we believe the serpent's lie that God's rule is tyrannical. The reality of God's rule is that is brings freedom, life and peace. But the kings of the earth speak of breaking chains and throwing off fetters. Moreover, not only do we reject God's rule, but we ourselves rule in the image of Satan's lie rather than in the image of God's rule. Human rule is to a great or lesser extent tyrannical and corrupt – whether in the home, marketplace or nation. That is significant for mission because it means people hear the good news as bad news. We announce the coming of God's rule – a rule that brings life and freedom. But people hear that announcement as threat. They reject it in favour of self-rule believing the lie that self-rule leads to freedom when in fact it leads to the slavery of sin.

From Eden onwards humanity has rejected God's kingship. But Psalm 2 continues with God declaring that he will install his king in Zion (Ps. 2:4–6). God will reassert his reign over this world through his anointed king. And God's anointed is the next to speak. He repeats God's promise, echoing the covenant with King David in 2 Samuel 7, that he is God's Son and God will give him the nations as an inheritance (Ps. 2:7–9). The writers of the New Testament saw this promise fulfilled in the resurrection of Jesus (Acts 13:32–33). When Jesus proclaimed the coming of the kingdom of God he is declaring that 'the time has come' for God to reassert his rule over the world (Mk. 1:14–15). Moreover, he is hinting that he himself is God's king, a fact borne out by his authority over people, spirits, sickness and sin (Mk. 1:16–2:12) as well as over nature and death (Mk. 4:35–5:43).

Finally in the Psalm the people of God speak in the person of the psalmist himself. They call on the nations to serve the LORD and submit to the Son (Ps. 2:10–12). The authority of the king is delegated to his people as they proclaim his rule (Rev. 2:27). This is our missionary message: kiss the Son lest you be destroyed when he comes.

But our message is also: 'Blessed are all who take refuge in him' (Ps. 2:12). For there is a twist in the story. When the king comes he does not come in triumph and glory. He comes in a hidden way. There is judgment at his coming, but the judgment falls on the king himself at the cross. People ask Malachi, 'Where is the God of justice?' (Mal. 2:17) When will God come and put things right? Malachi affirms that he is coming, but adds a warning: 'But who can endure the day of his coming? Who can stand when he appears?' (Mal. 3:2) The answer is no-one. The coming of God's king must mean conquest and judgment for all humanity. Except that the king comes twice. He will come in a glorious, triumphant way and dispense judgment. But first he comes in a hidden, gracious way and receives judgment in our place as our propitiatory sacrifice (see Mt. 13:24–30, 36–43, 47–50). The beauty of grace is that the king who is our greatest threat himself provides a refuge from himself.

Much of our evangelism takes an individual you-and-God approach: you have sinned, your sin cuts you off from God, but Jesus removes the consequences of sin so you can know God again. There is nothing incorrect about this story. But the Bible tells a much bigger, fuller story. It is the story of God creating a new humanity, reasserting his life-giving, liberating rule over the world, and bringing it to a climax in the triumph of his Son and the renewal of creation. The danger of the you-and-God message is that I remain at the centre. I am the almighty consumer, shopping around for what suits me best with God providing the best option for my religious life. God serves my spiritual needs while Tesco serves my grocery needs. In both cases, it would appear, the customer is always right. By contrast, an eschatological vision puts God firmly at the centre. The gospel tells the story of the kingdom of God.[2] The goal of the story is the glory of God and the climax of the story is 'God all in all' (1 Cor. 15:28).

The kingdom of God extends beyond my personal concerns to encompass the renewal of all things. Here is a message of hope for those suffering injustice, inequality and abuse. Take away eschatology and life has no meaning. That is the message of Ecclesiastes. Ecclesiastes is about living in a disordered world. View the world without God – look at what is simply 'under the sun' – and the conclusion is that everything is meaningless. But the book ends with the affirmation that God will impose moral order on this world. The final verse is: 'God will bring every deed into judgment, including every hidden thing, whether it is good or evil' (Ecc. 12:14). We need to incorporate eschatology into our apologetics. We do live in a disordered world in which the evil often prosper and the innocent suffer. We cannot pretend it is otherwise. But one day God will re-impose order on the world. The final judgment is the ultimate declaration that suffering matters and that evil is unacceptable.

That declaration is anticipated in the cross and resurrection. The resurrection is the promise that the godlessness and god-forsakenness of the cross is not the last word. God's kingdom is coming. Eternal life is coming. A new creation is coming. The American evangelist, Tony Campolo, describes a church meeting he once attended led by an old African-American pastor:

> He started his sermon real softly by saying, 'It was Friday; it was Friday and my Jesus was dead on the tree. But that was Friday, and Sunday's comin'!' One of the Deacons yelled, 'Preach, brother, preach!' It was all the encouragement he needed. He came on louder as he said, 'It was Friday and Mary was cryin' her eyes out. The disciples were runnin' in every direction, like sheep without a shepherd, but that was Friday, and Sunday's comin'!'
>
> The preacher kept going. He picked up the volume still more and shouted, 'It was Friday. The cynics were lookin' at the

world and sayin', "As things have been so shall they be. You can't change anything in this world; you can't change anything." But those cynics don't know that it was only Friday. Sunday's comin'! It was Friday, and on Friday those forces that oppress the poor and make the poor to suffer were in control. But that was Friday! Sunday's comin'!'

'It was Friday, and on Friday Pilate thought he had washed his hands of a lot of trouble. The Pharisees were struttin' around, laughin' and pokin' each other in the ribs. They thought they were back in charge of things. But they didn't know it was only Friday! Sunday's comin'!'

He kept on working that one phrase for a half hour, then an hour, then an hour and a quarter, then an hour and a half. Over and over he came at us, 'It's Friday, but Sunday's comin'!' By the time he had come to the end of the message . . . he had me and everybody else so worked up that I don't think any of us could have stood it much longer. At the end of his message he just yelled at the top of his lungs, 'It's FRIDAY!' and all 500 of us in that church yelled back with one accord, 'SUNDAY'S COMIN'!'[3]

The Goal of Mission: Disciples of the Cross

Meanwhile it is still Friday. History still bears the mark of the cross. The world continues to feel godless and godforsaken. And Christian discipleship still bears the mark of the cross. It is defined by the cross.

The goal of the Great Commission to 'make disciples of all nations, baptising them in the name of the Father and of the Son and of the Holy Spirit, and teaching them to obey everything I have commanded you' (Mt. 28:19–20). Already in Matthew Jesus has defined what it means to be a disciple. 'If anyone would come after me, he must deny himself and take up his cross and follow me' (Mt. 16:24). This statement comes in response to Peter's rebuke. Jesus has declared his coming death and Peter takes him aside, 'Never, Lord!' he said. 'This shall never happen to you!' (Mt. 16:22) Peter wants the glory of the kingdom without the cross. Jesus responds, literally, 'Go behind me, Satan', echoing his words 'Go, Satan' in the wilderness when Satan had previously offered him the kingdom without the cross (Mt. 4:8–10).

The pattern of New Testament discipleship is the pattern of suffering followed by glory reflecting the pattern of the cross and resurrection. Peter had learnt his lesson well. He says the Spirit predicted in the Old Testament 'the sufferings of Christ and the glories that would follow' (1 Pet. 1:11).

Christian discipleship is by definition to take up your cross and follow Christ; to live out the sacrificial love and submission of the cross. In 1 Peter 2 – 3 Peter outlines what it means for Christians to live good lives in a pagan world – a life with missiological implications as people glorify God (2:11–12). He explores Christian responsibility towards to the state (2:13–17), in the workplace (2:18–20) and within marriage (3:1–7). He talks about our responsibility when we suffer for going good (3:8–22). Central to all of this teaching is the example laid down by the cross (2:21–25). The cross exemplifies the calling that slaves have received (2:21) while wives and husbands are told to act 'in the same way' (3:1,7), that is, in the way of the cross. The cross is our pattern. Jesus did not retaliate against evil, but responded with good (2:23; 3:9). He died, the righteous for the unrighteous – and we are the unrighteous for whom he died. He responded to our rejection with an act that brings us to God (3:18). Now we respond to rejection with an eagerness to do good (3:13–17).

But the pattern of the cross is only half the picture. We follow the way of the cross in the hope of resurrection glory. Peter tells us to 'rejoice that you participate in the sufferings of Christ, so that you may be overjoyed when his glory is revealed' (1 Pet. 4:13). At the end of the letter Peter says he has written to testify to 'the true grace of God'. What is the true grace of God? It is the grace that Peter has defined in the previous verses: 'And the God of all grace, who called you to his eternal glory in Christ, after you have suffered a little while, will himself restore you and make you strong, firm and steadfast. To him be the power for ever and ever. Amen' (5:10–11). It is the ability to suffer for a little while in the hope of eternal glory and restoration.

Of course, there is an important sense in which through the Spirit we have resurrection life and power now. But resurrection power is given to us that we might live the life of the cross. It is power to be weak (2 Cor. 4:7–12; Phil. 3:10–11). Our resurrection life is a hidden life, revealed in conformity with Christ and his cross (Col. 3:1–4).

On 26 April 1518 at Heidelberg Martin Luther was called to account for the controversy his 95 theses had provoked. Luther produced a further 42 theses for the occasion – the so-called Heidelberg Disputation – in which he developed what he called 'a theology of the cross' (*theologia crucis*).[4] This was not about the saving significance of the cross, but about its significance for our faith and knowledge of God. 'He is not worth calling a theologian,' claimed Luther, 'who seeks to interpret the invisible things of God on the basis of the things that have been created' (Section 19). Creation, human reason, spiritual experiences and miracles do not reveal God. Or rather they reveal something of God, but the kind of knowledge they give puffs men up so that they never get beyond it. Is God then unknowable? If we cannot know God through what is visible then can we know him at all? Luther's answer is this: God is known through what is contrary. He is known in a hidden way. God's invisible attributes are revealed in suffering and the cross: glory in shame; wisdom in folly; power in weakness; victory in defeat. God is known through the message of the cross.

The theology of the cross is the opposite of theologies of glory. Theologies of glory are those which seek to understand God primarily on the basis of human reason, creation, spiritual experience or miracles. Any notions about God we might come to in this way are destroyed by the revelation of God in the cross. By choosing to be known indirectly through the cross, God hides himself from the arrogant. To recognise God in the absence of God; to recognise victory in defeat; to recognise glory in shame requires faith. It creates an epistemology of sovereign grace so that no one may boast before him; in which the foolish and weak shame the wise and strong (1 Cor. 1:18–31).

I want to suggest we should apply the same pattern to eschatology. We must reject eschatologies of glory which seek the glory and victory of the resurrection without accepting the reality of the cross. This was the mistake made by James and John; they wanted glory without suffering. But when they ask for positions of glory they are told that they must suffer along with the Christ (Mk. 10:35–45). When they come to Jesus, he asks them, 'What do you want me to do for you?' He uses exactly the same words in the following story when blind Bartimaeus is brought to him. Mark is drawing a deliberate parallel between the two incidents. Bartimaeus is blind and wants to see. But James and John, too, need to see: they need to see that following Christ involves a pattern of suffering followed by glory. Bartimaeus ends up following Jesus along the road, but in the second half of Mark's Gospel that has already been clearly defined as the road to the cross. Those with the ability to see recognise that following Jesus means following the way of the cross.

Instead of eschatologies of glory, we must embrace an eschatology of the cross which looks forward to glory and victory, while seeing them as present now in a hidden form as shame and weakness. This is true for both personal discipleship and social transformation. An eschatology of the cross functions as an eschatological proviso. The cross judges over-realised eschatologies of individual victory and success, such as those proposed by the prosperity gospel. 'We must go through many hardships to enter the kingdom of God' (Acts 14:22). And the cross judges over-realised eschatologies of social utopias and revolutionaries. Hope must be accompanied by patient endurance.

Paul says, 'I consider our present sufferings are not worth comparing with the glory that will be revealed in us' (Rom. 8:18). This verse comes in the middle of Romans 8 – a chapter about how you square the promises of the gospel with the realities of sin, suffering and death. The answer is in part that we are not yet what we will be. Like the rest of creation, we await our redemption. We have hope, 'but hope that is seen is no hope at all. Who hopes for what he already has? But if we hope for what we do not yet have, we wait for it patiently' (Rom. 8:24–25). Again and again in the New Testament the corollaries of hope are patience and long-suffering.

But patience and long-suffering are not common characteristics among Western Christians. Modern Westerners
expect good health as a norm. We call for public enquiries
because we think every disaster can be avoided. And we
Christians are not so very different. We expect God to keep
us healthy and safe. So when trouble comes – as Jesus promised it will (Jn. 16:33) – we not only struggle to cope with the
problem, we cannot make sense of what God is doing. Why
does he not answer my prayers? Is my faith too weak? The
result is that people struggling with turmoil in the circumstances of their life are beset at the same time with a crisis of
faith – a crisis that could have been avoided by a proper
eschatology. No wonder, then, that Paul prays that Christians
might realise 'the hope to which God has called us' (Eph.
1:18).

In 1 Corinthians 15 Paul asks why do 'I die every day' if the
dead are not raised? If there is no resurrection hope then the
logical thing to cry is: 'Let us eat and drink, for tomorrow we
die' (15:31–32). But if there is resurrection hope the logical
thing to conclude is: 'Therefore, my dear brothers, stand firm.
Let nothing move you. Always give yourselves fully to the
work of the Lord, because you know that your labour in the
Lord is not in vain' (15:58). Paul's missionary service is sustained by resurrection hope.

Neglecting resurrection hope leads to weak mission and
weak discipleship. Eschatology is central not only to the
message of mission, but also to the motivation of mission.
Many Christians today do live as if the dead are not raised.
Without hope we seek blessing in this earth. We do not live
as aliens and strangers. Without eschatology we are left with
a limp Christian existentialism in which immediate experience is everything. That may be a charismatic existentialism
with highs and healing. It may be a conservative existentialism with freedom from guilt and reassuring orthodoxy. It
may be a pietistic existentialism with leadings from God and
peace in my heart. But they all lack the rigour to meet the
inevitable demands of Christian discipleship. In contrast the
New Testament constantly redirects our attention to future
hope.

Do not store up for yourselves treasures on earth, where moth and rust destroy, and where thieves break in and steal. But store up for yourselves treasures in heaven, where moth and rust do not destroy, and where thieves do not break in and steal. For where your treasure is, there your heart will be also.

(Mt. 6:19–21)

Since, then, you have been raised with Christ, set your hearts on things above, where Christ is seated at the right hand of God. Set your minds on things above, not on earthly things. For you died, and your life is now hidden with Christ in God. When Christ, who is your life, appears, then you also will appear with him in glory.

(Col. 3:1–4)

Let us fix our eyes on Jesus, the author and perfecter of our faith, who for the joy set before him endured the cross, scorning its shame, and sat down at the right hand of the throne of God. Consider him who endured such opposition from sinful men, so that you will not grow weary and lose heart.

(Heb. 12:2–3)

9

Hell

The punishment of the age to come

Robin Parry

It might seem strange in a book about Christian hope for the future to include a chapter on hell. Hell is not, after all, something that anyone *hopes* for. It is, however, one important element of biblically based, orthodox Christian belief. To set forth a Christian vision of the future and its relevance for the present without considering the 'dark side' of that future would be misleading in the extreme.

In the modern West one will find versions (often unbiblical ones) of the concept of hell preserved in some elements of the entertainment industry. What is clear is that 'hell' still works well for us in 'fantasy' contexts (e.g., horror, fantasy books and movies, Heavy Metal music) but in non-fantasy contexts it is only ever found as a metaphor for horrific situations (e.g., 'war is hell'). Interestingly a reasonable number of people still claim to believe in hell. A Fox News poll (2005) found that 74 per cent of Americans believe in hell and a Mori poll commissioned by the BBC (2002) indicated that 32 per cent of people in Britain still believe in hell. Yet whilst many still profess such belief it seems to play a minimal role in their worldviews and lives. Hell has been effectively banished from 'real life' in the West.

Living in this context makes it easy for Christians to lose confidence in the biblical teaching on hell. A recent survey of nearly 9,000 members and clergy in the Church of England found that only 46 per cent say that they believe in hell, 34 per cent were uncertain and 20 per cent said that they did not believe. Even those who do believe in hell often silently drop the idea from their discourse. However, the New Testament is very clear in its warnings about the 'wrath to come' and to exorcise this element from our Christianity is to lose hold of an important thread in God's revelation.

The notion of hell needs recovering in church discourse and practise, but I also think we need to reflect biblically and theologically on the *nature* of hell as well as related questions.[1] This essay briefly sketches three (four?) different views on hell. I will not be recommending any one of them over against the others as my goal is rather to map the territory so that readers may reflect theologically on the issues for themselves. Central to *all the views* is the idea that hell is something to be avoided at all costs. Some of the views are more severe than others (and some are more theologically plausible than others) but *none* of them makes hell into something that is not awful and all have some claim to being Christian views (even though they cannot all be correct).

In the early church one may speak broadly in terms of three basic views of hell that could be found amongst Christian believers. One view was that hell is a place/state of eternal, conscious torment (ECT from hereon) inflicted by God on his enemies. A second view was that of hell-as-annihilation (HAA from hereon). The third view was that of hell as a place of corrective, restorative punishment (RP from hereon) from which ultimately all people will exit and be saved.[2] Historically ECT became the dominant doctrine of the church. However, in contemporary theology all three views of hell have their defenders.

The Classical View: Eternal, Conscious Torment

There can be no doubt that the classical, historical evangelical theology of hell was ECT. In this regard evangelicals simply embraced a theology of hell that can be traced right back to the early years of Christianity and which became the dominant Christian view from the time of Augustine onwards.

ECT has actually existed in many and various forms over the centuries. It is widely, though not universally, agreed by contemporary proponents of ECT that the biblical language of 'fire' and 'darkness' is not to be taken literally but there is disagreement on the state of the damned. Some would maintain that those in hell are in intense pain every moment of every day for all eternity. Others would propose that whilst hell is an awful state it is not one of *intense* suffering. However, the main horror of hell is its eternity. Few express this more strikingly than Jonathan Edwards in his famous 1741 sermon, 'Sinners in the Hands of an Angry God'.

> When you look forward, you shall see a long forever, a boundless duration before you, which will swallow up your thoughts, and amaze your soul; and you will absolutely despair of ever having any deliverance, any end, any mitigation, any rest at all. You will know certainly that you must wear out long ages, millions of millions of ages, in wrestling and conflicting with this almighty merciless vengeance; and then when you have so done, when so many ages have actually been spent by you in this manner, you will know that all is but a point to what remains. So that your punishment will indeed be infinite.

Some would argue that the damned are enraged against God as a result of their punishment. Some who take this view also argue that as anger at God for his just punishment is a sin the damned warrant yet further punishment which enrages them further still earning yet further punishment, and so on to eternity. Others are uncomfortable with the idea that those in hell continue to sin forever and prefer to think of them as acknowledging that their fate is one that is deserved. Some would even wish to speak of this acceptance of one's fate as a mode of being 'reconciled' to God.

The tradition certainly contains a stream of thought according to which the saved rejoice at the just punishment of those in hell. For instance, Jonathan Edwards can say, 'The glory of divine justice in the perdition of ungodly men, appears wonderful and glorious in the eyes of the saints and angels in heaven.' In this stream hell also serves to show the redeemed just how blessed their own state is. Edwards, in the sermon quoted above, goes on to say, 'When the saints in heaven shall look upon the damned in hell, it will serve to give them a greater sense of their own happiness. When they shall see how dreadful the anger of God is, it will make them the more prize his love.' That approach can still be found amongst some contemporary defenders of ECT but it is far more common to find that those who hold to ECT take no delight in the idea. Whilst acknowledging that such punishment is deserved and justified, they are deeply grieved that anyone should face hell.

The Case for ECT from Scripture

The simple reason that many evangelicals, past and present, embraced ECT is that they believe it to be biblical. The very plausible logic is that whilst we may not like the idea that God will punish people with eternal suffering we are not at liberty to reject a doctrine so clearly taught in Scripture. Several texts are worth mentioning in this regard

- Mark 9:47–48, 'It is better for you to enter the kingdom of God with one eye than with two eyes to be thrown into hell, "where their worm does not die and the fire is not quenched".'
- Matthew 25:46 – 'and these [the goats] will go away into eternal punishment but the righteous into eternal life'.
- 2 Thessalonians 1:6–9 – 'since God considers it just to repay with affliction those who afflict you . . . when the Lord Jesus is revealed from heaven with his mighty angels in flaming fire, inflicting vengeance on those who do not know God and on those who do not obey the gospel of our Lord Jesus. They will suffer the punishment of eternal destruction away from the presence of the Lord and the glory of his might.'
- Revelation 14:9–11 – 'If anyone worships the beast and its image . . ., he also will drink the wine of God's wrath, poured full strength into the cup of his anger, and he will be tormented with fire and sulphur in the presence of the holy angels and in the presence of the Lamb. And the smoke of their torment goes up forever and ever, and they shall have no rest, day or night.'

- Revelation 20:10, 15 – 'and the devil . . . was thrown into the lake of fire and sulphur where the beast and the false prophet were, and they will be tormented day and night for ever and ever . . . And if anyone's name was not found written in the book of life, he was thrown into the lake of fire.'

Biblical interpretation is never simply a matter of listing proof texts but it has to be admitted that the imagery of these texts is very striking. Defenders of ECT maintain that when the Second Temple Jewish understandings of eschatological punishment are examined we see that some Jews at the time of Jesus believed in ECT (e.g., Judith 16:17) and, given that background, it makes sense to take the biblical texts on post-mortem punishment as teaching ECT.

The case for ECT from reason

Whilst many Christians are willing to concede that the Bible teaches ECT and that the idea should therefore be embraced, it is true that many have struggled with it. At first blush it seems to be a terribly unjust form of punishment. Critics often appeal to our instinct that a human being is only capable of limited, finite crimes and, if the punishment should fit the crime, then ECT is a far more severe punishment than is warranted by retributive justice.

However, the believer in ECT may reply that this objection reveals a failure to appreciate the pure holiness of God and the utter depravity of our sin. God, being infinite and holy, has infinite honour. Any sin against God is an attack on his infinite honour and incurs an infinite demerit. The just punishment for a sin which incurs infinite demerit is an infinite punishment.

Some Reformed defenders of ECT have argued that God chooses creation to manifest the *fullness* of his glory. To do this he must manifest *both* the glory of his grace *and* the glory of his justice. Thus it is that punishing sinners in hell is necessary for the glory of God's justice to be manifest and his justice is no less glorious than his mercy. Not all defenders of ECT would endorse such reasoning.

In addition believers in ECT can point out that it is a doctrine that has driven evangelism and that its denial may serve to *undermine* motivation for evangelism even if not to remove it altogether.

The case for ECT from tradition

Belief in ECT, whilst not universal in the early church, can certainly be traced back to the earliest years and it became the majority view of Christianity. Most of the great theologians of the church embraced it, the Reformers all maintained it and the evangelical tradition has held it almost unswervingly until recent decades. Whilst the strength of the ECT tradition is not an argument to settle the issue it is a more important consideration than is often appreciated. We should be very cautious about quickly dismissing a doctrine that has been embraced by the greatest thinkers and the most spiritual practitioners of the faith. Of course, evangelicals will always be open to the possibility that they have misunderstood Scripture but it is reasonable to suggest that the burden of proof lies with those Christians who wish to dissent from the ECT tradition.

The Main Alternative: Annihilation

Belief in HAA was resisted for a long time within evangelical circles but whilst it still meets with considerable opposition in certain quarters it is now very much part of the contemporary evangelical scene. HAA comes in two basic versions. In one version people are annihilated immediately at death, whilst in the other they do suffer conscious torment in hell for a limited period before being annihilated.

The case for HAA from Scripture

Believers in HAA maintain that ECT is a misunderstanding of the Bible and that the biblical teaching on hell is that those in

hell are utterly destroyed. The biblical case involves a positive
case and a defensive case.

The positive case examines biblical texts which seem to speak
of hell as *destruction* or annihilation – 'the day of judgment and
destruction of the ungodly' (2 Pet. 3:7. cf. Phil. 3:19; 1 Thes. 5:3;
2 Thes. 1:9). God sent his Son so that people may have eternal
life and not *perish* (Jn. 3:16). It is further argued that the imagery
of fire implies that what is thrown into it is consumed. Consider
Hebrews 10:27 which speaks of, 'a fearful expectation of judgment, and a fury of fire that will *consume* the adversaries'.
Defenders of HAA also point out that in Scripture only God is
inherently immortal (1 Tim. 6:16) and that human immortality is
a gift of God (Jn. 3:16). Apart from this gift of eternal life the
damned will perish, fading away into nothingness.

The negative case seeks to argue that texts which *seem* to
speak of ECT do not *actually* teach ECT. For instance, it is often
argued that whilst the Bible speaks of an 'eternal punish*ment*'
(Mt. 25:46) this could easily refer to *a punishment with eternal
consequences* rather than to a process of eternal punish*ing*.

The case for HAA from reason

The main philosophical and theological arguments in defence
of HAA are actually objections to ECT. ECT is said to be an
unjust and an unloving punishment and consequently to be
deeply problematic for the Christian doctrine of God. HAA is
presented as an alternative that avoids these problems. Sin
warrants destruction and that is what sinners suffer. This punishment does not exceed the crime so it is not unjust. Also,
whilst ECT is hard to reconcile with God's love HAA is less so.
Whilst he wishes to save all sinners, God loves humans and so
allows them the dignity of choosing their ultimate destiny,
even if it is extinction. The awful possibility of annihilation is
a consequence of divine love.

ECT is also accused of assuming the unbiblical doctrine of
the innate immortality of the human soul. According to this
objection defenders of ECT wrongly assume that humans are
immortal and so their destiny either *has* to be eternal heaven or
eternal hell. HAA, on the other hand, assumes the natural

mortality of humans and that immortality is only a gift of God given to the redeemed. Now, in fact, most defenders of ECT do *not* believe that humans are essentially immortal – God does not keep people conscious in hell because he is *compelled* to by human nature. Rather, his justice requires that he preserve them in hell forever. This, however, creates another problem because God could punish people with an infinite punishment by annihilating them. Choosing to keep them consciously suffering in hell forever seems unnecessary for justice and, furthermore, utterly cruel.

The case for HAA from tradition

Whilst HAA has been a minority position it does have an ancient pedigree and can be traced through the history of the church. It has some eminent defenders past and present within the Protestant tradition and boasts some influential contemporary evangelical defenders.

A Minority Tradition: Restorative Punishment

Whilst RP can be found in parts of the early church it was more or less extinguished when some of Origen's other ideas were judged dangerous and his belief in RP became suspect by association. After the Reformation it resurfaced from time to time but has never been a mainstream view in any of the major Christian traditions. Christian universalism, which often accepts a RP view of hell, comes in numerous different versions. In this discussion we shall treat RP and universalism as interchangeable although, strictly speaking, they are not (see note 1).

The case for RP from Scripture

The biblical case for RP can proceed along two types of track – indirect and direct. The indirect track would seek to show that the teachings of Scripture, when considered as a whole, would indicate that hell should be understood as RP. At the most basic level the argument might go as follows:

(a) the Bible teaches that *all* people will be saved (e.g. Rom. 5:18; Col. 1:20; Phil. 2:11);

(b) the Bible teaches that some people *will* go to hell (e.g. Mt. 25:45; Rev. 20:10–15).

If we accept these teachings as inspired by God then how is it possible for both of them to be true? RP is presented as the solution to this dilemma. It is proposed that many will go to hell but at some point they will be delivered from it (through union with Christ) eventually emptying hell. Now this strategy clearly depends on successfully defending the controversial claim that certain biblical texts do teach that all people will be saved. If that hurdle is crossed then it also needs to fend off alternative ways of handling the tension between the two biblical teachings identified in (a) and (b). RP may not be the only way of handling that tension.[3]

A different, though compatible, indirect strategy is to argue that the biblical teaching on divine justice, wrath and punishment would incline us to understand it not merely as retributive but also as restorative. Punishments in the present age can be seen as anticipations of the punishment of the coming age (Jn. 3:18). If divine wrath now is both retributive *and corrective*, and it often seems to be, then hell could be seen in the same way.

The direct track would be to try to find biblical texts that could be said to explicitly endorse RP, which is not an easy task. The most plausible example that I have come across is the proposal that the lake of fire in Revelation 21–22 has an exit. Gregory MacDonald argues the following:

1. The two most severe hell passages in the whole Bible are Revelation 14:9–11 and 20:10–15.
2. However, when they are put in their literary context both have universalist postscripts (Rev. 15:2–4 and 21:23–27).
3. These postscripts lead us to interpret the fiery judgment as a RP from which people are later saved.

To take just one of the two passages to illustrate: Revelation 20:10–15 speaks of the unsaved being thrown into the lake of fire. The language is strong and, at face value, would seem to support ECT. However, in 21:23–27 we read of the 'nations' and the 'kings of the earth' entering the New Jerusalem through the ever-open gates. MacDonald points out that throughout Revelation the 'nations' and the 'kings of the earth' are always depicted as the opponents of Christ and his church and that they are those who have been thrown into the lake of fire. Thus, in MacDonald's view Revelation 21:23–27 is a direct portrayal of those condemned to hell being washed in the blood of the Lamb and then entering salvation.

The case for RP from reason

Universalists have the same objections to ECT as annihilationists (that ECT is unnecessary, unjust and unloving). They also have a battery of arguments to defend their universalism. At the most simple, the following two claims can be said to entail universalism:

1. God, being love, *wants* to save all humanity.
2. God, being all-powerful, *can* save all humanity.

He wants to and he can *so he will*. The obvious objection is that whilst God may wish to save all and may be able to save all it is possible that the cost of his doing so may be unacceptable to him. One version of this response is the classic Arminian objection that saving all people would require God to override freedom and that is unacceptable to him. If we choose to reject God forever then God will honour that choice. However, some Christian philosophers argue that God could save all people without violating human freewill. If such controversial claims are right then God could save everyone without undermining our freedom and so, according to the Universalist, he would do so.

The case for RP from tradition

When it comes to tradition the universalist is in a weaker position than ECT and HAA. There can be no question that most Christians past and present have not been universalists. The best that the universalist can hope for is to try and show that universalism/RP:

(a) has an ancient Christian pedigree and some respected con-temporary defenders even if it has never been more than a minority view;
(b) is not technically a heresy and is thus a *permitted* Christian view;
(c) does not contradict any of the central beliefs of Christian orthodoxy (e.g. Trinity, creation, atonement);
(d) can help the church to hold together traditional Christian beliefs (e.g. 'God wants to save everyone' and 'God will one day achieve all his purposes') better than is possible on traditional views of hell.

Three views on God's victory over evil

One way of bringing out the difference between the three views above is by asking how they make sense of the claim that one day God will be 'all in all' (1 Cor. 15:28). Defenders of ECT will maintain that the eternal punishment of the wicked in hell is the perfect balancing of sin and punishment. God is 'all in all' because his enemies will be defeated and his love and justice will reign unchallenged. Other defenders of ECT would add that the acknowledgment by those in hell of the justice of their punishment is part of this picture of future 'har-mony'.

Defenders of HAA worry that if people who are not recon-ciled to God remain in creation forever (i.e., in traditional hell) then God is not 'all in all'. Those who espouse HAA would maintain that God's annihilation of his enemies is the way in which he becomes 'all in all'.

Universalists maintain that God is only 'all in all' once that which opposes him is defeated and all his creatures are recon-ciled to him. On this view it is universal salvation that makes God's victory complete.

So is God's victory over his enemies complete when he justly punishes them (ECT), removes them from creation (HAA) or reconciles them to himself (RP)?

A Fourth View? Hell in History

The traditional debate about hell has taken an unexpected turn in some recent discussions. N.T. Wright, the evangelical Bishop of Durham, has argued in his influential book *Jesus and the Victory of God*[4] that all the gospel texts that have traditionally been taken to be about hell are actually about the destruction of Jerusalem and not about post-mortem punishment. Andrew Perriman's book *The Coming of the Son of Man: New Testament Eschatology for an Emerging Church*[5] takes this thesis even further and argues that the only passage in the Bible about *post-mortem* punishment is Revelation 21 – 22 and that, being heavily symbolic, should be treated with care. The suggestion that the passages Christians have always thought were about hell are really about historical judgments is quite disorientating and disturbing. The implications of these highly controversial views for a theology of hell are not immediately clear. Perriman clearly still leaves the lake of fire in place, although he seems to see debates about post-mortem punishment as engaging in a discussion the biblical writers were simply not interested in.

Does this represent a fourth view on hell? Perhaps so. It takes the warnings of coming judgment to refer primarily to something that happens *in history* and not post-mortem. However, those taking this approach could argue that whilst most of the fiery judgment texts do not refer *directly* to hell (in a classical sense) they still serve as types of *the final* judgment and can be used with care as an oblique window onto hell. *If* this was done then a defender of the fourth view could also defend one of the other three views on *final* judgment or they may prefer to maintain a strong agnosticism about the nature of final judgment.[6]

The Relevance of Hell for the Present Age

How does belief in hell impact living in the present age? To some extent this will depend on which of the views one adopts. However, there are some generic implications that can be noted in closing.

Hell and mission

The history of missions is full of stories of those who were driven to proclaim the gospel to save people from hell. Whilst saving people from eschatological punishment is only *one* biblical motivation for mission (and not necessarily the most important) it is a *biblical* motivation. It does not follow that evangelism will necessarily involve *telling people* that they must 'turn or burn', although that will be appropriate in some circumstances, but fear of hell still has a place in motivating those who proclaim the gospel and those who pray for the salvation of others.

Hell and holiness

Although not necessarily the primary motivation for holy living the New Testament writers often warned that the consequence of ungodliness and injustice was eschatological wrath (e.g. Gal. 5:19–21; Rev. 22:15). The early Christians were motivated in part by their awareness that sinners would experience divine punishment.

Hell and persecution

Divine judgment is a terrible thing but we must remember that it is also a word of salvation for victims. God punishing those who oppress the saints spells deliverance for the suffering church (2 Thes. 1:6-9; Rev. 15:2–4; 19:1–10). So the expectation of final judgment was and is a source of encouragement to those who suffer. Injustice will not prevail forever. The expectation that God will repay wrongs means that Christians (a) do not have to take vengeance into their own hands (Rom 12:17–21), and (b) are enabled to endure oppression.

Hell and Calvary

The cross was the end-time wrath of God poured out in the present age upon Christ, our representative. *In Christ* all humanity has suffered hell. *In Christ* all humanity has been raised to eternal life. Jesus stood with us in our hell, took it to its eschatological climax and exhausted it. As Moltmann wrote, 'Christ suffered the true and total hell of God-forsakenness for the reconciliation of the world.' So it is that all who are united to Christ, by the Spirit, through faith participate in his death (hell) and resurrection (eternal life).

All Christian reflection on hell needs to view it from Golgotha where God himself endured our God-forsakenness so that we might receive his life. This God is not indifferent to our human plight and has paid an immeasurable price to overcome it. This God is not merely the judge but also, in love, stood judged in our place. Thus the cross helps us to see, as Moltmann argues, that God, in Christ, descended into hell and stands with us in our God-forsakenness. We have hope because we know that even our current anticipations of hell can be broken open by resurrection.

10

Heaven

Justin Thacker

Introduction

> A priest walks into a pub, and says to the first man he meets,
> 'Do you want to go to heaven?'
> The man says, 'I do Father.'
> The priest says, 'Then stand over there against the wall.'
> The priest asks a second man, 'Do you want to go to heaven?'
> 'Certainly, Father,' the man replies.
> 'Then stand over there against the wall,' says the priest.
> Then the priest walks up to a third man and says, 'Do you want
> to go to heaven?'
> The third man replies, 'No, I don't Father.'
> The priest says, 'I don't believe this. You mean to tell me that
> when you die you don't want to go to heaven?'
> The man says, 'Oh, when I die, yes. I thought you were getting
> a group together to go right now.'

Such is the paradox of heaven. We want to go, but perhaps not
yet. With Paul, we are 'hard-pressed between the two' (Phil.
1:23 NRSV). Whilst Paul's ambivalence was out of a desire to
continue serving the church; for many of us, the ambivalence
stems from an uncertainty regarding the paradise that awaits.
Such uncertainty is not due to any ignorance regarding the relevant biblical images or theological concepts, nor is it due to a
lack of faith in the hope to which we are called. Rather it arises,
I would suggest, from our failure to experience sufficiently

what one theologian has called 'the invasion of the present by the power of what is yet to come'.[1] To a large extent, evangelical theologians agree on the nature of the paradise that awaits. They also agree that, in Christ, such eschatological hopes have been inaugurated. We struggle, though, with what this *means*. In what sense is it the case that we experience paradise in the harsh realities of our actual lives? The goal of this chapter is to outline a vision of paradise, drawn extensively from our biblically mandated experience of that paradise in the here and now. In short, I wish to describe the heaven to come, by detailing the heaven that has already arrived.

The New Heavens and New Earth

In contrast to the nature of hell (see previous chapter), contemporary evangelical theologians are of almost one voice in describing the nature of the paradise to come; although it must be said that we often disagree upon the route to that paradise. Much ink continues to be spilt over the existence and nature of a so-called 'intermediate state', and the precise timing and nature of the millennial reign. However, the subject of this chapter is not so much 'life after death', but rather, in N.T. Wright's memorable phrase, 'life *after* "life after death"'.[2] My topic is the life eternal of the age to come, the paradise that eventually summons us once Christ returns and the general resurrection of the dead has taken place. I will leave discussion of any intervening stages to another time and place.

When it comes to that final state, we find evangelical theologians in remarkable agreement. From a conservative, reformed perspective, Edward Donnelly states:

> Perhaps the great obstacle to a true appreciation of heaven is our inability to imagine our bodies there. Though we believe in the resurrection of the body, 'heaven' still brings to mind a realm which is immaterial, not physical in any real sense . . . Yet the Bible tells us that heaven is the ideal environment for them. At Christ's second coming this earth, which God

created for our habitation and his glory, will be restored and renewed . . . heaven and earth will come together in a wonderful unity.[3]

While, coming from a different theological constituency, Wright writes in a similar vein,

> Christians regularly speak of their hope in terms of 'going to heaven when they die'. One hears it in hymns . . . in prayers. The point seems to be that there is something called 'eternity', which is regularly spoken of as though it has only the loosest of connections with space and time, and one day we are going to step into this eternal existence . . . which has almost nothing to do with this earth and this present history . . . I suggest instead that what we find in the New Testament . . . is the Christian hope for a new, or renewed, heaven and a new, or renewed earth, with these two integrated together.[4]

There is, then, at least amongst British evangelical theologians, near universal agreement that the nature of the age to come is of an embodied existence in a renewed earth, in which heaven and earth are united or integrated. It must, of course, be emphasised that this has not always been the case. Indeed, for much of the last two thousand years, the predominant understanding has not been of an embodied, earthly paradise, but rather salvation in terms of a disembodied soul. At some point in church history, as John Colwell argues,

> Christian hope came to be expressed popularly, not in terms of the resurrection of the body, but in terms of the immortality of the soul . . . The last hundred years have witnessed widespread repudiation of this development, particularly amongst scholars of the New Testament.[5]

Donnelly, Wright and Colwell are absolutely correct to draw attention to the fact that such an embodied, earthly hope is frequently not how popular piety presents the life to come.

Martin Luther: death/birth.

It is common enough to find worship lyrics which speak of going to heaven when we die as if something different awaits us in the 'not yet'. Indeed, in talking of heaven as 'a place where we go', my own sermons have too often used terms that Wright and others would challenge. It is not the case, then, that thinking Christians do not believe in a renewed earth. It is rather that the dualistic forms of thought that imagine the hereafter in terms of a disembodied, spiritual existence are so ingrained within us, that it takes much conscious effort to resist them in our preaching, praying and singing.

One of the reasons, I suspect, for our reluctance to embrace a properly earthed concept of eternal life is that many of us still think we have no real idea of its nature. We trust in it as promise, but not as experience. So, Luther once wrote, 'As little as children know in their mother's womb about their birth, so little do we know about life everlasting.'[6] And Hal Lindsey has written, 'There's really very little said [in Scripture] about the nature of the new heaven and the new earth'; a point which, seemingly, has not deterred Lindsey from writing extensively about the subject himself.[7] In contrast, Wright specifically takes to task those who interpret the image in Revelation 21 in exclusively futuristic terms:

> Revelation is not all about 'the future', as though it were an Old Moore's Almanack for events yet to occur . . . A great many popular pictures of 'heaven', conceived as a purely future state (perhaps even up in the sky somewhere), are . . . misreadings of the wonderful picture-language by which Revelation describes the heavenly dimension of present reality.[8]

In the next few sections of this chapter, I shall draw on biblical passages and theological themes that indicate to us the nature of the paradise to come. But I shall describe that paradise by drawing attention to our present day encounter with it. In this way, the ideas generated combine future promise with present experience.[9]

Feasting in the Kingdom

> Touch me and see; for a ghost does not have flesh and bones as
> you see that I have.' And when he had said this, he showed
> them his hands and his feet. While in their joy they were disbe-
> lieving and still wondering, he said to them, 'Have you any-
> thing here to eat?' They gave him a piece of broiled fish, and he
> took it and ate in their presence.
>
> (Lk. 24:39–43 NRSV).

It is a commonplace of evangelical theology that the body of
the risen Christ provides us with the paradigm for our own
risen bodies, not least because this is the explicit proclamation of Paul in 1 Corinthians 15. Having said this, the precise
nature of that body (and therefore ours) remains somewhat
controversial. The quotation from Luke above clearly indicates its physical nature, but at the same time this body is
not immediately recognised, appears and disappears at will,
and seems to pass through walls. In response to these anom-
alies, Wright has described the resurrected body as
'transphysical', that is, not less physical than our bodies, but
more so.[10]

The significance, then, of the risen Jesus eating and drinking is that in the new heavens and new earth we will also
eat and drink. One of the images of heaven that Jesus presents is that of an eschatological banquet (Mt. 22:1–14; Lk.
14:16–24). We recall that the seven signs of John's Gospel are
not so much meant as a 'proof' of Jesus' claims, but rather
indicate that the anticipated kingdom of God has now
arrived in this person. Hence, the miracle at Cana illustrates
the nature of that kingdom: one flowing with the most glorious wine.

For this reason, the New Testament persistently points out
that a false asceticism gives no honour to God. In Colossians,
after chastising the church for such 'self-imposed piety, [false]
humility, and severe treatment of the body', Paul goes on to
say, 'Set your minds on things that are above, not on things
that are on earth, for you have died, and your life is hidden
with Christ in God' (Col. 3:2–3 NRSV) At first, this may appear

contradictory, for how can Paul attack asceticism yet subsequently encourage Christians to set their mind, not on things on earth, but on things above? Upon reflection, the problem is not Paul's, but ours.

Wedded to the dualistic notion that whatever is physical is bad, and whatever is spiritual is good, our reading of the passage creates a tension where there is none. Paul's exhortation is not so much contrasting the heavenly with the earthly, but rather what it means to be in Christ, with being apart from Christ. This is evident if we consider 'humility' which appears in both the list of vices (Col. 2:23) and virtues (Col. 3:12).[11] The contrast Paul draws concerns true and false expressions of what it means to be in Christ. Some of the Colossians pursued a severe asceticism and Paul reminds them that a life 'in Christ' is precisely the reverse of this. To be heavenly, to be in Christ, is to enjoy the good gifts of the earth, and to be earthly, to be apart from Christ, is to wrongly deny oneself such gifts.[12]

In a similar vein, it is no accident that Jesus demonstrates the nature of the new kingdom of God not by withdrawing from the world, but rather by celebrating its gifts. When his disciples are criticised for eating on the Sabbath, Jesus' response is to ask, 'The wedding guests cannot fast while the bridegroom is with them, can they?' (Mk. 2:19). Again, in Matthew 8 and 9, we witness nine miracles interrupted by a moment in which Jesus is seen eating and drinking with tax-collectors and sinners (Mt. 9:9–13). The miracles are not there to prove Christ's divinity, but rather demonstrate that the long-awaited kingdom has now arrived in him. Furthermore, this is characterised by the absence of disease, the presence of sight and speech, and, yes, feasting with redeemed sinners.[13]

In our present experience, when we truly enjoy our bodies through eating and drinking, we are not divorced from the kingdom of God, but rather enacting it. Hence, to describe a wonderful meal as 'heavenly' is not simply to speak metaphorically. To the extent that we enjoy these things as given by God for our fulfilment, we are, in the present, experiencing the kingdom come.[14]

Fellowship

A perennial question regarding our inheritance in the new earth concerns what our new bodies will look like? During the Middle Ages, this became a particularly troublesome question with a number of theologians converging on thirty years as the age at which all would be resurrected, whether or not they actually reached that age during their life.[15] At first the answer may appear comforting. At thirty, we are old enough to have developed intellectually and personally, yet not so old that our bodies appear less than attractive. Thirty also marks the moment when Jesus entered public life. However, what would a community of thirty year olds be like? What would it be like to live in a community without elderly folk, or children? Suddenly, such a community seems rather bland, something akin to an eternal parents' evening.

I have no idea what 'age' we will be in the new heavens and new earth. It may even be the case that the question, like that of marriage, is in some sense illegitimate. And one of the reasons for this is the strange non-recognisability of the risen Jesus. Given this facet of Jesus' resurrection appearances, the obvious question is whether we will know one another in the new earth? Some scholars, on the basis of texts such as 2 Samuel 12:23, argue that we will have no difficulties in recognising one another in the renewed earth. Donnelly writes, 'If God has given you a Christian husband and wife, parent or child, brother or friend, you can be sure that, whatever the parameters of your future relationship with them may be, the friendship will be closer than it is now.'[16]

Colleen McDannell and Bernhard Lang describe this as the anthropocentric view of heaven. It is heaven as the great meeting of friends, where God, if he appears at all, appears as the backdrop to our eternal reunion.[17] We must balance these assertions with Jesus' clear teaching regarding the inappropriateness of marriage relationships in heaven. On the one hand, we cannot imagine a heaven in which we do not know one another in the same way as now; and yet on the other, it is clear that those who have been married do not enjoy the same relationships in this renewed earth. How do we square this apparent circle?

In a sermon, Augustine once addressed the same question. He responded like this:

> Do you think that you will recognize me because you know me, and that you will not recognize my father whom you do not know? . . . You will know everybody. Those who will be there will not recognize each other because they will see their countenances; there will be mutual recognition because of greater knowledge. Thus, all will see and will see much more keenly . . . When they will be filled with God, they will see divinely.[18]

Our knowledge of one another, according to Augustine, will not be dependant, as it is in this life, on facial recognition; but rather we will know one another by means of divine inspiration. How might this work? In the here and now, we recognise others and enjoy relationships by utilising a range of concepts that enable us to categorise those with whom we are interacting. This is a stranger, a friend, a work colleague and so on. Furthermore, we have a standard set of behaviours that are appropriate for our children, partners, strangers and friends, and these behaviours are tied to the same range of concepts. One of the concepts we use is that of the fellow believer. I am sure I am not alone in knowing the joy of meeting an unknown brother or sister in Christ when I was not expecting it. Recently I found myself sitting on a bus sharing a wonderful conversation about the Lord with an elderly, Caribbean lady, despite never having met before. Our sole point of contact in these conversations is our shared love for Christ, and yet this alone can generate a very real and strong bond. In such a setting, the believer encountered is not seen as either a stranger or friend (for they are neither), but simply as a brother or sister in Christ.

In the new earth we will interact with one another primarily in terms of our oneness in Christ, that is, as brothers and sisters in him. This does not mean that our other concepts – strangers, friends, wife, husband, children, colleague – will no longer apply. I do think we will be able to say, 'Oh yes, we used to work together', or 'we were once married'. However, our shared identity in Christ will be so dominant that these other means of relating will simply become irrelevant. 'Yes, we once knew each other, but now we are brother and sister in Christ – and that is so much more'. In the same way that two people who met through work and get married now relate to each other primarily as husband and wife rather than as colleagues, so in the new earth we will relate as brothers and sisters in Christ, even though we once knew other forms of relationship.

Each time we have one of those strange encounters with another believer, we are experiencing both a foretaste, and the actuality of the renewed heaven and earth. Every moment of intimacy shared between believers now is predicated on the relationship we will share in Christ in the age to come. Whenever we are united in Christ, the family of God to which we look forward is experienced now. That is why our unity in the present builds the kingdom for the future. And this is also why a concept of Christianity in terms of saving my individual soul could not be further from the good news that Jesus proclaimed. We are saved, both now and then, as the body of Christ.

Facing God

Finally, we must address our relationship to God in the new earth. Paul tells us that 'we will see face to face' (1 Cor. 13:12); but what   precisely does this mean? In the Old Testament, to have the face of God directed towards one was an indication of God's pleasure. The psalmsist asks God not to turn his face away, associating his present gaze as divine acceptance (Ps. 27:9, 132:10).[19] However, in the New Testament, talk of God's face enables a more intimate and relational reading. Revelation and 1 Corinthians both talk of seeing God's face (Rev. 22:4, 1 Cor. 13:12). John tells us that we shall then 'see him as he is' (1 Jn. 3:2 NRSV). And the repeated emphasis of Revelation is that the point of the new heavens and new earth is that then God will be *with* his people (Rev. 21:3, 22, 23; 22:4, 5). This 'beatific vision' as it later came to be called has been the dominant motif in what is termed the theocentric view of heaven. Such views tend to take a fairly passive conception of activity in heaven, in which an endless praise service seems to be our chief task. Notwithstanding the image of continual singing in Revelation 5, is this indeed what will occupy us in the renewed heavens and earth?

To answer this question, we should consider how those New Testament passages that describe our eternal encounter with God function. Contrary to much popular teaching, Wright insists that the good news of the resurrection is not, 'You're going to heaven when you die', but rather, 'Jesus is raised, therefore God's new creation has begun and we've got a job to do.'[20]

So, what conclusions do the New Testament authors make when they outline our eternal unveiled proximity to God? Perhaps, the first place to begin is Paul's discussion in 1 Corinthians 13. 'For now we see in a mirror, dimly, but then we will see face to face. Now I know only in part; then I will know fully, even as I have been fully known. And now faith, hope, and love abide, these three; and the greatest of these is love (1 Cor. 13:12–13).' Despite its frequent usage in wedding services, 1 Corinthians 13 represents a bit of a tongue-lashing from Paul. The Corinthian church has become obsessed with spiritual ephemera to the exclusion of that which has lasting value, and Paul's concern is to outline that which really matters in contrast to that which does not.

No matter how astonishing and supernatural our present experience of God, whether by way of prophecy, tongues and revealed knowledge, these are all imperfect and partial manifestations in contrast to the lasting value of love. They remain genuine experiences of God, from God, for now; but, as Paul points out, we must not confuse them with the perfect, complete, 'face to face' experience that is to come. That 'face to face' experience will not be characterised by passing ephemera, but comprises perfect love. Therefore, in the present, enjoy and experience the temporal gifts which God has given, but not at the expense of the permanent deposit of love that is already ours. This is the priority which Paul is challenging the Corinthian church to get straight.[21] His use of 'face to face' terminology reminds us that present experience is not everything, a greater reality is to be revealed. We should spend our time and effort on that which will last, rather than on that which will pass away. We should neither overestimate nor underestimate our present experience, but rather re-evaluate it so that it focuses on God's priority: namely, love.

The promise of the beatific vision, far from encouraging us to neglect this world, or our struggle with sin, challenges us rather to continue and intensify that struggle with sin. Even in Revelation 21 – 22 where the grand vision of the new heavens and new earth is laid out, the stress remains on how we live in the present (Rev. 21:7–8, 27; 22:11–15). The message seems to be: this is what awaits those who persevere, therefore live lives that honour God. This is not Pelagianism, but rather a call to be who we are in the light of the hope to which we have been saved. Hence, the motif of the beatific vision, our full experience of God, serves in the New Testament to call us to repentance, to call us to love, to call us to continue to serve one another and the world that is in need.

A curious phrase that occurs in the middle of the wonderful vision of Revelation 22 proves particularly poignant at this point. Having spoken of the river of life, the throne of God and the Lamb, the glorious fruit and all that is there, we find this: 'But the throne of God and of the Lamb will be in it, and his servants will serve him' (Rev. 22:3). It echoes a similar verse in Revelation 7:15, but what is their point? Well, it is possible to interpret them both in terms of the elders and angels singing and praising God. This is entirely reasonable given that the same Greek verb, *latreuo*, is used for both service and worship. However, it is also possible to see here echoes of another vision, in Matthew 25:31–46, in which the Lamb is on his throne, with all his angels in attendance, and the nations before him, where reference is also made to those who served the King: 'for I was hungry and you gave me food, I was thirsty and you gave me something to drink, I was a stranger and you welcomed me, I was naked and you gave me clothing, I was sick and you took care of me, I was in prison and you visited me' (Mt. 25:35–36).[22]

If we recall the point that the king makes on that occasion that 'just as you did it to one of the least of these who are members of my family, you did it to me', then it becomes possible to identify a very real continuum between our practical service of the poor now, and our worship in terms of sung praise in the age to come. Presumably that continuum is at least partly related to the notion that both service of the poor and praise of God stem from a desire to give due worth to whomever we encounter. If this is the case, then the challenge to us is to worship with the angels in heaven not so much by singing songs, but by feeding the hungry. In this strange paradox, heaven on earth is experienced most where we least expect it: amongst the destitute, for is that not where we find Jesus?

Conclusion

The aim of this chapter was to write about heaven. Having written about the need to feed the poor, meeting strangers on buses and the blessings of good food, some might think I have neglected the task. However, I would maintain that whilst we can genuinely look forward to that which is to come, we can also begin to enjoy its first fruits now. And, moreover, that it is in the biblically mandated experience of God's kingdom in the present that we can gain the greatest insights into heaven's nature. Like Elisha's servant (2 Kgs. 6:17), and the two on the road to Emmaus, all that we require is for our eyes to be opened to that which is already before us.[23]

Hopeful Culture

11

Eschatology and Imagination

Seeing visions and dreaming dreams

Trevor Hart

Imagination, Faith and Hope

Imagination is essential to Christian believing and living, and to Christian theology. In 1948 the Anglican theologian Austin Farrer suggested, provocatively perhaps, that God's activity of revelation and the faith which it calls forth from us are from first to last matters of *imagination*. '(D)ivine truth', Farrer writes, 'is supernaturally communicated to men in an act of inspired thinking which falls into the shape of certain images.'[1] In other words, the way in which God makes himself known to us, and shares his redemptive purposes and promises for the world with us, is bound up with our capacity to *imagine*. Faith depends on our apprehending and holding in our 'mind's eye', as we would say, things which trespass far beyond the horizons of the things we can see and touch and hear.

We should note at once that Farrer has in mind here chiefly 'verbal images', rather than pictures or statues. He is thinking of the ways in which Scripture in particular furnishes a stock of images for picturing God, God's ways of dealing with the world, and God's purposes for it. So God is variously King, Shepherd, Father, Judge, Husband, Mother, Rock, Fortress; salvation is victory over an enemy, purification from stain, the execution of justice, healing from sickness, redemption from slavery, re-birth; God's promised future for his creation involves the resurrection of the dead, a second advent of Christ in the world, the defeat of Antichrist, a final judgment on human sin, the creation of a new heaven and new earth, and so on. Not all of these images have equal weight, and some will inform our interpretation of others. All are important, however, and – my main point here – all are *images* (albeit, as Farrer insists, *inspired* ones). They are ways of picturing or imagining what God, or God's purposes and actions, are like, drawing from the reservoir of our concrete experiences of life in the world.

The word 'picturing' here is very significant. We shouldn't, in a well-intentioned bid to insist on the priority of the Word for faith, overlook the fact that *visualisation* is vital to the way in which verbal images work. They are powerful precisely because they stimulate our imagining of concrete and often vivid states of affairs, and hence enable us to have some partial and provisional grasp, at least, on things many of which, strictly speaking, lie beyond anything we *can* as yet imagine (See, e.g., Eph. 3:16–20). We may see 'through a glass darkly', as the apostle Paul says (I Cor. 13:12), but we do 'see', and such seeing is vital to our faith.

If all this talk about imagination in the context of faith and theology makes some Christians restless or uncomfortable, or stirs up some deep-rooted resistance, as I suspect it may, then it is probably because we are falling into a trap set for us by our recent culture, and which is reflected clearly enough in much of our habitual use of the language of imagination in daily life. 'Don't worry,' we may say to reassure someone, 'you're imagining it' - which means in effect 'it's not real, and there's nothing to worry about'. Well, as Christians we certainly aren't going to have much truck with any suggestion that the God whom we know and worship, or our apprehension of God's ways with the world through Jesus Christ and the Holy Spirit are 'just our imagination (once again) running away with us'. Nor should we. And if that's the inevitable result of linking Christian faith to imagination then we had better steer clear of it.

However, this popular prejudice, which associates imagination automatically with the unreal or the false, doesn't stand up to the slightest scrutiny. Of course imagination *can* be a source of falsehoods and illusions (a lie is certainly a construct of the imagination, as is pretence, and fiction in all its rich variety). But that doesn't mean that this is its default setting, the extent of its repertoire, or its normal mode of operation. On the contrary, careful analyses of the subject suggest that the capacity for acts of imagination lie at the root of our most reliable and fruitful ways of engaging with the world, in the sciences as well as the arts and humanities, and furnish the conditions under which alone they are possible. In fact, whenever we are dealing with things lying beyond the very limited sphere of our immediate experience, we are compelled to be imaginative, to picture how things are, how things were, and how things may yet be. So, we should distinguish straight away between the 'imaginative' and what, for want of a better phrase, we might acknowledge as the merely 'imaginary'.

The stuff of Christian faith concerns things lying beyond our immediate experience. It should come as no surprise, then, that the Bible is a highly imaginative text. Through Scripture God seeks to take our imagining captive and thus draw us actively into the dynamics of his redeeming action, as participants in what the Bible itself refers to as 'life in all its fulness'. Sharing in this life, for instance, involves seeing ourselves as part of a story, a history of God's dealings with humankind, most of which happened long before we were born. It involves living daily in conscious communion with a God who, although he is known in and with and through all sorts of things, is not himself amenable to the physical 'seeing' which our culture so privileges, but must be discerned and 'seen' at work in the world and in our lives in a different sort of way. Similarly, the risen Jesus whom we worship and to whom we pray, though held to be present in our midst, is certainly not so physically, and our communion with him is intrinsically of an imaginative sort, informed by the Jesus we know so well from the gospel stories, the pattern of whose presence the eye of faith is now compelled to identify as a living reality confronting it and calling for a response. In these and many other

ways, faith is, as the writer to the Hebrews puts it, a matter of
dealing with 'things not seen' (Heb. 11:1); and that places it
securely within the territory where human imagination functions. And so it is that Scripture is filled to the brim with parable, story, poetry and other explicitly imaginative types of
writing. Indeed, more broadly, we might insist that Scripture
as a whole (while in fact it contains a wide variety of literary
types) consists of an appropriation by God of human realities
to capture our imagination and so transfigure the world,
granting us access to depths and dimensions of it which otherwise remain hidden and inaccessible to us.

Hebrews 11 also links faith decisively to another fundamentally imaginative human disposition of course; namely, hope.
Faith, it tells us, is 'being sure of what we hope for'. And hope,
as Paul observes elsewhere,[2] is all about things which are not
seen, not yet anyway. Faith has to do with all manner of things
which are essentially past and a matter of faithful remembrance, and with lots of other things which, while unseen, are
real enough and the regular object of our spiritual apprehension and activity. But Christian faith is above all a matter of
hope, of looking forward, of trusting in God's promises for the
future and living now in the light of them. And this again
drives home the truth that faith is root and branch an imaginative thing. Because our dealings with the future are very
obviously and indisputably of an imaginative sort. So, in the
rest of this chapter I want to consider the wider nature of
human hoping as an imaginative disposition, and then turn to
reflect on some ways in which the particular context and conditions of Christian hope, as hope invested in the God of the
resurrection, is finally distinct from any other sort.

Hope, Imagination and Action

Hope is certainly not a distinctively Christian thing, though the
Christian form of it does, as we shall see, have some vital distinctive aspects. Hope is, though, one of those things which, so
far as we can tell, marks out human beings among God's creatures. So much so, in fact, that one study of the subject suggests

that '*(h)ope comes close to being the very heart and centre of a human being*'.[3] Lack of hope, or hopelessness, must then in turn be a profoundly distorting and dehumanising force.[4] It comes as no surprise, therefore, that, in Dante's imagining of the scene, the portals of Hell are inscribed with the following chilling motto: 'ABANDON EVERY HOPE, ALL YOU WHO ENTER HERE'.[5] To abandon hope is indeed finally to abandon our humanity, and to be denied the only true basis for hope would be to have our distinctive human creatureliness taken away from us, and a hellish prospect indeed. As humans, it seems, we are not naturally stoical, but suffer instead from an inbuilt desire for reality and goodness. In the Christian account of things, of course, this same desire is itself distorted and twisted by sin, but its basic form remains identifiable. We do not, that is to say, put up passively and contentedly with our lot, whatever is given to us by our current state of affairs, but constantly crave more and better. In as much as what we thus crave is proper to our created nature, this might be deemed a fitting enjoyment and celebration of God's purpose and of the gift of creation itself; but this is to bring theology to bear too early in our account here. For now we may simply observe that human beings are naturally impatient with what confronts them, and imagination is the engine which drives and facilitates this impatience, granting human existence an essential outward and forward moving momentum. Whether it arises in the form of curiosity about what lies over the horizons of our knowledge, desire to enjoy more of the good things and the opportunities which life in the world grants us, or angry protest at the terrible pain, suffering and transience which blights so much of our experience of life in the world, imaginative reaching beyond the limits of what the given affords is a basic constituent of our humanity.

And such reaching is carried out of course, whether consciously or tacitly, in the expectation that it will be a worthwhile venture and not a futile one. We trust, in other words, that whatever fuller reality it is that as yet eludes our grasp will give itself to be known more completely, and that the knowing of it will be to our ultimate good. We step out 'looking forward to' an encounter with something worth pursuing, worth living and perhaps even dying for. This is the essence of hope in its most general form, a constant decision to move into the future, to transcend the present with its apparent limits and difficulties, expanding our perceived horizons of possibility. This does not, we ought to notice, make hope the logical opposite of fear. In fact, the two often fall together in our experience. Hope may be bolstered by patterns of past experience, but it faces a future which is, in principle, always unknown and open, and thus the source of possible failures, and even horrors and terrors. The realm of possibility is anything but secure, and our capacity for imagination has no default setting allied to the positives. The inscrutability of what may yet be therefore makes hopes and fears natural bedfellows rather than alternatives. Despite what we know may well be possible, and sometimes in the teeth of what we have every reason to expect as probable, hope is that imaginative disposition which refuses to submit, and steps up to the plate with its eyes wide open and fixed on a different set of possibilities which it perceives still lying within its grasp.

This, then is another feature of hope as an imaginative activity; it is essentially an active and committed disposition rather than a passive one. And it is a matter not of imagination alone, but of knowledge, passion and the exercise of will. Hope certainly entails a form of patient waiting for things which we do not yet see (see Rom. 8:25), but it is not the sort of waiting which stands idly by with its hands in its pockets, whistling and marking time. In its patience, hope nonetheless has a sense of urgency about it, and moves forward to seize and to embrace what it looks forward to. Hope is not daydreaming, but living now in the light of an anticipated future, yearning for it, and striving to see it come to pass. The Marxist philosopher Ernst Bloch gets this right when he describes the nature of hope as the imaginative intuition of a 'Real-Possible' in the world, 'a Not-Yet-Being of an expectable kind'.[6] Hope, that is to say, latches imaginatively on to some state of affairs which stretches (sometimes quite a long way) beyond the limits of what is currently the case, and perhaps what is currently possible. But its conviction that what it envisages is no mere illusion drives hope forward, energising its efforts to see its own vision realised, struggling to overcome what may sometimes seem to be insuperable obstacles, striving to find the way ahead even when that way cannot yet be seen clearly. In his magisterial study of language, George Steiner notes a link between our capacity for such hopeful disposition and the possession of a grammatical future tense. Our ability to act meaningfully in the light of an anticipated or hoped for future, he suggests, is closely tied to our ability to speak of that future, to 'speak it into existence' as it were, by describing it for ourselves and for others, and thus positing 'axiomatic fictions' (fictions, because as yet our account of them pertains to no actual state of affairs) which become the goals of and the inspirations for our action. 'We move forwards', he writes, poetically, 'in the slipstream of the statements we make about tomorrow morning.'[7]

Imagination for the Kingdom of God

This brings us to a convenient point at which we may turn and consider some of the distinctives of the hope which is proper to Christian faith. And our starting point is the observation that Christianity has its gaze fixed on a *transcendent* rather than a merely *immanent* source for its hope. Let's unpack that claim.

The wider pattern of human hope as an imaginative stretching or reaching outwards and forwards, as we have described it above, is in effect a matter of intuition. And what 'secular' hope (if we may call it that for the sake of convenience) intuits is some state of affairs which is, in principle, possible in the world as it exists under the conditions of nature and human history; possible, that is to say, within the normative scheme of things in the world as we know and experience it. Whether the object of our hoping is a change in the climate, an upturn in the fortunes of the England cricket team, or the abolition of global poverty in our lifetime, in other words, no matter how remarkable and surprising it may be, that hope will nonetheless be for something which is in principle possible and thus in principle accountable for in terms of the recognisable continuities of our world. Radical and perhaps unlikely changes may have to come about in order to secure it, but none of them will involve anything breaching or interrupting what the natural and human sciences between them have safely within the grasp of their descriptive and explanatory powers.

Western society as a whole has, in the last few centuries, played host to hope of this sort on a grand scale, though it has generally talked about it in terms of 'progress'. In brief, ever since the middle of the eighteenth century the predominant assumption has been that human reason, liberated from the bondage of prejudice, tradition and superstition, would bring humanity to a level of self-knowledge and self-control and a dominance over the forces of nature sufficient to see the advent of a new age of freedom, peace and prosperity. Progress in science, technology, economics, ethics and every other significant sphere of human learning was, it was generally supposed, inevitable, and thus it was only a matter of time before a Utopian future would arrive. In passing, we should note that the basic pattern of this way of thinking is far from self-evident (eastern cultures, for instance, seem not to manifest it to the same extent or in the same way), and its unrelenting grip on the western imagination seems likely to derive in fact in significant measure from the religious heritage of the Old and New Testaments, in which human history is pictured as leading towards a momentous goal in which all things will find their fulfilment. Secular modernism, it seems, has found it easier to air brush God out of this biblical picture than to dispense with the picture itself. Still haunted by what one writer has called the 'sense of an ending'[8] towards which all things are steadily moving, western hopes have effectively shifted their sights from a theological to an immanent and secular teleology, seeking meaning and fulfilment within history itself, rather than beyond or outside its limited range of possibilities.

It is difficult to deny, of course, that modernity has seen genuine progress in all sorts of scientific, technological, social and political areas. Few of us would want to return to a world without modern creature comforts and conveniences, let alone one which lacked such relatively recent luxuries as anaesthetic or the curative powers of modern medicine. And yet, as soon as we have said that, we are compelled to remind ourselves that many people do still live in just such a world, because while the technologies are now available, their benefits are not universally or evenly distributed. And, on a much more basic level, the human story is a very mixed one indeed, one in which progress in certain fields is matched by no apparent improvement whatever in others. In the face of the events which our wide format plasma TV screens transmit digitally twenty-four hours a day (with accompanying surround sound) into our air conditioned living rooms, the notion of moral progress, for instance, appears to be little more than a cruel joke. If anything, our enhanced capacities to 'do things' in and to the world just makes the atrocities we are inclined to commit more horrendous and more easily realised. Arguably, in this regard we have regressed rather than progressed.

The history of the last century is one littered with terrible pogroms, the industrial ruthlessness of carpet bombing, napalm strikes and threatened nuclear obliteration, hundreds of thousands of infant deaths from easily preventable diseases, and many other symptoms of an unjust global economics. Add to this the dawning realisation of our abiding fragility and powerlessness in the face of such spectres as HIV/Aids and bird flu, planetary warming and the destructive capacities of potential meteorite strikes, and it is little wonder that the myth of progress has run aground, being left high and dry on the sands of 'postmodern' despair. The idea that there is genuine hope for humanity or for our world seems fanciful when we take a long hard look at the evidence, and while ever our consideration is limited to the immanent capacities and possibilities of nature and history as we know them to be. In truth, this realisation is in any case just the admission on the larger scale of what every individual must finally face on the scale of his or her own existence – that all that is good and worthwhile in our life is to be consumed sooner or later by transience, snuffed out, returned to the dust whence it came. Death gets us all in the end. No amount of progress could ever deal with that. Extinction, personal or global, appears to be our inevitable lot.

'Who will deliver me from this body of death?' asks the apostle Paul, and then conveniently supplies the answer to his own question: 'Thanks be to God, who gives us the victory through our Lord, Jesus Christ!' (Rom. 7:24b–25a) This, of course, penetrates straight to the heart of what is different about Christian hope. As an imaginative apprehension of things to come, it is not constrained at all by the capacities and possibilities of the known world, but only by the promise of the God who lies beyond the world as well as being close to it. And this, of course, is the God who called the world itself into existence in the beginning, who filled the womb of the virgin with child, and who raised the crucified Jesus to new life. This is a God, in other words, who is unconstrained by what is possible for us or for the world he has made, a God with whom all things are possible, and a God who has promised to 'make all things new' (Rev. 21:5). Importantly, as Jesus' own resurrection from death indicates, this does not mean wiping the slate completely clean and beginning again from scratch, but a 'new creation' which is at the same time a radical re-making of this world and its history. Continuous with this world, the world of God's promised future does not emerge or evolve 'naturally' from it, but from a further act of God's grace on the cosmic scale. So, since its conditions lie wholly beyond the purview of anything we can currently *know*, we can only *imagine* what such a future existence will be like, and Scripture does so by picturing states of affairs which are, to borrow a cliché, 'this world – but not as we know it'. It will be a world in which all that is evil in this world will be purged and redressed, all that is lacking or hurting in this world made good, all that we properly value and celebrate in this world not just restored but (if we dare imagine it) bigger and better than anything we currently enjoy. Life in all its fullness indeed! In this sense, Christian hope is properly 'other wordly', because it has its sights fixed on a reality lying beyond the bounds and the possibilities of the world we now know, and on the faithfulness of the God who himself lies beyond that world, who promises to bring it to fulfilment, and whose promises can be trusted.

In another, vital sense, though, Christian hope is not 'other worldly' at all, but very much a matter of living expectantly in ways that transform the here and now. And here again, imagination is vitally important. Karl Marx famously complained that religious visions of a 'heavenly' future with God were deliberately engineered by those in power to dull the sensibilities of the masses (serving as an imaginative 'opiate'), and thereby to prevent them from rising up in violent protest against their current unjust and downtrodden circumstance. Perhaps there was some truth in that. But that's not the true nature of Christian hope. On the contrary, as theologian Jürgen Moltmann notes, trust in God's promise for the world 'causes not rest, but unrest, not patience, but impatience. It does not calm the unquiet heart, but is itself this unquiet heart in man. Those who hope in Christ can no longer put up with reality as it is, but begin to suffer under it, to contradict it.'[9]

Hope, as suggested earlier, is essentially something active, not passive. And this is no less true of Christian hope than any other. It is a matter not just of 'looking forward to', but of moving forward to discover the importance of God's promises for the here and now. To live by faith, as a disciple of Christ, as a citizen not just of this world but of the kingdom of God, is to live life in accordance with a reality which is not yet fully present, but which we imagine, long for and hope for, and which, in the meanwhile, we strive to make known already in the patterns of our being and acting in the church and in the world. That such living regularly contradicts the wider patterns of experience and 'common sense', and the expectations of society, does not and need not deter us, for it is founded, finally, not on our own sense of immediate possibility, or our capacity to intuit optimistic scenarios and opportunities lying within our long term grasp, but on the promise of God which takes as its premise our finitude, our brokenness and sin, and the apparent spiralling of our world towards extinction, and sets a limit to it. 'Let me worry about that', God says in effect; 'Behold, I am about to make all things new! Let me show you something of what it's going to look like when it's finished . . . Now, you go out there and start living now as though the job was already done.' That's the promise and the command which, as Christians, has taken our imagination – and thereby our hearts, minds and wills – entirely captive.

12

In God's Good Time

Music and the hope of the world

Russell Rook

Music, the Devil and the Deep Crystal Sea

My parents had always encouraged my musical interests – I
was a choirboy at an Anglican school and a trombone player in
a local Salvation Army band – in part, no doubt, because it
drew me further into the life of the church. And then, one fate-
ful summer's day, I discovered 'heavy metal'. Leaping high
above the mattress and twanging my air-guitar with a dem-
onic ferocity I found myself shouting the lyric, 'I am the
antichrist, come follow me! I am the antichrist, come follow
me!' It was at this inopportune moment that my mother
entered. As I brought my screaming serenade to an abrupt
finale and came to an unsteady standstill on the edge of the bed
my Mum began: 'Russell, there is plenty of evidence for the
antichrist in this world without you.' This devastating point
made, she added, 'Thank you very much,' and left the room.

For almost 2,000 years, music has been a perennial part of
church life and yet it is not too much to suggest that many
Christians still do not know what to make of it. The art-form
with which many Christians find themselves most at home,
can also render us all at sea. The place of music within biblical
revelation (the psalms contain more content on creation than
Genesis), its continual presence within the church's gatherings

(hardly a moment of church history has passed unaccompanied) and its useful vocabulary for exploring the mysteries of our faith (music regularly illustrates and informs our discussions of heaven, the Trinity and eschatology, to name but a few) have given the art-form an ecclesial ubiquity.

Yet, whether through our persistent attempts to distinguish the sacred from the secular (the Orthodox church's preference for vocal music distinguished her worship from the instrumental music of the pagans) our concerns that certain styles of music may undermine God's work in the world (remember the youth worker of yesteryear playing Beatles' songs backwards to unveil subliminal messages) or our fears for those whose musical tastes differ from our own (witness Jerry Lee Lewis, Johnny Cash, Jimmy Hendrix and other musicians whose work was considered Satanic), music is often eyed with considerable suspicion. Eschatologically speaking, music seems capable of conveying our greatest hopes and most terrible fears. It can transport us from the heights of heaven to the gates of hell.

In this chapter we will address the potential of music to communicate the hopes of humanity as expressed in the gospel. We begin with Augustine, for whom music holds both deep personal and theological resonances. Augustine uses a musical model to illustrate God's interaction with humanity in time. Having proved influential for musicians and theologians alike, we can observe and critique these ideas at close hand in the music of the church and the wider world. In particular, we will critique the notion that music brings us closer to God by facilitating an experience of timelessness. In the final section we will enlist the help of the contemporary theologian Jeremy Begbie. Combining Augustine's first thoughts with a more developed understanding of musical time, I will argue that music provides us with a unique and sophisticated language by which we can communicate and understand history as God's good time for creation.

Music, Augustine and the Time of Our Life

While many a theologian has expressed a love for music few have devoted as much time to the art-form as Augustine. In

his *Confessions* we witness a powerful personal testimony to
the theological potency of music. Having recounted, at
length, Augustine's personal struggles with faith, the book
details a mysterious musical introduction to Augustine's
acquiescence. In this moment, his somewhat circular debate
with the Almighty is permanently interrupted by the sound
of music:

> Whether it was the voice of a boy or a girl I cannot say, but
> again and again it repeated the refrain 'Take it and read, take it
> and read' . . . I stemmed my flood of tears and stood up, telling
> myself that this could only be a divine command to open my
> book of Scripture and read the first passage on which my eyes
> should fall.[1]

This strange musical interlude is the prelude to Augustine's
conversion. Coinciding with a period of renewed musical
interest in the life of the church (the singing of congregational
songs and psalms was becoming more widespread at this
time) music becomes part of the background noise of
Augustine's growing faith. The absence of music prior to his
conversion betrays a nervousness on Augustine's part; music
was still largely associated with pagan worship and ritual at
this time. However, following his decision, music takes on a
higher spiritual significance. It resolves tensions, mediates
mercy and communicates truth. Above all, it opens
humankind to the possibility of salvation, propels him
towards the goal of existence and anticipates the ultimate fulfilment of life itself.

In his later work, *De Musica*, Augustine ascribes music's
eschatological potency to its capacity to account for the
process of time.[2] Although fundamental to our every experience, the process of time's passing proves precarious to the
theologian and philosopher alike. While we can imagine a
world without the colour purple, the pyramids, aardvarks or
Belgium, it is impossible to imagine our world without time.
Theologians maintain that this says something about the
creator's relationship with creation. Creation is, quite literally, the time that God has made for his creatures. While

fundamental to it, time remains one of the most ephemeral aspects of creation. As Augustine himself attempts to explain, time is the process whereby the future (those events and objects which do not yet exist) come into the present (where they do exist) only to pass into the past (thus disappearing once more). This elusive process becomes easier to observe and understand through the language, structure and form of music.

As a singer begins to sing, the song exists in the performer's anticipation. As each note is sounded the music momentarily comes to life in the present, before passing away. Finally, while last notes fade to the ear, the music echoes on in the memory. In this, the song provides a parable of our own experience of time. We live in a state of continual anticipation never quite knowing what is around the corner. We invest prayer and effort in the hope that our aspirations will materialise and our fears be averted. At some point, these expectations are either realised or denied before, finally, becoming consigned to our memories.

As Augustine's theology and testimony reveal, music not only informs our understanding of time but also transforms our experiences of it. At a moment's notice, music can trigger a change in our mood or emotions. It can distract and surprise us, generate new understanding, and facilitate divine revelation. Whether through the pianist in the fancy restaurant, the organ prelude to a church service, the background 'muzak' in the elevator or the 'favourites' on our iPod, music has the ability to enhance our experience of time. In Augustine's case, music has the power to transform a restless seeker into a newborn worshipper.

Music, Augustine insists, harnesses humankind's God-given fusion of physical and spiritual reality. On the one hand, through the intake and outflow of breath, the singer utilises the physical processes by which life itself is sustained. On the other hand, once lodged in the memory the song transcends biology, becoming the property of the soul. Music moves us from the sensory world to a sense of the divine. Hence while the ear delights at the physical sounds, the soul loves music more for its timeless truth. In the here and now, Augustine argues, music is the gift of God's eternal presence.

Music, Timelessness and the Pursuit of the Perpetual Present

Augustine's experience of music accompanied his development as a theologian. In particular, music becomes a vindicating factor in his defence of the immortality of the soul. By enabling our understanding of time, music illustrates the soul's immunity to time's passing. While time is transient, each moment, whether the remembered past, experienced present or anticipated future is retained within the soul. This defining mark of our humanity is also our connection with the divine: although life appears fleeting, our mortal existence will one day give way to the timelessness of eternity. By giving voice to the passing of time and transporting us from the physical to the spiritual realm, music enables us to transcend temporal realities and encounter God in his timelessness. The impact of Augustine's thought, in this regard, has had a far reaching impact.

To this day, one of the highest compliments that can be paid to a musical piece or performance is that it is, 'timeless'. The notion that music can facilitate an experience of timelessness, and is thus subject to certain timeless characteristics, has been common throughout the centuries. Given its prominence in Augustine, it is somewhat unsurprising that church musicians have made much of this. I recently found myself in a discussion about contemporary music in evangelical and charismatic churches. 'The reason we repeat the same line, chorus or motif over and over again', one performer reported, 'is to disturb the congregation's sense of time so that they might be closer to God'. The theology behind this technique is clear. If God is timeless and we are his temporal creatures then our chances of experiencing his presence are increased if we can somehow remove ourselves from time. Augustine's model of musical time makes this journey possible. Their sense of time blurred by the pleasant monotony of these repetitive musical motifs, the congregation feels free from temporal confinement and limitations and more able to experience God's timeless presence.

This technique is not peculiar to contemporary church music in the evangelical and charismatic traditions. Influenced by the ancient and monastic art of plain song, the Orthodox composer John Tavener has used a similar range of techniques to the self same effect. The aleotoric nature of Tavener's music attempts to evoke an experience of eternity and thus provide a window on God. The music appears to deflect and even negate our sense of time. His works often lack an obvious direction, resist sudden changes and movement and attempt to avoid clearly defined beginnings and endings. The eternity which Tavener is drawn towards consists of a time without time.

This attraction to timelessness is not confined to church musicians. The minimalist movement, synonymous with John Adams, Philip Glass, Steve Reich and Michael Nyman, utilises the relentless repetition of different musical materials and motifs to suppress the sense of time's passing. One of the most popular and popularised of contemporary classical genres, the minimalists' techniques have been regularly commandeered by film composers, pop artists and jazz musicians alike. Within pop music, for instance, early 'rave' and 'house' music was a direct development of minimalism and these techniques continue to provide the vocabulary of current dance music. In this, dance music forms an exemplary expression of popular postmodern eschatology. Untied from time, and escaping both the pain of the past and the threat of the future, the 'clubber' is free to experience a perpetual presence, a never-ending now.

Before we become carried away by the timeless possibilities of music, a contrary argument demands our attention. For while Augustine is undoubtedly correct in asserting the revelatory and spiritual possibilities of music, his attempt to attribute timeless qualities to the art-form is as problematic as his teaching on the immortality of the soul. Augustine's promotion of timelessness threatens music, and time for that matter, with irrelevance. What began as an argument for the Creator's activity within, and ultimate purpose for, creation, eventually threatens God's connection with creation as a whole.

Upon reflection, the connection between music and time-lessness is tenuous, even illogical. Time is not simply the frame in which musical works of art appear. Time, as we said at the start, forms a crucial part of what music is. Beats and bars, rhythms and runs, crotchets and quavers all express different values of time. In short, music is always 'in time'. Whether gifted musicians or not, humans utilise these aspects of music to make the most of time. Whether in the counting of a child playing hide and seek, a group of burley men shouting, 'one, two, three, heave!' as they attempt to manoeuvre a heavy object or the runner coordinating the rhythm of his feet with the meter of his breathing, human beings use rhythm and tone, the fundamental building blocks of music, to understand and make the most of time.

While clever musical techniques may displace, stall or sus-pend our sense of time, they can ultimately only blur the boundaries. However much we become part of the music, we never lose contact with the timely reality of the physical world. In simple terms, the case for musical timelessness is under-mined by the fact that musical works have endings. Whether we are listening to a Wagner opera, or dancing the weekend away at a rave, the experience will eventually come to an end – we will applaud, or stop dancing, and go home. The loss of time proves as damaging to theology as it is to music. If God is timeless and we, in all our music making, are tied to time, how can our music ever reach the heavens? More worryingly still, how can a timeless God realistically intervene and direct our temporal world towards his own ends? Having identified music's revelatory capacity by its appropriation of time, Augustine's subsequent argument for music as the conveyer of timeless reality undermines the role of music in his own tes-timony and conversion.

Having outlined a theology of music to rival that of the pagans, Augustine is finally unable to square the circle. His error, in this arena at least, was to confuse the eternal God of the Bible with the timeless god of Greek antiquity. This latter char-acter is the God of Plato, a product of Greek religion and its phi-losophy. He is a permanent presence outside of the physical world, an undifferentiated being beyond the quotidian course of time and accessible only to the immortal soul. The former God is Triune, the one who makes, sustains and uses the physical world, a communion of persons in relationship one with another, whose eternity is not a denial of time but rather comprises a perfect time all of his own. Trinity does not deny time but comprises a perfect time of his own. It is in this context that Scripture speaks of a God who creates a dynamic world and proclaims it good. The possibility of creation's future development and perfection renders it good and it is the creation of time which enables God to move the world towards this ultimate end. As music is reliant upon temporality, so too everything we know and experience in creation takes place in God's good time.

Music, Begbie and the God Who's on Time.

Having recognised the importance of time to all that God has made and declared good, and having acknowledged the way in which God uses time to achieve his good purposes for creation, we turn now to the work of Jeremy Begbie. A contemporary pioneer of the relationship between music and theology, Begbie's work demonstrates how music enhances our appreciation of time. In this final section, I will outline a number of ways in which Begbie's work enables us to further understand the relationship between music, time and eschatology. The key to understanding music, in Begbie, comes, once again, through its appropriation of time: 'When we ask *how* music is temporal, we are confronted by an enormous range of temporal processes.'[3]

Firstly, a musical model of time enables us to grasp some of the complex ways in which God directs human history. In particular, music undermines the notion that God's activity in time is a matter of simple progression; this view blighted the modern era and has been the subject of considerable criticism in the last fifty years. For much of modernity, theology and philosophy equated the passing of time with the notion of progress. Either by man's intellectual evolution and/or God's growing intervention in human history, the world was considered to be marching relentlessly towards a new age or the kingdom of God. However, the consummation of these hopes and dreams never materialised and the twentieth century proved bloodier than any of the centuries that preceded it.

Musical time refutes the notion that all events occur as one simplistic progression. A piece of music, while always in time, is subject to many concurrent directions and developments. Themes introduced in one moment can be developed in the next. They can change key, become inverted, run backwards, or separate into secondary themes and are sometimes forgotten. Furthermore, the layering of musical materials such as harmony, instrumentation and rhythm can drive music in a number of multifarious directions at the same time. None of this makes time meaningless; instead, it contributes to the dynamism and destination of the piece. Eventually all works of music, whether progressive or regressive, random or mathematically constructed, improvised or composed, come to an end. It is then that we can more fully understand and interpret what we have heard.

Given that history is driven by the complex concoction of divine sovereignty and human freewill, it is unsurprising that human history is not fashioned through one linear movement, be it towards perpetual progress or entropic decline. An understanding of musical time helps to illustrate and affirm a Christian eschatology in this regard. Here, history is regarded as the unified outworking of every independent interaction between the creator and his creatures within time. In the same way that a symphony moves us towards a climax and conclusion through a multitude of melodies and motifs, memories and moods, so too God exercises and executes his plans for creation through many different concurrent and contingent movements. At times these progressions may appear contrary or regressive, yet each and every deferral, detour and delay contributes to the overall effect and destination of the work as a whole.

Secondly, music illustrates the nature of shock and surprise in God's plans for human history. In music, the future is not simply an extension of the present but often involves elements of surprise and discontinuity. Where linear models tend to downplay discordant interruptions, indirect routes and disturbing ruptures are an inherent and enriching part of great music. At any point, a composer is at liberty to introduce radically new schemes or materials to a work. These futuristic inventions may have little or no bearing upon what the audience have experienced so far but as the work evolves, materials which previously appeared surprising, eventually become part of the fabric of the whole. A moment which seemed shocking, or out of place, may turn out to be a prophetic glimpse of that which is yet to come.

A biblical eschatology must retain its scope for shock and surprise. While indebted to the numerous theologians who engineered an eschatological turn in twentieth-century theology, one remains cautious of attempts to tie eschatology down. Wolfhart Pannenberg's location of God's entire eschatological action in the resurrection of Christ and the popular attempts of novelist Tim LeHaye to outline the end-times narrative in advance, represent two, albeit very different, examples of what might be considered an overly prescriptive eschatology. The idea that we can bring closure to the story of time ahead of time would seem to remove God's capacity to surprise us. Even the most cursory glance at God's revelation in the Bible would suggest that this move is unwise. Furthermore, the event of the resurrection means that we, like those disciples in the final moments of the gospels, should remain alert, for the risen Jesus is willing, able and likely to surprise us.

Thirdly, music helps us to understand that all of time is meaningful for God. Begbie accounts for a musical work through a series of ever-widening time bands, or waves. In micro form, a musical wave can account for the smallest amount of musical material, determining the distance between two semiquavers, or the period it takes to sound a single note or chord. All of these waves are encompassed within broader waves and in time within the piece as a whole. Within the wider work no musical moment is unimportant and no movement is arbitrary. Each note relates to every other note and every musical fragment, whether noticed or unnoticed, remembered or forgotten, expected or unexpected fulfils a vital role in the overall event. Eschatologically speaking,

Christian theology frames each and every moment of history within the wider story of creation. As a result our own life's story finds its meaning within the story of the community of creation and, ultimately, in the story of the creator himself. Furthermore, each event that occurs within created time will contribute something to creation's final end and consummation. For as Scripture tells us, at the end, nothing good will be lost and Christ will be all in all.

Finally, music provides an insight into the consummation of history in time. All great works of music finish with a flourish. It is the grand finale of a piece which enables the audience to interpret the work as a whole. Likewise, the fact that created time is directed towards a definite ending provides history with the possibility of purpose and ultimate meaning. In addition, music may enable us to imagine something of life on the other side of time's fulfilment. For many, the popular conception of heaven seems somewhat unattractive. The idea of a permanent existence with no potential for growth or development, expectation or hope is deeply problematic. How can heaven be the fulfilment of the Christian hope if in heaven there is nothing less to hope for?

While a symphony may have a grand finale, towards which every musical material is directed, a song, for instance, rarely takes such a form. As with most forms of music, songs rely upon repetition and recapitulation for their development. Following this model might we re-imagine heaven as an eternal remembrance and anticipation of all that God has done and continues to do. As part of God's own Triune life, heaven marks the beginning of an infinitely new series of eternal possibilities. With this we come to what is no doubt the most fitting end to this discussion on music and eschatology, for as Jonathan Edwards wrote, 'when I think of heaven all I can imagine is people sweetly singing'.[4]

13

Eschatology and Pop Culture

It's the end of the world as we know it

Krish Kandiah

It's the End of the World as we Know it . . . and I Feel Fine

These days it is not just the sombre street evangelist with his sandwich board that proclaims the impending doom of planet earth. There is a whole subgenre of science fiction that pronounces that the end of the world is nigh. From alien invasion to global meltdown to nuclear holocaust, there is a whole range of doomsday scenarios for us to choose from, as we relax in the comfort of our ergonomically designed reclining cinema seats. And it is not only the silver screen that is affecting our vision of the future. When we choose our pension plan, shop on credit, turn on the playstation, and recycle our plastics, our subconscious conceptions of the future seep out into our day to day lives. The church may have abandoned sandwich boards, but there are new dangers and opportunities before us in the way in which we interact with the question of the future.

The Future's so Bright, I Gotta Wear Shades

The cult television show *Star Trek* is a powerful visual aid for the way that our culture used to visualise the future.[1] With a bright gleaming starship Enterprise conquering the universe ahead of it, the original series made in the late 1960s projected an optimistic view of the future based on the triumph of technology. At a popular level there is still a great legacy of confidence in science and technology to solve many of the problems of our society. Reliance on pioneering surgery to help improve weight loss and remove wrinkles, faith in cleaner cars, faster computers, new food groups and additives to improve our life expectancy are all remnants of a modernist view of science and technology. *Star Trek – The Next Generation* which was made twenty years after the original series, did not project quite such an overwhelmingly optimistic outlook of the future. In this series, a more vulnerable captain, a ship's counsellor and a more multicultural cast, time warps, a virtual reality deck and the introduction of other beings over whom we were not superior, began to reflect the shift in culture towards postmodernism. Contrary to Stanley Grenz who saw *The Next Generation* as thoroughly postmodern, there is, however, still a bright gleaming spaceship that solves most of the problems it encounters through superior technology.

The Future's not what it used to be

Our contemporary culture retains the optimism about the possibility of scientific solutions to the ills of society but also expresses pessimism towards the effects and the dangers of the power of the technical. We are in a transition stage in the overlap between two competing worldviews, which indicates that we cannot yet be defined as totally postmodern. A view of the future at its most postmodern however is vividly reflected in films such as Ridley Scott's *Blade Runner* (1982) where technological disintegration is portrayed as a foreboding danger. Other films that take up this theme include *12 Monkeys* (1995), *Terminator* (1984), *The Matrix* (1999) and *I-Robot* (2004). The overwhelming confidence in human ability to conquer the challenges of nature and create a shining New Atlantis[2] have gone, replaced instead by a dystopian pessimism.

These films all demonstrate a frankensteinian fear of the machinery made to serve us rising up and becoming our masters. They are instantly recognisable as postmodern because the aesthetic of the future is not the bright glistening glow of a hygienic, technically superior world but rather a murky, grungy, dysfunctional mess of wires, computer screens, pollution and dirt. Film-makers love to capitalise on the fear and uncertainty that come from the changes occurring in our technocultures. The idea of networked computer technology developing a level of artificial intelligence that becomes self-aware and sentient is a wellworn theme in contemporary science fiction movies. Couple it with the ways that new technologies have been utilised by terrorists to co-ordinate their atrocities, and even seemingly innocent technologies such as mobile phones and airliners become potential tools of terror. It is no wonder that we are so easily unnerved about the impact of scientific progress on our society.

This fear of technology is nothing new. When the television was first introduced, many people feared that the people on the screen were actually spying on them in their homes. Under Ned Ludd, the English textile workers of the nineteenth century destroyed the machines they saw as robbing them of their livelihoods. Mary Shelley's *Frankenstein* was written shortly after the trials that sent many of those first Luddites to the penal colonies or to the gallows. If *Frankenstein* was the very first science fiction novel then even at the genre's inception we are being warned of the dangers of unaccountable scientism.

The apocalyptic bent in our society is also evident in other aspects of today's culture. We are so fearful of the untold damage we have wrought on the environment, it is unsurprising that this inconvenient truth is raised in movies such as the *Day after Tomorrow* (2004) where the effects of global warming are vividly displayed through the latest computer generated imagery. But thirty-two years earlier these same themes were also raised by the film *Silent Running* (1972). We have played God too easily and too often, and our creations, whether in the form of 'genetically modified crops' or biological weapons, have now come to life in the dystopian nightmares of films like *Outbreak* (1995), *Gattaca* (1997) and *Children of Men* (2006).

Although the fear of technology and pessimism are nothing new, Anthony Giddens argues that our contemporary world has new risk parameters largely or completely unknown to previous eras. These include high-consequence risks, deriving from the globalised character of the social systems of modernity. Our outlook on the world

> is apocalyptic, not because it is inevitably heading towards calamity, but because it introduces risks which previous generations had not had to face . . . so long as nuclear weapons remain. . . so long as science and technology continue to be involved with the creation of novel weaponry, the risk of massively destructive warfare will persist.[3]

He goes on to argue that this often produces a fatalistic view of the future where 'living in the modern world is more like being aboard a careering juggernaut rather than being in a carefully controlled motor car'.[4] For Giddens the smooth drive to the future was modernity's promise of progress whereas in postmodernity, the future is the inevitable destruction that awaits a runaway world,[5] where technology and nature are out of control.

The doomsday scenarios prevalent in contemporary movies reveal our state of panic as we face the future. Many are experiencing what Alvin Toffler described as 'future-shock'.[6] The risks of modern life and the increasingly negative views of the future contribute to an escalated emphasis upon the immediate. The present takes priority over the future as it is hoped that tomorrow never comes for it only brings disaster.

Future-shock is not only affecting our views of politics, ecology and technology. Closer to home, marriage and its promises for better or worse, and for richer or poorer, till death do us part, are readily exchanged for serial monogamy or another one-night stand. Zygmunt Bauman, the noted sociologist, describes how 'with the new frailty of family structures, many a family life expectation is shorter than the individual life expectation of any of its members'[7] This is a complete reversal of the picture of family dynasties that would last throughout generations. Our relationships are like hearts etched onto the sand quickly washed away by the liquidity of modern life, where immediate gratification takes precedence over the long term security of the family name.

Our culture's focus on the present at the expense of the future is also impacting our financial stability. Recent statistics from Credit Action portray that because average consumer borrowing via credit cards, motor and retail finance deals, overdrafts and unsecured personal loans has risen to unprecedented levels, UK personal debt has exceeded £1¼ trillion and is increasing by around £1 million every four minutes.[8] Bauman comments:

> The work ethic has been replaced by a consumer ethic; the savings-book culture of delayed gratification has been replaced by the credit-card culture that "takes the waiting out of wanting". The resulting looming financial catastrophe of "buy now-pay later" can be coped with by projecting it into the far off never never land of the future.[9]

Nostalgia isn't what it used to be

When the future is so bleak, that every effort is made to avoid looking forward, pining for the past becomes a welcome distraction. The French philosopher Baudrillard argues that 'when the real is no longer what it used to be, nostalgia assumes its full meaning'. In today's culture, nostalgia is no longer a pastime just for the elderly. Film versions of classic television shows such as the *Dukes of Hazzard* (2005), *Magic Roundabout* (2005), *Starsky and Hutch* (2004), *Charlie's Angels* (2002 and 2003), *Scooby Doo* (2002) and *Bewitched* (2006), are targeting a much younger audience as an effective deterrent for future-shock. Needless to say, most of these films are dismissed by critics as artistic disasters, but they provide comfort cinema, offering the reassurance of old characters from better days. However this optimistic pining for the past is treated with a similar cynicism and scepticism as optimistic views of the future. John Webster argued that postmodernity 'characteristically rejects any idea that human existence in time constitutes an ordered whole, history is dispersed into a

non-sequential, non-developmental, non-utopian, non-eschato-
logical scatter of elements'.[10] This paralysing disconnection with
past and future is one of the main features of postmodernism.

Stuck in a Moment

And so our culture is stranded in the present with this moment
in time being all that really matters. In *Last Kiss* (2006) directed
by and starring Zach Braff, a successful architect is just about to
turn thirty and experiences a crisis of hope. Despite having a
great job, a beautiful and understanding girlfriend, close
friends and a baby on the way he loses any vision for his future.
In desperation he embarks on a kamikaze relationship, having
an affair with a college student ten years his junior. The film
highlights the phenomenon that many people, whilst believing
they can be perpetually adolescent,[11] are experiencing the
struggle for meaning for life whilst still in relative youth, and a
new term has been coined: the 'quarter-life crisis'[12]

If the future is bleak, the past is a joke and the present does
not measure up to expectations, then the stage is set for a
retelling of the Christian story for this generation. This story
has an alternative ending to the narrative being offered by our
culture, which challenges the symptoms of postmodern
future-shock that can be seen not only in our culture, but also
in our church: pining, pessimism, paralysis and panic.

Pining

Bert Hoedemaker argues that there are two extreme positions
in ecclesiological typologies. Firstly, there is the church that
defines its existence because of its beginnings.[13] This type of
church can develop a nostalgic view of the past which pines
after bygone days when the church was healthy, or experiencing revival, rather than engaging with the issues of the present
and future. Secondly, there is the church which is defined by
its emergence. This type of church exists because of the goals
and anticipations it pines for, regardless of its past or present.

Now the church must live in the tension of being faithful to the historic and apostolic faith and also of being a foretaste of the coming kingdom of God. We must look back to the biblical past to normalise the formulation of our faith and yet we must also look to God's promised future to set the agenda of how this faith should be expressed.

The danger comes when one of these anchor points is lost. If our view is only backwards, we can find it easy to latch on to specific historical expressions of the cultural life of the church and make them normative for the church. Too many of our churches are time machines transporting us backward to a point in history where we deemed that Christianity was healthy. For some churches this is a puritan expression of faith, for others it is 1970s revival meetings. But this may simply be another expression of our culture's pining after the past. If our view is only to the future we lose the anchoring point of our Christian heritage. Many churches are driven solely by their mission statements, numerical targets, building projects, or the fashionable fluctuations in social trends rather than the unchanging apostolic gospel.

In a culture which seeks satisfaction through nostalgic television reruns or which seeks security through the reprinting of the annuals that appeared in our youth when life seemed much simpler, or which seeks intimacy and identity through a rekindled interest in genealogies and genes reunited, the church has a tremendous opportunity. Into this context the Christian faith can offer a story that can encompass all of the little stories of individual lives. The gospel of creation, fall, redemption and consummation provides a framework in which our longing for the past, and our quest to find security and identity can be truly satisfied. Rather than simply pandering to the immediate felt needs of our audience, we can offer a family with both a history and a destiny. Our story offers an alternative ending to the global doomsday scenarios but also to individual life narratives.

Pessimism

The mood of the Christian missions movement of the nineteenth century can be summed up by the slogan of the Student

Volunteer Movement, 'The evangelization of the world in this generation.' The uninhibited spirit of optimism is obvious, and in hindsight begs the question whether that optimism was based on a confidence in the authority of the triune God or in the cultural and political ascendancy of Christendom at the time. That optimism is no longer present in the western church, in fact there seems to be a sense of pessimism, even defeatism. Many of us are happy for our churches and even our individual spiritual lives to survive rather than thrive. We resist the challenge to be part of the conversion of our neighbour, let alone the conversion of the world. Mission agencies comment how they are finding it increasingly difficult to motivate churches in the UK to take global mission seriously, some blaming it on the primacy of the survivalist tendency.

But historically it is precisely when the church was forced to survive, that it began actually to thrive. The current experience of the church increasingly feeling marginalized and on the periphery of the political process offers us the opportunity to demonstrate that our confidence is in the gospel and not on the church's privilege and power in society. Decrease in church attendance can be an important time of winnowing out those that are cultural Christians and those that truly believe. It forces us to reconsider how we can effectively reach out to those around us. It provides us with the impetus of urgency. It enables us to learn again to trust God's sovereignty and will. This optimism can be witnessed in the bold humility of the early church; incredibly bold in the face of the imperial power that stood against it, humbly assuming no power of its own except reliance on the Almighty. This is the optimism we need to recapture again in order to demonstrate the gospel of grace in our time. In our powerlessness we need to recapture the spirit of Paul who could write, 'I am not ashamed of the gospel, because it is the power of God for the salvation of everyone who believes '(Rom. 1:16).

Paralysis

At a popular level the pessimism in western culture is revealed in its desire for perpetual adolescence. This manifests itself in the avoidance of commitment; increased consumerism, and an unwillingness to learn from the past or face up to the challenges of the future. This paralysis leads to escapism into the virtual worlds of games, chatrooms or music, and the sociologists often relate this to cocooning – the attempt to isolate ourselves from the stresses of the world by socialising less and retreating into our homes more. This cyclical process of diminishing social confidence was first called 'cocooning' in the 1990s by Faith Popcorn – a fantastically appropriately named trend forecaster. It has been a commercially significant observation as the stay-at-home entertainment sector has sky-rocketed through DVD sales, internet relationships and digital television shopping. It may be that 'it's the end of the world as we know it', but in front of my plasma screen, snugly protected from the ills of the world, I feel fine.

This sense of retreat into a safe cocoon has been experienced by the church too. We have become happy to focus our activities in-house providing services for members only. We become fearful of crossing paths with people from non-faith or other-faith backgrounds. We have become self-absorbed, apathetic and paralysed. There are glimmers of activism in the world and in the church: the Make Poverty History campaign or the response to the 2005 tsunami, for example, but in general there is still a pessimistic trend. The church needs to provide more than just a safe haven. It can meet the world's need for a place where social inhibitions are broken down and real intimacy can be forged through the love of Christ. However, a church that ends there is as paralysed as the world. We are called to action and it is through action that we reach maturity. Moreover, the paralysis inherent in our culture provides the very opportunity for the church to be spurred into action to demonstrate its hope more clearly. Churches that take the initiative in urban renewal, forging links with other culture groups, or providing services for the young and the elderly will not go unnoticed.

Panic

The western world is finally beginning to take the environment seriously as a moral rather than a political issue. Concern for reducing our carbon footprint, lowering our consumption of energy, recycling, cutting down our waste and land fill usage are becoming mainstream issues for responsible citizens in the western world. Christians should feel excited that our calling to be good stewards of the planet is being facilitated by environmental concerns becoming part of everyday life. The danger is that our motivation for creation care is being shaped by the panic-driven agenda of the environmental lobby rather than a confident trust in our creator's sustaining of the planet and our responsibility to be caretakers of creation. This same panic-driven mentality can also seep into our lives when it comes to making money, finding a partner or even doing evangelism or chasing church growth.

Shared concerns with the world around actually bring us opportunities to relate better and partner with individuals and organisations with the same agenda. They offer a great point of contact with our society and so our hope in God in the midst of this environmental crisis, for example, offers a powerful opportunity and apologetic as we work alongside others for the sake of God's planet. The panic that drives much environmentalism can be countered by the confident active church that discharges faithfully its call to care for the world out of a hope that a better one is coming.

The Future's Bright . . .

The overriding answer to the ills of future-shock: pining, pessimism, paralysis and panic, can be summarised by the Christian concept of hope. Lesslie Newbigin writing about evangelistic opportunities in the inner city focuses on the hope that the gospel brings into the despair of many housing estates:

> in all our preaching . . . about the hope which the gospel makes possible, we have to keep steadily in view the fact that what the gospel offers is not just hope for the individual but hope for the world. Concretely I think this means that the congregation must be so deeply and intimately involved in the secular concerns of

the neighbourhood that it becomes clear to everyone that no one and nothing is outside the range of God's love in Jesus. Christ's message, the original Gospel was about the coming of the kingdom of God, that is to say God's kingly rule over the whole of his creation and the whole of human kind. That is the only authentic Gospel.[14]

Newbigin's approach emphasises communal hope. This challenges the individualistic nature of the progress offered by modernity and also the pessimistic fatalism of postmodernity. The congregation as eschatological foretaste challenges the rejection of attempts to narrate past, present and future into a meaningful whole as without some conception of hope it is difficult to continue living. The gospel provides a bold vision of the future with the coming of God's kingdom, and the local congregation is to provide tangible evidence of this reality. This future-fuelled emphasis coheres well with Jürgen Moltman's theology which argues, 'Christianity is eschatology, is hope, forward looking and forward moving, and therefore also revolutionising and transforming.'[15] The London Institute for Contemporary Christianity's Imagine project offers a much needed wake-up call to the pessimistic paralysis of much contemporary evangelicalism. Mark Greene comments that even with drastically reduced church attendance there are still 4.5 million people attending church at least once a month.[16] The biblical imagery of the church as the salt of the earth hints at the minority making major impact. With roughly 7 per cent of the population connecting in some way to the church there is an incredible opportunity for mobilisation. If this sleeping giant can be woken from its inactivity there is great hope of significant cultural change.

In light of the doomsday scenarios, the short termism of investments both financial and relational, the hope of the gospel offers an exciting alternative ending to the narrative that drives many of our friends and neighbours. In the quirky film *Big Fish* (2003) Ewan McGregor's character is given a glimpse of the future and sees in a witch's eye the way he is destined to die. Rather than sending him into shock it provides the basis of a fearless approach to life. We have the incredible privilege of knowing how the story ends and our future hope is a great security for us as we face tomorrow. This security is not to be wasted in a cocoon of self-indulgence but instead it is to form the basis of risky living for the sake of the gospel in our world today. Knowing how our story ends means we need not be overwhelmed by the various dangers and adventures that come our way. In a dark world a little hope goes a long way. Our great hope for tomorrow is the powerful antidote our world needs today.

14

Eschatology and Politics

Luke Bretherton

Introduction

There are a number of temptations besetting Christians as they act politically in the contemporary context. They are dangerous because in relation to the political dimensions of Christian mission and ministry, these temptations constitute a turning away from faithful witness to Jesus Christ. I want to suggest here how understanding the relationship between eschatology and politics helps inoculate us against these temptations.

In this chapter I want to do four things:

1. Outline the biblical foundations of eschatology and how these relate to the political vocation of the church.
2. Describe some of the ways in which these foundations have developed historically, notably in the work of Augustine and Joachim of Fiore, identifying the political projects these historical strands have sponsored.
3. Give an account of eschatology, salvation and political witness, showing how this account works with and develops particular strands within the Bible and the historical tradition.
4. Outline how this vision addresses three pressing political temptations facing Christians in the contemporary context.

Biblical Foundations

There is not the space here for a full review of the Bible in relation to eschatology and politics. However, some key texts and
trajectories can be mapped.

Old Testament

How the end relates to the beginning is crucial for understanding the relationship between eschatology and politics. In
canonical readings of Scripture this involves asking, what is
the relationship between Genesis and Revelation? Genesis
gives us a number of key themes that shape how the end
relates to the beginning. First, all humans are created by God
so there are no sub-humans or natural slaves. This first theme
is spelled out most obviously in relation to Adam. All humans
are portrayed as having their origin in Adam and so, in the
first instance, we all belong to the same family and are equal in
status both in relation to each other and in relation to God.

Second, while humanity is one, it is properly divided up into
different societies or nations that through their inter-relation-
ship form the unity of humankind. Creation is not static, but
ordered and mandated to develop in particular ways: it is a
garden to be cultivated. Just as the beasts of the field and the
birds of the air do not remain an undifferentiated mass, neither
does humanity. There is a proper process of differentiation and
development. This is a central theme of Genesis 10 in which the
Table of Nations portrays a process of differentiation that
involves taking up goods of creation – notably, kinship, land
and language – and enabling them to be drawn into, ordered
within and serve on-going patterns of personal relationship
directed to communion with God. The Tower of Babel story
underscores this. If one aspect of the mandate to multiply given
in Genesis 1.28 is fulfilled by the differentiation of humanity
into nations, then the refusal of humans to 'scatter' or spread
abroad (Gen. 11:4) constitutes a rebellion against God's purposes for creation. Diversity in unity of relationship to God is
the way in which creation is to be properly ordered, all other
attempts at unity constitute different kinds of totalitarianism,

which seek to centralise control and make everybody the same. Genesis 11 emphasises that the proper ordering of humanity involves differentiation into different polities and thence the ordering of these different 'nations' eschatologically to fulfilment in communion with God and each other.

Third, these different nations are not part of the natural order but are contingent, historical formations whose political, social and economic arrangements are not written in stone; rather, they should be open to change and development. In short, we do not have to settle for the status quo. While part of God's providential ordering of creation, nations are not part of the creation order in the same way as the changing of the seasons or the boundaries of the water and the land. They are political communities, the result of historical processes and can be changed for the better (or for the worse).

Fourth, God is acting to redeem and perfect this good but fallen creation, and God's primary act of redemption involves the calling of a particular people who are to show other fallen nations the pattern of what creation healed and perfected might look like. The particular election of Israel is to be the means by which the nations would hear of God's rule and know what was required. Thus, it can be argued, that the real contrast is not between Israel and the nations, but between godly patterns of life and idolatrous, dehumanising patterns. Conversely, those nations that do not fear God and refuse to learn from Israel come under judgment (e.g. Ezra 25–32). Indeed, the conception of the nations as under judgment in Jewish prophetic literature must be set within an overarching vision of eschatological hope for the nations who are envisaged as coming to sit at the Messianic banquet. It is this vision that is taken up, affirmed and developed in the New Testament. Thus, for example, Revelation envisages all nations as under God's Lordship and the role of the church, like that of Israel, is not to be vindicated but to be a witness that serves to bring the nations to acknowledge the true God.

New Testament

One of the terms used most frequently by Jesus in the synoptic gospels to describe what he was proclaiming was 'the kingdom of God' (e.g., Mt. 24:14; 28; Lk. 11:20). The kingdom of God denotes the sphere of God's active rule wherein God is at work redeeming and perfecting creation. Jesus' ministry is about demonstrating how the present state of things relates to the realm being established by God. What Jesus does and says acts as an invitation to anticipate now what will be the case in the coming kingdom. Washing feet and crucifixion spell out the nature of the king and his rule, while raising up the lowly, bringing down the proud, filling the hungry with good things and letting the oppressed go free constitutes the pattern of life that is to be lived in this kingdom (Lk. 1:51–55; 4:18–19).

The kingdom of God is but one among many ways in which the New Testament speaks about, and calls us to bear witness to, the good news that the time of the Lord's favour is upon us. The ways Scripture speaks forth what the life, death and resurrection of Jesus Christ establishes are abundant. In addition to the kingdom of God, there are also the images of Sabbath rest (Heb. 4:1–11; Rev. 14:13), new creation (Rom. 8:19–23; 2 Cor. 5:17; 2 Pet. 3; Rev. 21), eternal life (e.g., Mt. 19:29, Mk. 10.30, Lk. 18.18–25, Jn. 3.16), the Messianic banquet (Mt. 8:11, 11:19; Mk. 14:25; Lk. 6:21, 14; Rev 7:17, 21:4), and the garden-city of God or New Jerusalem (Rev 21 – 22). What we hope for involves the renewal and transformation of all creation and not its annihilation (Isa. 65; Rom. 8:19–23; 2 Cor. 5:17; 2 Pet. 3; Rev. 21). And Jesus Christ is the concrete revelation of what this all looks like. He is our memory of the future.

While we live in a suffering and fallen society, we look to that time when this pattern of life will be fully disclosed and, in the power of the Holy Spirit, we may anticipate this Christ-shaped life now. There is, to use the theological jargon, an eschatological tension: there is a tension between the ways in which the kingdom of God is set in motion by Jesus' life, death and resurrection and the ways in which God's kingdom is not yet fully manifest because we still await the full disclosure of God's rule when Christ returns. Thus, we are to act in order to maintain, restore and fulfil the creation order but we should not expect its fullness now and recognise all our attempts to live out the kingdom are touched by sin. Yet to feed the destitute, to give a voice to the voiceless, to reconcile enemies, to comfort the afflicted or to bring physical healing is to taste the meal that Christ hosts. To discern the concrete ways in which such things are prohibited from happening is to be hungry and thirsty for the Messianic banquet. As Christians we are to live as those participating in the kingdom of God, as those who are anticipating the new creation now. As the vision of the New Jerusalem reminds us, this kind of eschatologically-orientated living is intrinsically a political form of life. Our destiny is a life lived with others in communion with God, the life of the *polis* or political community of God.

In order to encapsulate the intrinsically political dimensions of the Christian life and its eschatological orientation, one of the key terms the New Testament writers used to describe the church was as an *ekklesia*. The term carries a strong political connotation for it originally meant the public assembly of a city. The church was the *ekklesia* of God – the public assembly called together by God to deliberate about welfare in the city of God, a city that encompassed the whole of creation and was directed to the good of all.

Historical Strands and Political Projects

We find several key biblical themes:

- creation is good but fallen: open to its future perfection;
- the unity and equality of humankind;
- the proper differentiation of humans into different political communities which are orientated beyond themselves to communion with God and each other;
- the calling of a particular people who are to show a fallen world what creation healed and perfected might look like;
- the judgment and relativisation of present social, economic and political arrangements by the coming of a Messiah;
- the inauguration of God's kingdom in and through Christ's death and resurrection.

These are taken up and developed in various ways in the history of the church. The book of Revelation has been very important in this respect. By assessing different responses to Revelation 21 and the vision of the New Jerusalem we can illustrate some different historical approaches to eschatology and the different political visions these responses have fostered.

One of the most influential figures who directly links eschatology and politics is St Augustine of Hippo (354–430), the greatest of the Latin Church Fathers. Augustine divides human societies in two: there is the city of God – which combines both the true, invisible church in this age and the New Jerusalem of the age to come – and the earthly city (*City of God* xx.17). Within Augustine's theology the visible church is as much part of the earthly city, and thus directed to prideful ends, as any other part of a society. We should therefore be suspicious of any attempt to identify our particular take on Christianity as somehow the embodiment of the New Jerusalem now. The visible church is always a field of wheat and tares, combining the earthly city and the city of God and so cannot be separated until the last judgment.

Augustine believes that humans are naturally social animals who find fulfilment in a polity of some kind. Contrary to much other political thought, though, he argues that the political societies we see around us are neither natural nor fulfilling because they are fallen and orientated away from the true end of human being – communion with God – and towards their own prideful, self-destructive ends. For Augustine, as the only true peace and justice is to be found in the city of God, earthly politics is about enabling a limited peace. On an Augustinian account we can side neither with those who take an overly positive view of human nature and the possibilities of what politics can achieve, nor with postmodern thinkers in taking too pessimistic a view and who question the very possibilities of justice.

For Augustine, politics is about negotiating what is necessary for a tolerable earthly peace to exist within which the gospel can be preached and which the city of God makes use of for a time. Politics is not an end in itself, but serves an end – communion with God – beyond itself. Political authority is about establishing the conditions for human flourishing. It is liberal in the sense that it warrants the limitation of the state and a modest view of what politics can achieve. As such, Augustine would be deeply suspicious of either the idea of a Christian society, or any project of liberation through politics alone, and alert to the dangers of identifying the best society (by which is often meant the most 'successful' society at a particular moment in history – such as the British Empire once, or America now) with a Christian society. All political formations and structures of governance are provisional and tend towards oppression, while at the same time, whether it be a democracy or a monarchy, any political formation may enable a shadow of justice and the limited good of an earthly peace. This is not to say that there is no difference between the Roman Empire and a band of brigands, to refer to Augustine's famous jibe (*City of God* iv.4), but it is to say that the peace of all other societies is different in kind from the just and certain peace of the true society found in the city of God (*City of God* xv.21). Augustine's vision, of the New Jerusalem as a wholly distinct political society that will only be fully realised at Christ's return, sponsors a chastened pursuit of common goods and a limited earthly peace.

Augustine's understanding of the relationship between eschatology and politics dominated medieval political thought in the West. However, from the thirteenth century onwards other views began to be influential. Key among these was that of Joachim of Fiore (c.1135–1202). Joachim broke with Augustine in a number of ways, one of which was to see human history as the arena in which the New Jerusalem would be made fully manifest. In contrast to Augustine's essentially pessimistic view of human endeavour this side of Christ's return, Joachim had a more positive view. He divided history into three ages: the age of the Father (which refers to the period of the Old Covenant), the age of the Son (which began with the period of the New Testament) and the final age, the age of the Holy Spirit (which was immanent). This last age would be preceded by a period of persecution and the reign of the anti-Christ. At the same time, the age of the Spirit would be anticipated by an outburst of renewal.

A Joachite view of history has sponsored a variety of millenarian or apocalyptic movements that identify themselves

with the age of the Spirit and all who oppose them as agents of
the anti-Christ. Some of these take a direct political form. The
sixteenth-century Anabaptists are an example. They sought to
establish the New Jerusalem in Münster, Germany – an
episode that ended in its violent collapse and suppression.
Another example is the seventeenth-century radical politics of
the 'Diggers' and 'Fifth Monarchists' in England during the
English Civil War, who many see as proto-communists and
who envisaged the earth as a common treasury to be shared by
all. Their utopian vision was attempted in practice in the
American Colonies in places such as New Haven, Connecticut,
the design of which was modelled on the New Jerusalem.
They also find an echo in William Blake's hymn *Jerusalem* that
envisages the New Jerusalem built in England's green and
pleasant land. In the modern period this Joachite tradition
informed the post-millennialism of those such as Walter
Rauschenbusch (1861–1918) who advocated a 'social gospel'
and who saw in modern scientific, economic and political
developments, and the reform they enabled, the heralds of the
last age. One could even go so far as to interpret all modern
utopian politics and schemes – from modernist urban archi-
tects to Marxist revolutionaries – as attempts to build the New
Jerusalem now.

A Joachite approach tends to hold that the New Jerusalem is
an outgrowth of human history and that we can be certain as
to the end and direction of history. It is thus ready to pass judgment on the worth or otherwise of present political arrange-
ment. By contrast, an Augustinian approach holds that the
New Jerusalem is an irruption of the divine from outside
human history, an act of grace that surpasses all that precedes
it and changes the terms and conditions of the politics and
social life that follows it. The paradigmatic and definitive
event is, of course, the resurrection of Jesus Christ, but just
because the Christ has come it does not mean God ceases to act
in human history. Precisely because Christ has come, the Spirit
can break open the kingdom of God among us in ways that are
over and beyond human construction and developments within history. By implication we can never be certain what direction history is going in, and so an Augustinian approach is

more open ended and less absolutist in its judgments on present political arrangements. If the Augustinian tradition sponsors a more reformist approach to politics, ready to see both good and bad in any polity, yet at the same time pursuing change and open to God's acts of grace, then the Joachite tradition tends to be more radical and revolutionary, for a particular polity is either for or against the end of history it confidently predicts. However, both see a direct link between eschatology and present political arrangements.

There is a third approach that is more Joachite than Augustinian but which tends to wholly spiritualise the New Jerusalem, decoupling eschatology and politics by rendering the New Jerusalem either an inner or an other worldly reality. Some mystics, for example, envisage the coming of the New Jerusalem as a renewal of the inner spiritual life. In the modern period, many premillennial eschatologies, such as those influenced by Nelson Darby, tend to make the New Jerusalem a wholly otherworldly reality so that it becomes 'pie in the sky when you die'. Politics is something to be avoided, for at its best it is a pointless activity for those who will enjoy the 'rapture' and at its worst it is the vehicle of the anti-Christ. Such a view is articulated in the popular Left Behind series of novels. While a premillennial eschatology has often sponsored evangelistic activism, it has tended to breed political quietism and even withdrawal, directly undercutting the New Testament's conception of the kingdom of God and its implications for earthly political life.

Eschatology, Salvation and Pursuit of the Common Good

As is probably already clear I think that an Augustinian approach is closer to the Scriptural witness and helps us relate eschatology and politics in more faithful ways and resist the temptations that beset us in the contemporary context. What are these temptations?

The *first temptation* is to let the church be constructed by the modern bureaucratic state as either just another interest group seeking a share of public money or just another constituency within civil society who can foster social cohesion and make up the deficiencies of the welfare state by helping to deliver social welfare. The former reduces the church to a client of the state's patronage and the latter co-opts the church in a new form of establishment, one where the state sets the terms and conditions, and thence controls the relationship.

The *second temptation* is for Christians to construct themselves as part of what the philosopher Charles Taylor calls the 'politics of recognition'. This entails re-framing Christian political witness in terms of either multiculturalism - the church becoming just another minority identity group demanding recognition for its way of life as equally valid in relation to all others – or the rhetoric of rights – the church decomposing itself into a collective of individual rights bearers seeking freedom of religious expression.

The *third temptation* is to let Christianity be constructed by the market as a product to be consumed or commodity to be bought and sold so that in the religious marketplace Christianity is simply another lifestyle choice, interchangeable with or equivalent to any other.

All these temptations situate the church in a competitive and conflictual relationship with other groups in society – be they from other faiths or no faith. The result is that instead of seeing others as neighbours to be loved, they emerge as enemies who are to be demonised, defended from, and ultimately defeated so that Christianity either gains the lions' share of the public purse, or is the primary partner of the state, or is the dominant cultural force, shaping 'our' way of life, or wins the largest market share. Evidence for the entrapment of Christians within these temptations is witnessed whenever Christians establish oppositional identities where it is easier to say what they are against rather than what they are for.

An Augustinian approach identifies these three temptations as forms of pride and as attempts to create a peace in the church and pursue justice for the church by prideful means. A Joachite approach legitimises these prideful temptations by casting all who oppose the church as agents of the anti-Christ or forces of oppression. Likewise, an Augustinian approach helps us see that those who are different from us are not necessarily our enemy or competitor but are themselves a field of wheat and tares, containing good and bad elements.

There is, however, more at work in the three temptations that simply occasions of pride. Each of the three temptations is a refusal of the relationship between creation and eschatology set out above. First, this is because these temptations situate the church in a relationship of rivalry and competition with others, so we constantly find ourselves denying that all humans are created by God by demonising or scapegoating others and so treating them as sub-humans, not worthy of respect. In our relations with others we must always remember that we live in a common world. The ground of this common world is neither technological nor economic globalisation but the hospitality we receive from Christ establishes the grounds for friendship and justice in a fallen world. Just as in Adam we were one family, so in Christ, we may be one again. On the one hand, we must resist all attempts to deny humans share a common world with a moral order all may conform to and, on the other, we must protect those most in danger of being excluded from the human community as unworthy of human life or as sub-human, whether they are a foetus, a refugee, or someone in Guantanamo Bay prison.

Second, these temptations recapitulate Babel by refusing to uphold an eschatological vision of diversity in unity orientated towards communion with God. They are each an attempt to create unity by making everything the same. The bureaucratic state instrumentalises religions, making them equal units serving the cohesion and needs of the nation-state. The politics of recognition turns different religions into nothing more than identity badges jostling for respect. The market commodifies everything, melting all things into interchangeable units of exchange that can be bought and sold.

In creation, by contrast, differentiation and particularity are seen as good and each kind of thing has its own intrinsic value. This relates to humanity and human relationship in the following way. Each of us is like all other humans, a creature of God. Yet this sameness is only ever experienced in the particularity of creaturely relations – that is, we are not God-like, everywhere all at once. Rather, to be human is to exist in the created limits of time and space. The particularity of creatures is, to a large extent, constituted by their place; that is, our social, economic, political and historical location in creation. Relations between particular creatures necessarily involve limits and points of exchange at both an individual and communal level. Such limits form the basis and pattern of the relations of gift and reception that constitute what it means to be human in the image of God. Therefore, while we are the same as all other creatures, we are more like some persons than others and we are also like no other person; each person is unique. This basic structure of human being is at once assumed and affirmed in the incarnation. Jesus is human; Jesus is unique; and Jesus, as a historical person is more like some than others. As Oliver O'Donovan notes:

> It is essential to our humanity that there should be always foreigners, human beings from another community who have an alternative way of organising the task and privilege of being human, so that our imaginations are refreshed and our sense of cultural possibilities renewed.[1]

In short, we need others to be Other in order that we may all be human.

Third, these temptations are a refusal to accept the eschatological horizon of history. They accept that the terms and conditions of contemporary social, political and economic relations are 'natural' or set in stone. By placing ourselves as necessarily in competition with others and by acting to protect 'our' way of life, we turn the gift of faith into a possession. Instead, we must repent and turn away from our participation in systems and structures of idolatrous security; we must learn to value how others decentre and disrupt our sedentary lives and our refusal to live as pilgrims within the earthly city. The now/not-yet, eschatological fault-line at the heart of the Christian life renders all forms of human society – familial as well as political – provisional, secondary and penultimate in relation to the ultimate and perfect form of human society: communion with God in the New Jerusalem. We should not settle for less.

Fourth, these temptations constitute a denial of God's action to redeem and perfect our good but fallen creation. By forming oppositional identities and demonising others we deny the truth that no one is beyond the bounds of salvation, not even the terrorist or paedophile (in saying this I am not advocating abandoning caution or discernment; it is rather that all our action must be orientated to the possibility that even our worst enemy might at some point be our friend). All are part of the human family and invited to salvation in Christ. We are called to extend this invitation. However, our invitation and hospitality to those who are strangers to God must be done in the light of our own experiences as strangers who have been graciously welcomed by God. We are the recipients of God's abundant and costly hospitality of us through the death and resurrection of Jesus Christ. Thus, openness to the stranger requires constant remembrance of our strangeness to God and God's hospitality of us.

In summary, all three temptations are in effect forms of apostasy. They constitute a denial of the unity of creation in and through the Word or Logos, the healing and reconciliation of all things in Jesus' life, death and resurrection, and the drawing of the whole cosmos, including all the peoples and nations, into communion with the Father through Christ in the power of the Spirit. These temptations are a refusal to point to the reality that Christ established a common world all humanity is part of and may now, through Christ, participate in fully. In the light of this, the most important political task of the church in the contemporary context is to, where possible, uphold the possibility of a common life shared with others and where necessary build bridges in order to foster common action in pursuit of the common good.

The apologetic implication of this is that Christian moral and political claims are neither reduced to ecclesiastical house rules, nor dismissed as special pleading by a vocal minority. Instead, they can be heard as claims to tell the truth about the human condition in the light of its coming future and fulfilment, seen most clearly in the person of Jesus Christ. Thankfully, examples of the kind of political witness abound and can be seen in the fair-trade movement, the campaign against human trafficking and in the participation of churches in the work of the Citizens' Organizing Foundation in London and Birmingham. Let us seek these and other examples out and learn from them and so learn what faithful political witness involves today.

15

Eschatology Goes to Work

Darrell Cosden

Does our daily work matter much in the grand scheme of things? Does the specific work we do each day, including the routines and results, the processes and the products count for something in any ultimate sense? Can 'secular' work make a lasting difference from the perspective of eternity? The answer to each of these questions can be yes, but only if our ultimate Christian hope can be shown to apply in some way to our daily work and working life.

This, however, will require that Christians have a robust eschatology. For these are in fact questions about God's intended end, eternal goal, and ultimate purpose for the whole of creation – a creation encompassing our work. Thus, as the theologian Miroslav Volf argues, and as we shall explore in this chapter – the 'significance of secular work depends upon the value of creation, and the value of creation depends upon its final destiny'.[1]

Popular understandings of eschatology, however, seldom, if ever, tackle such issues. When the average Christian thinks about eschatology at all, the topics that arise most often are the soul's destiny in heaven or hell, the timing of Christ's return and how human history will end. Yet a full-bodied eschatology, while obviously concerned with human salvation and Christ's return, will not be content with these doctrines as popularly depicted. It will instead probe deeper into our foundational Christian beliefs including the resurrection of Christ (and of the dead at his return), the coming new creation, and the makeup of final salvation. It also will explore some of the less often recognised implications for creation that flow from these foundational beliefs. For example, it will ask what the resurrection means for the whole material creation and not simply for persons. In seeking to understand the cosmic scope of salvation, it will identify those aspects of creation that will be renewed in the new heaven and new earth. It will wish to comprehend whether our work too might 'get saved' in the end along with us. Yet sadly these are mostly ignored within popular eschatology.

In short, to find out if there is any real hope for 'the work of our hands', our eschatology must 'go to work'. For eschatology was always intended by God to transform the way we live now. It was intended to show us the meaning and value of ordinary life which is lived faithfully. That is, eschatology was intended to work for those of us who spend so much of life at work.

Yet when eschatology goes to work it is not simply our *experience* of work itself or life in the workplace that changes. Rather, when eschatology goes to work everything changes. Our understanding of what the spiritual life entails is transformed, for our understanding of God's purpose for humanity within creation changes (personal eschatology). Likewise, when eschatology goes to work we find that the shape and future of human culture more broadly changes (historical eschatology). And ultimately, when eschatology goes to work, we discover that the result is as large as creation itself for the whole of creation changes too (cosmic eschatology). Christian hope is not just concerned with our subjective experience of life. It is ultimately a genuine hope for the future of all created reality, which includes our work.

But dare we claim that our work has some connection with salvation – the ultimate salvation of people, of history and of the whole cosmos? I believe so, for this does not mean that we are saved by our work(s). Rather, it is the belief that as creation is saved with us, so too are our work(s). And it is this latter claim that we shall now explore.

In the final analysis, in order to show that our 'secular' work is significant and valuable we need to consider it from the perspective of eternity. As Christians know, the question of eternal destiny is what ultimately matters, for eternity is the last word. Thus, to experience work in the present as in some way ultimately meaningful we need to show that work will find a home in eternity. That is, our work too must 'get saved'. Yet to demonstrate as biblical the notion that our work experiences salvation, that things are saved and not simply people, we will begin not with a biblical study of work itself. Rather, we start with a study of Romans 8 which describes to us the future salvation of the whole creation in Christ (cosmic eschatology). We start here because the destiny of our work is bound up with the future of creation since our work, as we will see towards the end of this chapter, is integral to creation.

Having started with the end in view, the destiny of creation itself, we will then be in a position to consider the future of our work by peering through this lens of cosmic eschatology backward to the future/end of human history and culture as depicted in Revelation 21 – 22 (historical eschatology). Finally, from this vantage point, we will be suitably oriented to cast back along this creational trajectory even further to the very beginning, to the opening chapters of Genesis to consider the meaningful though eventually disrupted purpose of humanity (personal eschatology) which includes at its centre our work.

The Future of Creation (Romans 8)[2]

Eschatology uses the term glorification when referring to salvation's final state or goal. When Christians typically speak or sing about glorification it usually involves directing praise to God/Jesus – he gets 'all the glory'. We often forget, however, that 'glory' is likewise the hope and goal that humans and the natural world together anticipate. According to Christian teaching, we receive the glory too.

This is what Romans 8 teaches – that the material creation will be glorified. Importantly, as we will see, this glorification (which is salvation) happens by means of resurrection. At first, this may seem odd. However, the fact that human and non-human glorification is a necessary part of Jesus' own glorification, and hence

God's final salvation of the material creation, is good news for the world of work.

Romans 8:1 begins by declaring boldly that for those of us 'in Christ Jesus' there is 'now no condemnation'. Our glorification (the opposite of condemnation, vv. 17–18), which is also called our freedom (v. 2), is possible because the Son took on a physical way of life that is modelled in the 'likeness of sinful man' (v. 3). And as our representative, Jesus then became for us a sin offering (v. 3) so that the 'righteous requirements of the law' would be fully met (v. 4). But, interestingly, these requirements are not met – as we might have expected the text to say – 'in him'. Rather, righteousness is met 'in us' who now live according to the Spirit (v. 4). The text begins, of course, with the condition that firstly we must be 'in Christ' (v. 1), 'in accordance with the Spirit' (v. 5).

As puzzling as this may seem, it is in fact this 'layering', or multiple levels of inclusion using the preposition 'in', that becomes the key to understanding the theology of resurrection (glorification/salvation) that is contained in this chapter. For Paul, to be 'in' Christ is to understand the future hope of creation (v. 21). The importance of this 'inclusive layering' will become clearer, however, as we explore further.

Further on in the text we find that we who are controlled by the Spirit, who have the Spirit of Christ 'in' us, though our 'body is dead' (subject to the principle of death) 'due to sin', nevertheless our 'spirit is alive' (vv. 9–10). However, lest we be tempted to think that this implies an immaterial salvation, in verse 11 Paul says that if we have the Spirit 'in' us, 'he who raised Christ from the dead will also give life to [our] mortal bodies'.

And why is this important? Because without our physical resurrection, there is no hope for the wider non-human creation, and thus salvation would be incomplete since Christ would not truly be God's 'heir' to creation (v. 17).

Then in the culmination of the section on 'sonship' (vv. 12–17), we find the first direct promise that we who are mere creatures will 'share in his [Christ's] glory'. Immediately following, in verse 18, we find what again might seem strange to us at first. The future glory which is Christ's will be revealed (or realised in creation) not directly by Jesus, but rather indirectly through or, as the text says, 'in us'.[3] But how is this possible?

Beginning in verse 19, we see that the whole creation 'waits in eager expectation' for what turns out to be its salvation. Non-human reality is also the object of God's final salvation and will be vindicated and thus *justified* as being ultimately valuable. Though for effect, and to emphasise creation's genuine right to salvation, Paul personifies this natural but non-human world. He describes it as waiting, even groaning (v. 22), in frustration (v. 20) because it is trapped in bondage to decay – permeated by sin and death (v. 21).

According to verse 21, however, the salvation of the material universe, which is here called liberation in parallel to human freedom, does not come directly through Christ at his glorious return, as we might have expected. Rather, salvation will come to the whole of the non-human creation only when 'brought into the glorious freedom of the children of God' which is, as verse 23 states, the 'redemption of our bodies'.

Of course, our resurrection only comes to us 'in Christ'. But the text is careful here to make *our* redemption the focus and means by which redemption comes to the rest of the physical creation.

The ordering of these ideas – creation is 'in us' as we are 'in Christ' – is theologically important. The non-human creation, of course, did not fall into sin by its own choice. Apparently, here in reference to Genesis 3, it is God, 'in hope that the creation itself will be liberated', who 'subjected [creation] to frustration' (vv. 20–21). But why would God tie creation's salvation, its glorious destiny to human choice and destiny? In what way is the non-human creation 'in' humanity?

To answer the question we must return to Genesis. Being made from 'the dust of the earth', Adam, was, first and foremost, a natural creation. He was necessarily bound up with, and as part of, the physical creation. Yet he was also given a special calling within creation to be more than this; to be God's image and his responsible representative. Because of his unique identity uniting both heaven (the image of God) and earth (the rest of creation), when Adam fell he took with him that which he was naturally, physical creation, and that which he was responsible for, the non-human creation. In this same way, as is evident in Colossians and 1 Corinthians 15, the salvation brought by the last Adam, Christ, must also extend to the rest of the material creation.

Yet Romans 8, rather than focusing in this way on Christ's work, focuses instead on us. It is we who are 'in Christ', and consequently characterise the new humanity (the image of God completed). As a result, it is we who take on the work of bringing the non-human creation to its glorification, the 'glorious' destiny which is its salvation.

The salvation and 'liberation' (v. 21), which is the hope of creation, will be brought or ushered 'in us' towards our own glory, which is our physical resurrection 'in Christ'. Since nature co-inheres 'in us', our salvation and glorification become creation's own salvation and glorious transformation.

That this transforming salvation of the natural world would include the results of our work follows by implication. Our work, in that it has further shaped nature, is as much a part of nature as God's original creation. Unless we are to understand work as 'un-natural', a result of the curse, and this would surely be a misunderstanding, then we must infer that our work, as part of creation, experiences salvation along with us.

The Future of Human History and Culture (Revelation 21 – 22)[4]

If this is correct we would expect to find further evidence elsewhere in Scripture, and this is what we find when we look at the eschatological culmination of human history and culture depicted in Revelation 21 and 22. Here we see that the coming glory does in fact preserve and transform what humans have done in creation through our work.[5]

Revelation 21 begins with the vision of a new heaven and a new earth (v. 1) which is actually a uniting of heaven and earth into a new creation. In this vision the dwelling place of God and the dwelling place of humanity become one new 'city', one new integrated creation in which God and humanity in all its fullness find a new eternal home (v. 3).

The image of the 'heavenly Jerusalem' emphasises this unity, along with its continuity and discontinuity with this creation (v. 2). So, for example, unlike initial creation, the new creation has no sea, which in this context symbolises destructive evil and with it the possibility of a reversion to chaos (v. 1).[6] It is also 'new' because now, unlike even the Garden of Eden before the Fall, all persons of the triune God will live continually and permanently in it with us (v. 3). Fear will cease since there will be no more pain or loss. Indeed, death itself and all that flows from it will be gone. A 'new creation order' will have arrived (v. 4). The presence of Christ here does not replace the old order, but rather makes everything new (v. 5).

Jesus himself is this salvation. He is 'the Alpha and the Omega, the Beginning and the End' (v. 6). And although the historical temple (the location and thus promise of God's full presence with us) will be missing, it will nevertheless be present in Jesus himself. His body will embody the temple and, as the presence and glory of God, he will enable us to see things the way they really are so that we can appropriately live out our new life in his presence (vv. 22–23).

Yet the New Jerusalem is not only a divine city, heaven coming to earth. It is also quite earthly. In contrast to the prostitute of Babylon (Rev. 17–18), it is depicted as the bride, the wife of the Lamb (v. 9). It is thus creation, all be it the perfected and glorified creation (vv. 15–21) that has been taken by Christ to heaven. Here it is expressed as the fullness of saved humanity (and thus the cosmos therein) symbolised by the twelve tribes of Israel and the twelve apostles (vv. 12–14).

Importantly for its inhabitants, it is also a city of glorious possibilities. It will be forever open (v. 25), include the best of human culture and contain achievements past and possibly ongoing (v. 26). It will thus include everything that we have accomplished through our own work. For what we have done, our 'splendour', will be brought and put on display as part of the 'glory and honour of the nations' (vv. 24–26). While the city is always open, nothing or nobody still permeated by the old order of things will be allowed to enter (v. 27). Only that which has been purified in Christ and listed in his book of life will find its freedom here (cf. Rom. 8).

That there is genuine continuity between the current and future creation, and that humanity – and not simply God – shapes its new reality is further vividly expressed through the very image chosen to describe this new heaven and new earth. The image is a city. One might have thought that the pre-Fall Garden of Eden, what God created alone, would have been a more fitting image. Although many Christians have thought that heaven is simply a return to Eden, this is not the case in this vision. Here a city, at best an ambivalent product of human work (Gen. 4:17), represents the future of God's and our new created reality.

But this is not just any city; it is called Jerusalem, the city of God. But even this is at best an uncertain symbol for Christians. For, although Jerusalem is a symbol of hope throughout the Bible, it nevertheless became a place of terror for Christians since humanity crucified Christ there.

Both as city and as Jerusalem, the new creation is a transformed and now holy place (v. 2). The vision suggests that God is pleased to gather up, transform, and include not just his 'pure' creation but also the genuine additions to the created reality that we have brought about through our own transforming actions, or work.

Of course, God does still gather up and take into the new creation his own pristine creation. And he gives it a central place. With its mention of the 'river of the water of life' (v. 1) and the 'tree of life' beside it (v. 2), Revelation 22 makes clear reference to the garden of Eden. This garden-city gathers up and preserves within it the glory of the unspoiled creation. Here the natural is not destroyed or replaced but set free. Yet the garden is not fenced off but stands in the middle of the city to make the city what it is – a place of life and healing (v. 2).

In this city, characterised by healing and life (v. 2), even the nations (human political creations and cultural achievements) find restoration and fulfillment. The great 'work' mandate given in the garden (which we shall explore below) is thus fulfilled (Gen. 1:26–30).

The new is much more than the garden ever was. On the one hand, it is more because of what God brings to it, his full presence, total healing and transformative restoration. On the other hand, it is more because of what we bring to it, the products of human culture which are the results of our working activities. These are some of the building blocks that God uses to build his and our new home.

Eschatological salvation then, changes creation. It transforms the fallen nature of which we are a part and in so doing transforms the full spectrum of created reality. This transformation includes and makes a place for healed historical human cultural achievement. Although not perfect now, once transformed our work 'gets saved'.

Human Purpose in Eschatological Perspective

But how does eschatology going to work both cosmically and historically bring hope, and in fact change to what I have called personal eschatology? Eschatology is not just concerned with salvation in the 'end', meaning the end of time. Rather, it likewise addresses the 'end' in the sense that creation, here we have in mind particularly humanity, is brought to completion. This means completing the creational goal and purpose for which people were created. Eschatology then is about salvation to something and not just from something.

The question is, therefore, for what purpose are we saved, both now and ultimately? But of course, this question depends at least in part upon a prior one. Why were we created in the first place?

Obviously, this is a very complex question and we have neither the time nor space here to explore all the answers that we might give. We are complex beings and God's purposes for us are multifaceted – from our appointed roles and commissions, to our relationship with God and with others, humans as created by God are unique. Yet, we can discern at least an essential part of the answer both biblically and for the purpose of the essay with a brief examination of the initial creation narrative found in the opening chapters of Genesis.

If Scripture gives a succinct picture of human purpose generally, it is found in these texts. And it is repeated and reaffirmed several times and indeed is the sub-text throughout the

Genesis 1 – 11 narrative.[7] Importantly, this purpose is precisely what we have seen brought to fulfilment with the end of history in Revelation 21 – 22. Clearly our purpose, that for which we were created, matters in the grand scheme of things.

So what is it? Why were we created? Genesis 1:26–30 says God created people, the community of male and female humanity to be his image. And bound up with imaging or reflecting the active and creating God, we find in Genesis 1 and 2 that our mandate is to steward and work creatively as God's apprentices within creation. We will do this by adding to and bringing about further structure and order to the creation (2:19–20). And as we have already seen, this is so that we might in Christ ultimately usher creation to its goal or completion, which is its freedom to be a fitting, harmonious and natural home for God, humanity, and everything else that makes up creation.

In Genesis we find that God appoints humankind to 'rule over the fish of the sea and the birds of the air, over the livestock, over all the earth and over all the creatures that move along the ground' (v. 26). He wants humankind to begin to be productive (fruitful) and to reproduce so as to fill and administrate, lead and manage the earth in a way that reflects his own creative working (vv. 28–30). Creation in Genesis is complete, but not in the sense of being the finished product. Rather it is complete in the sense that everything is there to be developed, to be worked toward its ultimate eschatological goal.

This reading of the Genesis 1 narrative is reinforced in the parallel creation account in Genesis 2. In verses 4–5 the narrative says that God created the earth and the heavens, but initially did not put anything in it. Why, because as yet 'there was no man to work the ground'. No shrub nor plant nor garden was made because there was nobody there yet to carefully work it into what God intended it to become. Indeed, human purpose could not be made any clearer than in Genesis 2:15 – 'The Lord God took the man and put him in the Garden of Eden to work it and to take care of it.'

Of course, had we looked at Genesis before Romans 8 and Revelation 21 – 22, we might have been tempted to think that this calling to mission was oriented only, or even primarily to the initial creation, and that it had nothing to do with eschatology. However, having already seen the end-goal of creation, we are able now to understand that the beginning too is part of a larger eschatological trajectory – a trajectory that from eschatological beginning to end is permeated with reference to the purpose, value and indeed future of our daily work.

So does the 'secular' work you do each day, including the routines and results, the processes and the products count for something in any ultimate sense or make any lasting difference from the perspective of eternity? Yes they do, for as we have seen, our work is integral to God's purposes both in this life and the next. In the end, our initially God-given purpose to work is caught up in, and reaffirmed by, God's saving of human history, when God will finally save, transform, and glorify the whole of creation. In short, when eschatology goes to work everything changes.

Hopeful World

16

Living for the Future

The end of ethics

Elliyal Q
for ther.

John E. Colwell

It is common, in chapters such as this, to offer an enigmatic title that is then explained in the sub-title. In this instance a title has been chosen for me, so the sub-title is the remaining opportunity for enigma. To speak of 'the end of ethics' is deliberately ambiguous: clearly, 'end' might mean 'finish' and might mean 'fulfilment'. There is another ambiguity, however, with respect to an understanding of 'ethics'. This latter ambiguity might be far less obvious to a contemporary reader, since overwhelmingly for modernity and for postmodernity, and for Christians as much as for non-Christians inhabiting these contexts, ethics is a matter of decision making. We think 'ethics' means the study of moral choices in response to moral dilemmas. Should Christians be pacifists? Should Christians be vegetarians? In what circumstances might abortion be justified? In what circumstances might the withdrawal or withholding of medical treatment be justified? Is re-marriage after divorce truly marriage? What constitutes a marriage in the first place? Can cohabitation ever be reckoned as marriage? Can a covenant partnership between two people of the same sex be reckoned as marriage? Should Christians drive cars and contribute to impending environmental disaster? Should Christians take flights for foreign holidays and contribute to impending environmental disaster? Such moral dilemmas are the stuff of ethics according to popular thinking and, as the examples demonstrate, they constitute the stuff of Christian ethics according to popular Christian thinking.

Indeed, for Christians such dilemmas surely have a sharp theological, rather than merely moral, focus: Christians know that the world is not yet as God ultimately desires the world to be; Christians know that the world is fallen, and that they themselves within it are fallen; Christians know that the world and the people who indwell it require something more radical than more effective environmental programmes, citizenship awareness courses, or better education; Christians know that the world and its peoples need redemption rather than mere improvement. And though Christians hope for this redemption and await it with expectant assurance, they know that this 'end' is not yet and therefore, here and now, they expect to be disturbed by moral dilemmas, they expect there to be 'wars and rumours of wars' (Mt. 24:6), they expect there to be 'famines and earthquakes in various places' (Mt. 24:7), they expect pain, they expect the signs and symptoms of this world's corruption as they look for 'a new heaven and a new earth, the home of righteousness' (2 Pet. 3:13).

And since Christians know what others do not know (or do not yet know), they bring certain distinctives to ethical debate: though they bring a healthy awareness of human and worldly corruption, they also bring a confidence in the original goodness and purposefulness of creation; they bring an awareness of God's will as revealed in Scripture; they bring a recognition that God's ultimate good is not yet available, that the best we can achieve in any dilemma is always less than God's best, that our best but inadequate strivings for the good are embraced and qualified by God's mercy; and they bring hope, ultimate hope but also penultimate hope, beyond every human moral dilemma.

To think of ethics as a series of moral dilemmas consequent upon our own fallenness and the fallenness of creation promotes a corresponding idea of the eschatological 'end' as the termination of this fallen context and the absence of such dilemmas. The final coming of God's kingdom will put an end to sin and to sinfulness. Corruption, suffering, sickness, and death will be no more. There will, therefore, be no more medical dilemmas to trouble us: no ectopic pregnancies or malformed foetuses; no cancer, multiple sclerosis, or Parkinson's disease, and therefore no cause to ponder the morality of gene therapy or stem-cell research; as children of the resurrection we will no longer be married or given in marriage (Lk. 20:35–36), so there will be no possibility of adultery, no divorce; there will be no death so there will be no pertinence to questions of a 'good death', of euthanasia; all of creation will be made new, and there will be no more possibility of pollution, exploitation, or abuse. And perhaps more significantly, we too will be changed, the work of new creation in us will be completed, rendering us beyond and above temptation – though, of course, with all these dilemmas removed, with the devil and his angels consigned to the lake of fire (Mt. 25:41; cf. Rev. 20:10), there will be nothing to tempt us in any case. All will be tranquil, undisturbed and undisturbing, in this God-given Utopia, this restored paradise. There will be no moral dilemma. Ethics will be ended.

This (rather caricatured) depiction of the age to come is not, I suspect, uncommon amongst evangelical Christians – and there are plenty of passages of Scripture which, though admittedly metaphorical, prompt such musings. Occasionally we may pause to ponder the apparent incongruities of such perfection – if there's no more sea are there no more whales; if the wolf lies down with the lamb how will it retain its physical fitness (Isa. 11:6); if there is no need can there be any care, selflessness, or generosity; or (and more seriously), if every ball is a perfect leg-break, met by a perfect cover-drive, intercepted by a perfect catch, what will be the point of cricket – how unimaginably and unremittingly boring. But the truly profound flaw in all such musings concerning the age to come is the commonly unnoticed omission throughout of any mention of Christ. Hope that is distinctively Christian is not a hope for some humanistically conceived Utopia – it is hope for Christ himself; he is the end of all things, the one through whom and for whom all things were created (Col. 1.16), the one in whom all things will be brought together (Eph. 1:10). Christians do not hope for the coming of something but for the coming of someone – his coming, and the outcomes of his coming, may be metaphorically expressed (indeed, it cannot be other than metaphorically expressed) but it is not thereby defined, encapsulated, or exhausted. The end for Christian faith, hope, and love is Christ himself, a person rather than Utopia, a completion rather than a termination.

And consequently, since this projection of a Utopian end is inadequate, humanistic, and Christ-less, the dilemma-focused understanding of ethics from which, in part, it originates must similarly be deemed inadequate, humanistic, and Christ-less. Since Christ is the sole and authentic end of all things, he is the sole and authentic end of ethics, the goal and sum of the 'good', the only true and final definition of true humanity. And he is this not as the definition of what we are called to avoid or to decide against, but rather as the definition of what the Father invites us to become and to be in the Son and through the power of the Spirit.

That Enlightenment and post-Enlightenment ethics tend to be dilemma focused is at least in part an outcome of its inherent goal-less-ness (or effective Godlessness). The desire to dispense with all external authority and to assume the competence of the individual thinker tended to relegate any notion of 'god' to the margins of creation's beginnings or, more radically (and consistently), to abandon notions of 'god' entirely. But reduce the notion of Creator to that of 'watchmaker',[1] the original maker and designer of all things, and you conclude the present effective independence and self-sufficiency of all things: the Universe is no longer recognised as wholly and continually dependent upon its Creator. And jettison any notion of 'god' other than as the distant source of all things and you jeopardise any sense of the purposefulness and connectedness of all things: any meaning to life becomes self-generated and, more often than not, self-bounded.

At least the Scottish philosopher David Hume (1711–1776) had the wit and honesty to recognise that in such a disconnected and self-contained universe morality could consist of no more than the expression of an individual's or a society's approval or disapproval.[2] Notions of 'self-evident rights' are celebrated in the American Declaration of Independence and

other hugely influential documents of the modern era. These
have proved modernity's best attempt at a self-contained and
self-generated foundation for the recognition of obligation,
but the notion of 'self-evidence' is problematic. If something
is 'evident' it is evident to someone, and that person's perceptions are culturally shaped. Perhaps the recognition of a
'right' itself derives from a vaguely remembered (and no
longer sustainable) notion of purposefulness. More commonly (and following Hume), modern and postmodern
cultures assess the rightness or wrongness of an act according
to its foreseeable outcome (in ethical theory, this is called 'consequentialism'). There are problems with this, however: outcomes cannot be infallibly foreseen; our assessment of what
constitutes a good or bad outcome is peculiarly our own; and
that I act rightly on certain occasions does not of itself constitute me a good person (bad people sometimes act rightly).
Consequentialism, therefore, reduces morality to a series of
discrete and disconnected decisions; it assumes the connectedness and purposefulness of isolated actions without reference to any connectedness or purposefulness of life as a
whole; it is solely dilemma focused.[3]

When a lawyer asked Jesus concerning the greatest commandment we cannot know the form of reply he expected. As
contemporary Christians, shaped inevitably by the assumptions of modernity and postmodernity as much as by the
gospel story, we would most likely seek some clearly defined
principle or absolute rule to direct our actions in specific situations – as the original question perhaps suggests, a rule of
right acting rather than a goal of right living. Jesus will not be
beguiled by our 'enlightened' disconnectedness – the greatest
commandment focuses on the agent rather than the action; it is
both personal and all-encompassing:

> Jesus replied: "'Love the Lord your God with all your heart and
> with all your soul and with all your mind.' This is the first and
> greatest commandment. And the second is like it: 'Love your
> neighbour as yourself.' All the Law and the Prophets hang on
> these two commandments.
>
> (Mt. 22:37–40)

Christian faith attests the Triune God, as narrated in the gospel story, as the true source and goal of all creation. Human life, together with every particular of creation, is purposeful not purposeless, meaningful and not meaningless. It is connected and continuous not disconnected and discrete. Jesus Christ, the true source of creation, is creation's true goal. He is the beginning and the end. He himself is the command and invitation of God to us and to the whole of creation. The 'good' that is the goal of life is not some absolute and detached principle of right action or good behaviour, it is God himself (Mt. 19:17), the one made known in Christ, the one narrated in the gospel story. To love God, and to love all else in the context of this love of God, is the goal of human life.

Christian ethics, therefore, is not primarily concerned with a series of questions about right action (and such truly right actions can never be considered as discrete and discontinuous), but is primarily concerned with right being, a proper orientation of life, a life ordered to this goal which is the true God. Similarly sin, properly conceived, is not primarily a series of wrong actions (whether discrete and continuous or not), but is primarily a matter of disorder and disorientation, a refusal to love God, to glorify God, to return thanks to God. (Rom. 1:21)

The theme of love, of course, is difficult in a contemporary context: in English the word can be used to convey a range of passions, desires, and preferences, often rendering the term trivial and unsuited for theological and ethical precision. Perhaps this is not solely a contemporary problem: attempts to differentiate with absolute clarity a range of Greek words, all of which could be translated as 'love', are less than persuasive; and the word most commonly taken to signify distinctively Christian love had a far wider range of significances at the time. The New Testament solves this problem, as should we, by defining the word with a narrative or, at least, the summary of a narrative:

> This is love: not that we loved God, but that he loved us and sent his Son as an atoning sacrifice for our sins.
>
> (1 Jn. 4.10)

The love that is the greatest commandment, the whole of the law, the sum of the virtues, is defined in the gospel story; it is the nature of God himself; it is the eternal covenant love between the Father and the Son, eternally mediated by the Spirit; it is this divine love incarnated amongst us, narrated in the gospels, and signified throughout Scripture; it is cross-shaped and resurrection radiant; it is all embracing and utterly beyond us. Human affection can be humanly achieved but this love is all embracing, all consuming, wholly self-giving, utterly gracious. Love is firstly divine and therefore beyond the creature. We cannot generate this love merely by effort and discipline; it comes to us as gift; it is the fruit of the Spirit; it is generated within us through his indwelling. And, as Jesus indicates, he dwells in us as we dwell in him; the branches bear fruit by being part of the vine (Jn. 15.4).

The Holy Spirit is the mediator of the life and love of the Father and the Son in the life of the Christian, and, contrary to some common contemporary assumptions, the Holy Spirit mediates that presence and power in a mediate manner, through the instrumentality and agency of created things and created people. The apostle Paul met the risen Jesus on the road to Damascus but he was baptised and instructed by Ananias (Acts 9:1–19). Such 'unmediated' visions are rare: more commonly the Holy Spirit mediates his transforming presence in our lives through the ordinary, ordered, and ordained means of the people of God, the church. The word of God read, heard, and preached, the gospel sacraments of Holy Baptism and Holy Communion, the ministrations of the church's ministers, and the fellowship of the church itself – these are the ordinary, ordered and ordained means through which we come to indwell him and he comes to indwell us and to shape us. It is here, through these means, that he has promised to meet us. He can, of course, meet us and shape us elsewhere and through other means – his promises are not his prison – but he has promised to meet us here, through these means, and it is highly perverse to ignore this promise and arrogantly to seek to bypass these means.[4]

We indwell Christ, then, by indwelling the church and its sacramental life, and through this indwelling he, by his Spirit,

indwells us and shapes us. Though he was never to complete
the work, the Swiss theologian Karl Barth (1886–1968), when
pondering an 'Ethics of Reconciliation', purposed to focus on
the Lord's Prayer, on Baptism, on the Lord's Supper, as our
proper ethical response to the gospel.[5] It would be hard to
imagine anything further removed from the dilemma-focused
ethics of modernity and postmodernity with which this chapter began – but in Barth we find an ethic that is distinctively
Christian because it is radically focused on Christ, on what he
has done, and what, by his Spirit, he continues to do among us
and within us.

The covenant love that is the eternal nature of the Triune
God, the gratuitous and self-sacrificing love that is narrated in
the gospel story, takes form within us as we are indwelt by the
Spirit and as we indwell the life of the Christian community.
This love, then, is a gift, that which we receive through this
indwelling. And, as such a gift given in this manner, it is also
a habit, a growing characteristic of life, a mark of identity. The
classic Christian text on Christian love (*caritas*) as a gift, as a
virtue, as a habit, occurs in the *Summa Theologica* of Thomas
Aquinas (c.1225–1274): both parts of the second volume of this
unfinished work are devoted to an account of Christian virtue
and Christian living, with Christian love (*caritas*) as the sum
and perfection of the virtues and of the Christian life.[6] For
Thomas Aquinas the goal of human life is not our general
flourishing within society but the eschatological goal of seeing
God, of a vision that is finally transforming, a participation in
the divine life and the divine nature. Only the love that comes
to us as God's gift, as grace, can order our lives to this ultimate
goal. Here, therefore, we have the clearest eschatological
account of ethics and ethical account of eschatology: the 'end'
of ethics is to see God and to see God is the 'end' of ethics. God
and God alone is the greatest good and to desire God, to love
God, to participate in God, is the only true goal of human life,
the only true ethic.

Of course, a life directed towards this goal will still face the
common dilemmas that are symptomatic of our present fallen
existence. Such dilemmas, however, no longer confront us as
discrete and disconnected ethical issues if our life is rightly

directed. Instead, when understood within the connectedness of a life directed towards God, the 'good' is no longer identified with discrete responses to discrete dilemmas. Rather, it is identified with God, with the basic orientation of the life within which such dilemmas are encountered.

As Thomas Aquinas notes, even in eternity we will not be able to love God as much as God is loveable, only God himself is capable of loving God as much as God is loveable, but we will be able to love God as much as it is possible for the creature to love God. Here and now even this possibility remains beyond us (or, better, ahead of us), God hasn't finished his work in us yet, we are still being shaped by the Spirit in the habit of love, we are still capable of being distracted by the cares and corruptions of a fallen world, we are still beset with temptation – or as John Calvin puts it:

> this restoration does not take place in one moment or one day or one year; but through continual and sometimes even slow advances God wipes out in his elect the corruptions of the flesh, cleanses them from guilt, consecrates them to himself as temples renewing all their minds to true purity that they may practice repentance throughout their lives and know that this warfare will end only at death.[7]

Jesus was tempted. Temptation in and of itself is not sin. Being confronted by the moral dilemmas symptomatic of a fallen world is not sin. We know that 'this warfare will end only at death', or, more precisely, at the coming of Christ and the end of this age, but this must not deter us or deflect us from the expectation of a growth in love, from the expectation that his love will be perfected in us (1 Jn. 4:17–18). But the nature of our context and our own nature militates against the possibility of an absolute perfection here and now. Certainly we are called here and now to anticipate a perfecting of love, to anticipate the eschatological future which is Christ himself, but even were we to love God without wavering and to love all else in the context of this unwavering love for God, the dilemmas symptomatic of this world's fallenness, dilemmas such as those listed earlier in this chapter, remain. And they are genuine dilemmas: in this

fallen context the possibility of the absolute good, unequivocally doing the right thing, simply is not available to us (and
perhaps isn't even available here and now to God). All we can
do here and now is provisional; all we can do here and now is
under God's mercy.

In this present context it is inevitable that we will make mis-
takes, that with hindsight we may recognise a better course of
action, that there will be that which we regret. All this is symptomatic of our present imperfection and the world's present
imperfection, and even were we already perfect the world's
imperfection would remain and so would the inevitable dilemmas. But our lives are not a disconnected series of discrete
dilemmas, each pregnant with the possibility of failure and
regret; our lives are oriented to an eschatological goal that is
Christ himself. He alone is good and the measure of the good.
Oriented to him our lives are not a disoriented catalogue of
regrets but are ordered by mercy, grace and trust.

Were Christian ethics to be reduced to a series of discrete
dilemmas, then the end of this age would constitute the 'end'
of ethics in the sense of the termination of such dilemmas. But
since Christian ethics is focused on Christ, since he himself is
the goal and 'end' of ethics and of all things, the 'end' cannot
signify a termination but rather a completion and fulfilment.
The apostle Paul writes to the Corinthians of love, with faith
and hope, as 'remaining' or 'enduring' (1 Cor. 13:13), and this
reference raises two final considerations.

In the first place, and as anticipated earlier in this chapter,
the love that is distinctively Christian love (because it is distinctively God's love) is the sum of the virtues . God is simple,
undivided, absolute unity; God's 'perfections' (or attributes)
are not a series of rival and competing dispositions but rather
complementary ways in which we perceive his single, undivided nature. Similarly, the gifts of the Spirit are not a series of
distinct and separate outcomes of the Spirit's indwelling;
Christian virtue is single and undivided; Christian love is the
sum of Christian virtues. It is, of course, possible to be coura-
geous without being prudent, to be temperate without being
just, perhaps it is even possible to be hopeful without being
faithful, but the manner of love which is distinctively God's

love and distinctively Christian love includes and perfects every virtue. Any love that is not at the same time faithful and hopeful, therefore, is something less than the love into which we are invited. Similarly, any faithfulness or hopefulness that is not truly loving is something less than that envisaged by Paul in this passage. Even justice, temperance, prudence, and fortitude are only perfected as they are outworkings of this love and oriented to its goal. Here again it should be plain that the manner of love that is Christian love is not vague, sentimental, or content-less but content-full and utterly demanding.

And finally love, together with the faithfulness and hopefulness that are its inherent expressions, remains and endures in eternity. This may appear puzzling. That love should endure, as God's eternal nature in which we come by the Spirit to participate is what we would expect. But in what sense might faithfulness and hopefulness endure in eternity? Surely faith will be replaced by sight and there will be no more for which to hope? Here, then, lies the significance of understanding these Greek words in terms of faithfulness and hopefulness rather than merely faith and hope: faith will be replaced by sight but faithfulness, as an aspect and outworking of love (or lovingness), and as our continuing and perfected orientation to the one in whom we have placed our trust, endures; every hope will have reached its fulfilment but hopefulness, as an aspect and outworking of love, and as our continuing and perfected orientation to the one who is our hope, endures. Faithfulness and hopefulness are not discrete and separate virtues, they are aspects and outworkings of love and, as such, they do not end or terminate at the coming of Christ, they rather reach their end or fulfilment. The age to come is not a static but an absolute dynamic: the perfection of our participation in God; the perfection of God's participation in us by the Spirit; the perfection of love; the perfection of every virtue; the end of ethics.

17

Eschatology and the Environment

And there was no longer any sea . . .

Ruth Valerio

Introduction

'So what about where it says, "and there was no longer any sea"?', said the man to me on his way out. His question was nothing new. I can almost guarantee that whenever I talk to Christians about ecological issues the first question asked will be regarding the future and the 'end of the world'. There is no doubt that eschatology is of immense significance when considering ecological concerns: if the world is going to be destroyed, then why should we bother?

Indeed, as the chapters in this book have demonstrated, eschatology is vitally important for all areas of our lives as Christians: we are future-oriented people with our sights set on – and our lives irrevocably changed by – our future hope in Jesus Christ. Theology in general, and environmental theology in particular, must therefore reflect that for, as Jürgen Moltmann says, 'from first to last, and not merely in the epilogue, Christianity is eschatology, is hope, forward looking and forward moving, and therefore also revolutionizing and transforming the present'.[1] If this is the case then we must ask ourselves what light does that future goal shed on our beautiful, but suffering, world and what should our response to it be?

Any discussion on eschatology and the environment tends to focus on certain key biblical texts, in particular 2 Peter 3:10, which has been read as saying that the earth will be destroyed by fire, and Revelation 21:1, which uses Isaiah's language of there being 'a new heaven and a new earth'. These texts are crucial to our understanding of the relevance of eschatology to environmental concerns, but before we look at them – and other key texts – in more detail, we must take a step back and see where they fit within the overall scheme of salvation that we see in the Bible. In other words, I want in this chapter to develop an ecological theology that is oriented in a Christ-centred eschatology and, from that, to consider how we must live as a consequence.

Creator of Heaven and Earth

We start, of course, with the declaration that, 'in the beginning God created the heavens and the earth' (Gen. 1:1). There are several things to note when we consider a doctrine of creation. The first is the Christian affirmation that the creator God is the Trinity: Father, Son and Holy Spirit were all involved in creating the world (Col. 1:16 talks of Christ's involvement). The significance of the Trinity in creation, as Gunton highlights, is that God did not need the world as such, because he was already a loving communion of persons. Instead, the world is something that he has made 'simply for its own sake'.[2] And so, God looked at the whole of what he had made and said it was 'very good' (Gen. 1:31). The world and all its inhabitants, therefore, have intrinsic value. It is good in and of itself and not just because it serves human needs.[3]

The second thing to note is that creation is never considered to be a finished work: rather, it is a dynamic process; a project to be completed. As Gunton says, 'it has somewhere to go'.[4] Middleton and Walsh notice that the usual refrain, 'and there was evening and there was morning – the first [second, third, etc.] day', is missing from the end of the seventh day. Why? Because we are still in the seventh day: 'God's work of unfolding and developing the inbuilt potential of creation throughout human history' is continuing.[5] To put this in theological terms, creation has a telos, a goal, and Colossians 1:16 explains this more: creation exists for the sake of Christ.

Thirdly, the place of humanity in God's plans for creation is crucial. Here a careful balance must be struck. On the one hand, we must never forget that we are a part of creation; formed from the earth on the same day as other animals; living within the same ecosystems and sharing the same food (Gen. 1:29–30). And yet, alone of all that God created, humans are made 'in the image of God' (Gen. 1:26–27). The Hebrew grammar of this verse carries the sense of, 'let us make humanity in our own image, in our likeness, so that they may rule over'. It is almost as if God had in his mind (so to speak!) that he would create mankind in order that they might look after the rest of what he made.[6] The idea here comes from the nations around Israel in which the king was thought to be the representative of the gods and, in this sense, was described as the gods' 'image', representing the presence of the gods in the midst of the people. We, therefore, as the image of God, are to be God's representatives on earth; placed here to 'take care' (Gen. 2:15) of the rest of creation and enable it to fulfil its purpose of existing for God's glory.

That purpose, however, was thwarted by the Fall as 'sin entered the world' (Rom. 5:12). The narrative of Genesis 3 relays graphically how the relational harmony that was to exist between God and his creation, and between human and non-human creation, was broken. Theologically, the Fall explains why the world is as it is: why there is sickness and decay; conflict, pain, suffering and destruction.

Old Testament Hope

God steps into this situation and, in the story of Noah, we see his first step towards putting to rights what has gone wrong with his creation. What is of particular note here is the covenant that God instigates in Genesis 9. Since Sunday-school days I have been taught that this was a covenant with Noah, but a closer look at the text reveals that the covenant was actually between God and Noah and all living creatures of every kind on the earth (v.16). In fact, we are told this five times as if to make the point! God acts relationally not only towards humans, but towards all living things.

However, things get no better after Noah, and the rest of the Old Testament is the story of how God calls the nation of Israel into being, in order to carry out his plans for putting right what has gone wrong. This is not the place to give a full treatment of the ecological understanding of the Old Testament.[7] We must recognise, however, the importance that the land plays in Israel's understanding of herself and of her relationship with her God. So, for example, not only is care for the land included alongside the care for people demonstrated in the Sabbath prescriptions of Leviticus 25, but indeed the state of the land actually becomes a mirror for the state of the people's relationship with Yahweh and their practice of justice and compassion (e.g. Deut. 30:15–16; Jer. 5:23–25).

Of particular importance to this chapter is the development of Israel's hopes during and after the exile, as seen in the Old Testament prophets. Whilst the prophets often painted a picture of the future using somewhat bizarre and lurid language (called 'apocalyptic'), actually their hopes were thoroughly 'this-worldly' and earthly. Their hope was for a time when God would come and destroy their enemies and establish his kingdom fully on this earth (see, for example, Isaiah 60 and Ezekiel 36). Then, as Tom Wright says, 'when this god became king, the whole world, the world of space and time, would at last be put to rights.'[8] It is in this context – in Isaiah 65:17 – that we first meet the description of the future in terms of 'new heavens and new earth'. Here, clearly, a very physical and earthly existence is imagined, with house building and vineyard planting a regular occurrence!

The Scope of Salvation

It is within this cultural context and understanding that Jesus came calling people to repent and believe because, 'the kingdom of God is near' (Mk. 1:15). This chapter is not the place to look in depth at Jesus' message of the kingdom of God and all that

that entails, but suffice it to say that this kingdom was good news (Lk. 4:43) and it was good news because the salvation that Jesus brought was personal, social, physical, economic, political and spiritual.[9] Theologically speaking, where Israel had so spectacularly failed, Jesus came to continue and fulfil in himself God's plans for his creation. To quote Gunton: 'God re-inaugurates the project of creation by means of the life, death, resurrection and ascension of Jesus.'[10]

There are some key texts in the New Testament that spell this out more fully. One of these is Romans 8:18–25. Paul has been going through a sustained explanation of the dire problem which faces the human race and God's amazing solution to this problem, offered freely in his grace to all who will receive it. In this passage he reaches the conclusion that the implications of his discussion reach beyond the salvation of human beings to include the whole cosmos. Using language reminiscent of Isaiah 26:16–18, Paul describes the whole of God's creation as 'groaning as in the pains of childbirth' as it waits to be 'liberated from its bondage to decay and brought into the freedom of the glory of the children of God'.[11]

What a wonderful picture this is! Here is no theology that sees salvation in terms of us humans being whisked off to heaven while the rest of creation is destroyed: no, all of what God has made is to share in the destiny of God's children. The emphasis is still on human beings, as it is only people who are described as being 'children/sons of God' (vv. 19, 21), and yet the freedom that is waiting for those children of God is going to have far-reaching effects into the whole of God's creation. Here we have a succinct summary of creation-fall-redemption: the world that God created good became corrupt, but, through Christ and by the Holy Spirit, will be enabled to reach its fulfilment as God's glory is revealed in the children of God.

What this seems to mean is not so much that creation will share in that glory, but that, when the future becomes a full and present reality, as Jesus returns to this earth and God's children are resurrected into their new bodies, God's children will be set free to rule as they were always called to do, thus bringing freedom to creation instead of slavery.[12]

Cosmic, Man!

Another passage with a vision of salvation that extends to the whole cosmos is Colossians 1:15–20. This is one of the most remarkable passages in the New Testament; possibly a poem or liturgical hymn that was already in circulation, which Paul has taken and used here for his purposes. In this passage we find the clearest description of Christ's involvement in the creation of the world – an amazingly bold statement given that the man Jesus could have been living on the earth only as recently as twenty years before Paul says these words.[13]

What we have here is a description of the centrality of Christ in his relationship both to God and to his creation. In this passage, using language reminiscent of that used of Wisdom in Old Testament and wider Jewish literature, the person Jesus is described as being the pre-existent Son, who was the agent of creation. All things that have been made were made both by him and for him. Thus, 'Christ is both prior to and supreme over creation, for he is its Lord. All things have been created in him as the sphere and through him as the agent'.[14] Christ's role in creation, however, is not only a past event, for he is involved now in sustaining creation; ensuring that 'all things hold together' (v.17; the perfect tense used here would be more correctly translated as stating that in him, 'all things have been held together').

These two little words, 'all things' are crucially important for Paul's theology here (and see also Eph. 1:9–10). As Wright points out, there is a definite article at the start of this phrase giving it the sense of 'the all things', or 'the totality'.[15] Here we see the movement that is at work in Paul's theological understanding: all things, the totality of creation, have been created through Christ; all things are sustained and held together in Christ; and now all things have been reconciled to God through Christ, in whom is the fullness of God. Thus, again, we see a picture of God's plans for salvation that include the whole of creation, not just human beings. Verse 20, the climax of this passage, is startling in what it claims. I have always been taught that Jesus' blood on the cross was shed so that I, and countless others, could be 'saved' and brought back (reconciled) into a relationship with God. That still very much holds true, but in this verse Paul is saying that the blood Jesus shed on the cross was for the sake, not just of people, but of all things that have been created, so that all things might be reconciled to God. Personally, I find that very humbling.

Refiner's Fire

If that is the case, then, what about the earth being destroyed? This view finds a key text in 2 Peter 3:3–13. The author of 2 Peter is writing his letter with a specific aim in mind: to counteract a group of teachers who are proving influential.[16] Throughout the letter, therefore, the author is rhetorically arguing against them. In particular, this group seemed to be teaching that the Parousia – Christ's promised return – was not going to happen: the first generation of Christians had now died and so what the first apostles taught had been a lie. Rather than there being some cataclysmic event that would usher in the return of Christ and bring the final judgment, history would simply continue as it always had done (3:4). Because there would be no final judgment, argued these teachers, people were free to live their lives how they wanted, and clearly this led to all manner of ungodly behaviour (2:14–15, 18–19).

The author's aim, therefore, is to demonstrate the false nature of these claims and impress on them that God's judgment is indeed a reality, even if we do not know the exact time of its occurring. Verse 10 of chapter 3 is the culmination of his argument. It is sad then that this verse also, 'represents perhaps the most egrerious mistranslation in the entire New Testament'![17] This mistranslation revolves around the understanding of what will happen to 'the earth and everything in it'. The KJV (along with the AV, RV, RSV and JB) bases its translation on a variant manuscript reading that uses the word, *katakaesetai*, 'will be burnt up'. However, there is now near-uniform agreement amongst New Testament scholars that the most original reading of the various manuscripts uses instead the word, *eurethesetai*, 'will be found', from which we get our word, 'eureka!'.[18] The NIV follows this in its translation, 'will be laid bare'.

What is being said here, therefore, is not that the eschatological fire will come and destroy the earth, but that it will come to purify the earth so that what is bad will be burnt up, but what is good will be left. Thus Peter is emphasising the eschatological coming of Jesus and the judgment that he will bring.

That this does not mean the complete destruction of the earth can be seen in the parallel that the author gives with the flood in Noah's day (3:6). Although he uses the word 'destroyed', we know, of course, that the world was not completely annihilated through the flood; rather, what was evil was destroyed and what was good was preserved.[19] In this infamous passage of 2 Peter 3, then, we see an indication that, through the eschatological judgment, there will be continuity between this world and the next. As Bouma-Prediger rightly says, 'creation is not ephemeral and unimportant – some way station until the eschaton – but rather our home, now and always.'[20]

New or New?

2 Peter 3 focuses on the judgment of the wicked, but it doesn't leave it there and points forward to what happens after that judgment: the creation of a new heaven and a new earth. To look at this more, let us turn to the final pages in the Bible and, in particular, to the verse that this chapter takes its heading from: Revelation 21:1. These concluding chapters form the climax to the visions that John has been given, which have revealed to him, from a God-centred perspective, both what is going on in the events of his own day and what is to happen in the eschatological future.[21]

The visions of John have been the source of much controversy over the years. What we have to remember with these amazing pictures is that they are fixed securely within the Jewish apocalyptic tradition and, as such, they are not meant to be taken literally, but rather as powerful images symbolically conveying essential theological truths about both the present and the future.[22]

So what then of the description of the eschatological future in terms of 'new heaven and new earth'. The key thing we need to note is that there are two Greek words for our one English word, 'new'. The first word, *neos*, denotes something that is completely, quantitatively new: in other words, if I get a new car or house then that is totally different to the car or house I had previously. The second word, *kainos*, denotes something that is qualitatively new. So, if I were to tell you that I had a new kitchen you would assume that I hadn't completely bulldozed my old one and rebuilt it, but rather that I had kept the basic structure and had repainted the walls, installed new units, etc. It is this word, *kainos*, that is used with reference to the heavens and earth (and also, incidentally, in the description, 'New Testament'). Because of this, many scholars now prefer to speak in terms of the 'renewed heavens and the renewed earth'.

Thus Revelation 21:1, as we've seen with 2 Peter 3, is stating that there is continuity between this world and the next. The world we live in now is not going to be completely destroyed; rather, as Ladd says, salvation, 'always places man on a redeemed earth, not in a heavenly realm removed from earthly existence'.[23] We have to be careful here not to swing the pendulum too far lest we miss the radical discontinuity with the present that the future breaking-in of God is going to bring. The reality is, we simply have no language to describe what that renewed existence is going to be like.[24] But, we can rest assured: those images of floating in a white, ethereal existence are simply not what the Bible pictures!

What we see instead, in the next verse, is a picture of the heavenly city coming down from heaven to earth (not us going up from earth to heaven). This is a holistic vision of the new creation, 'in which "heaven" and "earth", the twin halves of created reality, are at last united. Always intended for one another, they are by this means to be remade, and to become the place where the living god will dwell among his people for ever.'[25]

So What?

And so we come full circle, starting with God creating the heavens and the earth and finishing with those two realities being united. But so what? If the one argument says, 'the world is going to be destroyed so why bother with it now?', does the other argument say, 'the world is going to be remade so why worry about it now?'?

It is interesting to note that the author of 2 Peter draws precisely the opposite conclusion as chapter 3 continues. Instead, he asks the crucial question, 'what kind of people ought you to be?' (v.11) and then goes on to stress that, because we are looking forward to our eschatological future, so we should be 'holy and godly in all our conduct'.[26] We want to be people who are fit to live in this renewed world! This same conclusion is drawn by Paul in 1 Corinthians 15. He has here been engaging in a lengthy explanation of the resurrection of Christ and of the final resurrection of all believers. His conclusion is that, 'therefore', the Corinthians should give themselves fully to the work of the Lord because, in the Lord, that labour is not in vain (v.58). Because there is a continuity between this life and the future, so what is done 'in the Lord' now will not be burned up with the dross, but will endure for eternity.[27]

The implications of this are immense. In terms of ecological care, it challenges us to live our lives in such a way that we enable the rest of creation to fulfil its eschatological goal. This sounds very lofty and noble, but the reality is that we cannot espouse the eschatological theology that has been argued for in this chapter without it impacting our day-to-day living. So, for example, if I buy meat from animals that have been intensively farmed or if I buy vegetables that have needed the land to be drenched in chemicals to grow them, or flown thousands of miles across the world, then I am not living in a way that enables 'creation's praise of the creator'.[28] On the other hand, if I buy my electricity from a 'green' supplier, take efforts to reduce the amount of packaging I use, press my local MP to support political reforms aimed at reducing carbon-dioxide emissions and plant some trees on the green areas around my house then I am engaging in actions that will last into the future.[29]

In all of this there is no denial of the central position that humanity occupies, both in terms of our position within creation as the only aspect that images God and in terms of our need for salvation. As Gunton says, 'we human creatures are the centre of the world's problems, and only by our redirection will the whole creation be set free'.[30] Thus, nothing in what is being said argues against the need either for evangelism or for human-focused social care.[31] However, if my theology tells me that salvation in Christ extends beyond people, then my actions must likewise reflect that too.

And so, in conclusion, we see that we are to live as children of the future; living our lives now in the light of what we know the future holds; guaranteed by the working of the Holy Spirit (Eph. 1:13–14). Bauckham and Hart describe this in terms of 'realised anticipations' of that future and argue forcibly that we must recognise the presence of the new creation already within the old by 'radical involvement in the world'.[32] As we do that – through our gospel proclamation, our social concern and our caring for the rest of creation – so we will begin to experience the new creation, inaugurated by Jesus' life, death and resurrection.

Perhaps no one expresses this better than G.K. Chesterton:

> On the third day the friends of Christ coming at daybreak to the place found the grave empty and the stone rolled away. In varying ways they realised the new wonder; but even they hardly realised that the world had died in the night. What they were looking at was the first day of a new creation, with a new heaven and a new earth; and in the semblance of the gardener God walked again in the garden, in the cool not of the evening, but the dawn.[33]

18

We are but Shadows of our Future Selves

Ann and Douglas Holt

'What time is it? What time is it?' and then two minutes later 'What time is it, daddy? Are we nearly there?' We are all familiar with the questions, and the impatience that lies behind them, of the child on a long journey. The questions asked of the heavenly Father are, perhaps, no less pressing and, what's more, are important for all of us on the journey of life. They are part of a suite of questions, according to N.T. Wright; whose answers help inform the worldview of every human being. We are living at a time that Andrew Kirk describes as the 'cult of the post' – postmodern, post-colonial, post-history, post-Christian and so it goes on, the attempt to make sense of a fast moving and often confusing state of affairs today,[1] by looking to the phenomena of the past while hoping that life is proceeding in some meaningful direction for the future. What we are describing is eschatological tension! Living in the now while remembering what has been and anticipating the not yet.

Postmodern culture is critical of the past and uncertain about the future. Paradoxically however, to the postmodernist the fragmentation of cultural norms appears so very certain! It might also give us pause for thought that postmodernity seems very clear about its past, with all its very misleading behavioural norms, unhelpful theologies and overarching metanarratives. So we are meant to be very distant from the misguided youth of our human story, climbing out of the immature behaviour patterns of ancient times and of the so-called Middle Ages, and becoming fully human now as autonomous, self-inventing, re-inventing individuals. We are, apparently, wiser than our forebears, knowing what we know about science, maths and the material universe. Our future is out of the hands of our dictatorial ancestors who told such tall stories, and is now in our very own hands, as we create a brave, new world on our own. We have rid ourselves of the 'God delusion' in favour of the secular magic worked by the stories of our celebrity culture.

That the above itself represents a grand meta-narrative with similarities to all previous proud and brave attempts to give life meaning seems only to be evidence for the ubiquity of story-telling in the determined human effort to make sense of life by looking backwards, outwards and forwards. On the basis of Christian presuppositions, this chapter attempts some of that for us in today's world. It invites us, in the words of Eugene Peterson, to 'live into the Story'[2] or to cite Wright again, to become 'act 5 Christians' whose aim is to live their lives and so find fulfilment in finding their place in the trajectory of acts 1 to 4 of the Judaeo-Christian Story while anticipating what is to come in the final act 6, namely the renewal of the heavens and the earth. To live in such a way requires us to 'access the historical memory of what God has done and continues to do'[3] as well as renewing our imagination about what God will do in the future. We are both shadows of our past and future selves.

No Dead End, or What the Hope of Easter Does to Us

Funerals are difficult for everyone, but young people can find them particularly stark and disconcerting. We were standing at the graveside as the coffin of a twenty-one year old whose life had been cut short prematurely by a particularly vigorous cancer was lowered. Very quietly, almost under her breath, one of her friends whispered 'Is this it? Is this all there is?' There is nothing like death for focusing the mind on the purpose of life, on what it means to be human. Sadly the general cynicism regarding any big idea or story that gives meaning or identity means that our society is 'only really comfortable with the domestic narrative, the ordinary which is reflected in our tastes in drama and literature. Ours is the culture of the TV soap typified by the mundane, the Street, the local pub. Such ordinariness makes no demands but it also places a burden. Bit by bit our landscape is flattened.'[4] It is culturally deadening and young people in particular, accompanied by those embarking on a mid-life crisis, have to 'find ways of rupturing the ordinary through the next exciting thing – whether a new pair of shoes, a career change, a violent crime, a drug induced high, a new marriage . . . We develop distorted hungers for the evermore exciting.[5] This is the place where Christian hope needs to be articulated.

The Christian vision of hope enables us to think of time and eternity as largely continuous and, more importantly, as being related to one another as dimensions of reality, given by God for our delight and learning. As Christians, eternity is in our minds, and it provides the context for our understanding and interpretation of creation. We, too, look back, out and forward, but with a different perspective from that of committed postmodernists or even the average person at the graveside. This material world we see around us is not all there is. Indeed, it has a past, a present and a future, but that past, present and future do not stand alone, disconnected. They stand in close relationship with another life, with eternity, and with death and resurrection. Which is where Jesus Christ enters so strongly. We cannot speak of our own development without speaking of Jesus Christ too. From our perspective, history is not merely the long, slow story of our growing up as a race, the so-called 'progress' view of history. As authors, the question posed to one of us in the classroom is as real today as it was then. What's more, it changed our lives! 'Why does the fact that you are a Christian not make a difference to the way you teach History?' Now there's a show stopper! It was this question that brought us together in the first place. Having realised that she was locked in to a progressive view of history that is engraved in many a text book, Ann went to Douglas for help. Marriage followed nine months later and so did some life changing thinking about the hopefulness of creation, the fall, redemption and the future. While progress remains an undeniable aspect of our worldview, we insist that there is also a centre to history. At that centre is the death and resurrection of Jesus Christ, an event which both takes place in and transcends history, an event which opens our eyes to an eternal view of the world. And it is from that point of view – namely from eternity – that we want to see everything that happens here on earth. That is what we call 'realised eschatology'. Jesus is the meeting point of what has been, what is and what is to come and he is the Way to be followed, not a goal to be achieved.

In some ways, therefore, the death and resurrection of Jesus are in themselves the eschaton, the last thing in the series of life, the thing beyond which nothing else can happen. Not quite and not exactly, but his death and resurrection become, for Christian thinking, the beginning, centre and end of all our attention. Here begins, in a way unknown even in earlier Judaism, a story of life being restored, of this life not being the sum total of all there is, of life beyond death. The eschaton, the last in the series, almost seems to reach back into time and into human history and in Jesus' resurrection, shows itself for what it is, namely another dimension. This reality stretches beyond the immediacy of the material world and, in so doing, gives the material world new meaning, a richer, deeper texture than it had before. It makes the most of human potential, that ambition so beloved of education and industry alike. Eternity, deposited in our minds by God himself, becomes real and determining for us through the events of Easter. Tom Torrance puts it powerfully in his book *Space, Time and Resurrection*:

> It is essentially in this way that the incarnation and resurrection of Jesus Christ came to be accepted by the early church and classical theology . . . That God Himself had become man was an offence to the Jew and folly to the Greek; that Jesus Christ rose from the dead was deemed to be utterly incredible. Yet the incarnation and resurrection forced themselves upon the mind of the Church against the grain of people's convictions, . . . and

they took root within the Church only through a seismic restructuring of religious and intellectual belief.[6]

Strangely, then, the death of Jesus is not the end but proves to be the door that opens on to a new realm. This new dimension changes our view of everything that is, was and one day will be. The incarnation and resurrection of Jesus is the last event in that it fundamentally alters all other events, relating them to life beyond death and to eternity. To live Christianly is then to live believing in life after death, certainly, but in such a way that *that* life then changes everything in *this* life now.

'When He appears, we shall be like Him' (1 Jn. 3:2). In part John's line is an allusion to Christ's second coming. However, it can also refer to this life and the way we live now. This is where the eschatological rubber hits the road and takes us a stage further than the reactions at a funeral. Christ has risen and appeared to us so that our future is 'alive' in us now. Around Easter, we usually remind ourselves that following Jesus means following him on the way to glory and that means via the way of the cross. Another way of putting it is to say that greatness comes to those who genuinely serve others. The essential link between humility and power is made by Christ on the cross. The redemptive work of the cross demands a renewed sense of vocation and a willingness to rejoice in servanthood, to become the means by which God meets human needs in the here and now.

But travelling this way is not all service, with greatness to come. We live the whole of life purposefully and in hope now. The last thing in the series is just that, but it also changes the series. Ask anyone a question about that most recent funeral they have attended, and mostly the answer will make some reference to a life beyond the grave. In part, this may only illustrate a psychological 'bent' on the part of modern day mourners, but it could also indicate a much bigger conclusion too. We travel in hope, we live in hope, and whatever we hope for in the future does have some impact on our lives today. The future reaches back to influence the present. This is what Christian hope does and we need to think about how it does it.

In therapy, clients are reminded, or should be, that they cannot change the past. What they can change is their response to the past, which is in the present. In turn, this intervention may transform their future. The past can, in a sense, reach forward into the present and even the future and change them. Similarly, the future, in its own way, can also influence the present. That way is called hope.

A Whole New End, or What Christian Hope Does to the World

As creatures made in God's image, we too create. In particular, we create human culture, we give it direction, and we are history-formers. In doing all this, we express what is in us. We make things in our image, collectively as well as individually, and we keep on 'mimicking' God. We may do that well or poorly, in full knowledge of his good will for us, or in ignorance of that, but we cannot not do it. Whatever we think God is like and whatever we think God likes, we will reproduce. So producing an array of paralysing choice, a machine with built-in obsolescence, a mind-numbing selection of television programmes, etc. tells us quite a lot about what 'god' looks like to many if not most of our contemporaries. Since the Second World War, in the West, we have been so intent on economic prosperity that everything has been reduced to, and is measured in terms of, economic survival or economic success. In the Government's White Paper, 'Every Child Matters' the adjective attached to well-being is 'economic'. This 'economism' as Brian Walsh describes it has captured our imaginations. 'It is in the air everywhere and sadly the Church supplies no gas mask'.[7] Our imagination of happiness and fulfilment has been shaped by a constant stream of cultural images. Advertising is adept at turning luxuries in to necessities and has placed us on to a hedonistic treadmill. Yet the work of the Economist, Richard Layard, demonstrates that we are no happier than we were 50 years ago. Despite a considerable increase in disposable income people report no greater satisfaction in their lives.

Sometimes the ground shifts, however, and the signs are there. People are no longer impressed with the endless talk about GDP. They are looking for new 'measures', for new signs of hope. It was the late Lesslie Newbigin urging Christians to preach the gospel of the kingdom by being a hermeneutic of this gospel in our communal and individual lives who said:

> We have a gospel to proclaim . . . we have to proclaim it as part of the conversation that shapes public doctrine. It must be heard in the conversation of psychiatrists, educators, scientists, politicians. We have to proclaim it NOT as a package of estimable values but the truth about what is the case, about what every human being and every human society will have to reckon with (on that day).[8]

In Christian hope, we are charged to worship a 'god' who looks very different from the gods of this world. The future which reaches back to influence the past and change the present for Christians is in the hands of a truly wise and loving God who has understood the end from the beginning, unlike many of us human beings, who never 'begin at the end'. To begin with the end is to look to the desired future, to see God and remain open to his guidance in our flexibly laid plans today. Take the field of Education from which we both come. Teachers can, we suppose, teach their subjects for years on end, and take no thought for where the world, this country, their city/town/village and their own students are going. Such a lack of historical intelligence is clearly possible. But once described, once noted, once named, can it really remain a desired approach to the business of teaching? Can we go on not caring about our students' development for long?

Most teachers are forced into looking to the future, then, even if they might naturally fight shy of it. They develop that toned desire to see their students do well, they plan accordingly, they talk about what comes next, about life after the exams; they in fact constantly direct their students' minds to the future. Some may even point to an end beyond the grave. Education as preparation for death in the midst of life! It becomes natural for a good teacher to look at least some way into the future, open herself to that future and allow it to influence her in the content, structure or style of her teaching. The good teacher may not look to the eschaton, in fully Christian terms, but she will have and share an historical consciousness with her students, and place the learning in a context of past, present and future, the past, present and future of the learner and of the subject. To do otherwise is to imprison the learner in the present, and no-one wants that from a teacher. Real learning occurs when we face something new, when we learn how to change.

As with good teachers, parents also share a natural affinity with eschatology. They are never out of touch with the past of their children. They live with them in the present and they have a dream for them for the future. It may not climb much higher than wanting a better pair of shoes. It may not be much different from selfish ambition. It may fall into keeping up with the Joneses. But it is there in all parents. Parents, made in the image of God, want to do well by their children, to enable them to learn and grow, to encourage their learning and to live with a vision of a better life, however inarticulately this may be expressed. Likewise, as Christians we have no choice but to learn. We need to grow intellectually, physically, morally, spiritually. Our life and our skills are not given to us in a finished package at birth. Throughout our lives we grow and mature. In this way, the future influences how we live in the present and perhaps even how we deal with the past. To do so we not only need knowledge of the Bible (the first four acts of the play) but we need to know the world were God has placed us. Good teachers and parents, made in the image of God, know this intuitively.

Christians live with more than an intuition. They live with an eschatological understanding of the world. Its past, its present and its future are intimately bound up together. The last thing in the series is the eschaton, also known as the kingdom of God, where lions and lambs lie down together and so do the enemies along the street. That vision of the peaceable rule of God guides Christians to a greater or lesser extent and keeps the future always open. However closed it may seem, however closed off it may seem – and it seemed pretty closed for Jesus Christ especially in the run up to what we call Good Friday – it always remains open. The challenge is to live with great passion and conviction, remaining open and flexible, aware that in this life we are but shadows of our future selves. We must not stray into the heresy that the body will pass away permanently after death and that we will only reappear as some type of disembodied wraith. 'I believe in the resurrection of the body and the life everlasting' There are no disembodied spirits in the Creed. The shadow, that part of us which has not been fully revealed, is what we are now, not what we will be then! It is now that we are to be the forerunners and the first fruits of the new age. True spirituality is not about escaping this world to some other place where we will be for ever. This world is our home. We are not passing through. We are shaping the building blocks of eternity. That is why this gospel shapes the world and explains why we are here. We are here to care for a creation that is waiting 'in eager expectation for the sons of God to be revealed' (Rom. 8).

That caring involves creating, adapting, developing, being co-creators with God – 're-imagining Eden and Edening the imagination'. To be human, in the image of God, is to shape the world, to judge, to decide not just interpret. We are to be stewards of all things, time, energy, health, family life, buildings as well as natural things. Our work becomes a gift from God, a sacred task, whether it is repairing a tap, making a bed or teaching a class. Our work is a divine service to others. It is to be balanced by rest and play. Work can become idolatry or an addiction and even leisure can become a consumptive activity for those with no eschatological understanding. To enter into God's rest is an act of trust, a place of praise where we can glimpse the world as it will be. It is here that we become fully human. In this moment God renews our imaginations, enabling us to become artistic in the way he intends us to be, to image the One whom Picasso described as the 'greatest artist'. Have you ever thought that the way we dress is an aspect of imaging God? We have no business looking dull and even worse being dull. In the words of Dorothy Sayers 'How could we have made the whole drama so pedestrian?' 'If the

Christian faith produces good families, good businesses, good art, good books and good politics then people will notice that the kingdom of heaven is at hand. We are not to divorce anything from the transforming presence of God, past, present and future'.[9]

When we are surrounded by despair, often masquerading as hedonistic selfishness, our task is to keep going; to work towards the 'Isaiah agenda', as Raymond Fung puts it, of a world where children do not die, old people live in dignity, those who build houses live in them and those who plant vineyards eat the fruit.[10] It sounds so simple but this is the genuinely happy ending to life's story and currently so counter cultural in many parts of the world. We do not live in a time of perfection and wholeness but nor do we live in a time of total failure and pain. Sin and holiness permeate every dimension of our lives in this time of eschatological tension. 'Prayer may be blasphemous and bricklaying may be holy. Sermons may be treacherous and jokes may be healing'.[11]

It is a time in which we can bring about, in the words of Francis Schaeffer, 'substantial healing'. The wheat and the tares grow together and we live in the time before the final winnowing. The kingdom is already here but much of what God has promised still lies ahead of us. We live by his promise in a time of sanctification and preparation for living in the new heavens and the new earth that God will bring about. We need to be patient. God has bought us time to prepare. In time, sin will be destroyed in the refiner's fire, not the destructive fire of annihilation but the purifying fire of judgement. At the centre of the new earth is not a garden as at the beginning, but a city, imaged in human culture as a place where and a time when we raise our children, make a proper living, act politically . . . be responsible in every way. The story goes that when asked what he would do today if Jesus were coming tomorrow, Martin Luther replied 'plant a tree'. In other words he would have got on with life hopefully in the midst of despair. And Jesus *is* coming again and at that time he will accept our imperfect works, including planting trees, and make them perfect.

Closing in Prayer, or What Only Hope Can Say

Consider the eschatology of those who wrote this prayer on a scrap of paper in Ravensbruck concentration camp in the early 1940s:

> O Lord, remember not only the men and women of good will,
> but also those of ill will.
> But do not remember
> all the suffering they have inflicted upon us.
> Remember the fruits we brought forth thanks to this suffering:
> Our comradeship, our loyalty, our humility,
> the courage, the generosity, the greatness of heart
> which has grown out of this.
> And when they come to judgment,
> let all the fruits we have borne be their forgiveness.
> Amen.[12]

We both understand and fail to understand this prayer. Its words mean a great deal to us, knowing, as we do, some who have suffered unbelievably in the last thirty years of Northern Ireland and some who have suffered in the recent violence of the London bombings here in England. So we can grasp what the words were intended to convey, and hear in this Jewish prayer the most profound echoes of Christian eschatology. At another level, we know we have not got as far as this yet. We have heard the call of God from his future and have sought to respond obediently. But not that much! Certainly not yet! We could wish that we had! For the prayer expresses such a wide and broad casting of the net of God's loving handling and holding of the world and its future. Imagine this prayer on a nat-ional and global level and you have the influence of God's future on our present AND on our past. There is a long way to travel on this journey, in this 'between time'. Our mission is 'less about the transportation of God from one place to another and more about the identification of a God who is already there'[13] with us on the journey. Only he really knows what time it is and how far we have to go on the journey. But he has allowed us to catch sight of the destination, a new heaven and a new earth. Meanwhile we need lives that are the signs of great hope of that day when,

> The Kingdom of the world has become the Kingdom of our Lord and of His Christ, and He shall reign for ever and ever.
> (Rev. 11:15)

Glossary

Adventist: Someone who believes in the future second coming of Christ.

Amillennialism: The view that the 'thousand years' spoken of in Rev. 20:1–6 is not to be read literally and that the Church is currently living in the 'millennial' period (compare *postmillennial; premillennial*)

Anabaptist: Member of one of several radical movements stemming from the Reformation. An emphasis on a strong separation between church and state and the claim that baptism is reserved for believers only.

Annihilationism: Belief that those who are not saved will be destroyed/annihilated, rather than suffering eternally in hell.

Apocalypse; apocalyptic: 'Apocalyptic' describes a form of Jewish literature with a strong emphasis on divine revelation and often highly symbolic pictures of the spiritual battle between God and the forces of evil as a way of interpreting current history. An 'apocalypse' is a book of this form; 'The Apocalypse' is another term for the book of Revelation, the last book of the Bible, which displays features of this form.

Apostasy: When someone who has been a disciple of Christ denies him and abandons the Christian path.

Armageddon: A predicted climactic final battle between the forces of good and evil. See Rev. 16:16.

Arminian: The view that God wants to save all people, that Christ died for all people and offers grace to all. Human free choice, rather than God's election, is the ultimate reason why some are not saved.

Canonical reading: Modern school of biblical interpretation that stresses the unity of the Bible, and so looks for connections between books, and for meaning in the overarching structure of the biblical books.

Catechetical, Catechesis: 'Catechesis' is the process of preparing new converts for baptism (or church children for confirmation), and particularly the instruction in basic Christian belief and behaviour that is part of the preparation.

Dispensationalism: A way of reading the Bible that divides history up into a number (classically seven) of different 'dispensations', in each of which God deals differently with people.

Docestism: Early heresy teaching that Jesus was not really human, but just appeared to be.

Dystopia; dystopian: Converse of 'Utopia'; an imagined future or fictional state in which everything is warped and wrong.

End times: Period during which various events supposedly related to the return of Christ (e.g., *rapture, tribulation*) occur.

Enlightenment: Period in Western culture, reaching its height during the eighteenth century, that stressed the possibility of reason to solve human problems, and rejected inherited traditions and practices.

Epistemology: The philosophical study of knowledge (e.g., What is 'knowledge'? What can we know? How can we know it?).

Eschatology; eschatological: The study of the 'last things': the return of Christ, death, judgement, etc.

Existentialism: Western philosophy of the nineteenth and twentieth centuries that sees the particular experienced existence of each human being as decisive to understanding the world.

Fundamentalist: Traditionally, Christian believer, mostly from the United States, who accepts and emphasises the beliefs outlined in a series of publications entitled *The Fundamentals*. These stressed a very conservative Protestant faith.

Futurist: A way of interpreting the book of Revelation which sees it as a prediction of future events, describing what will happen in the *end times*.

Gentiles: Non-Jewish people.

Gnosticism: Early Christian heresy which regarded the material world as evil, and saw salvation as escape from the material world, achieved through the possession of secret knowledge.

Hellenistic: Related to the Greek culture of the Eastern Mediterranean area in the centuries following the conquests of Alexander the Great.

Historicist: A way of interpreting the book of Revelation as if it were a prediction of the course of history from the time of Christ until the *end times*.

Magisterial reformers: Mainstream reformers at the time of the Reformation who believed that the state had a role in reforming the church, including Luther, Calvin and Knox.

Metanarrative: A grand 'story' that controls the way in which those who embrace it understand and interpret the world.

Millenarian: Focussed on the *millennium*.

Millennium: The thousand year period of Christ's rule and perfect human society spoken of in Rev. 20:1–6.

Modernity: Western cultural movement coming to full fruition in the early twentieth century, focussed on the primacy of science as a way of understanding the world, and a rejection of tradition.

Patristic: Related to the 'Church Fathers', the leaders and theologians who wrote in the first few centuries of the history of the church.

Pelagianism: A fifth-century heresy teaching, opposed by Augustine, that taught that human beings can and must attain perfection by their own efforts.

Postmillennial: Believing that the second coming of Christ will occur after the *millennium*. Compare *amillennial; premillennial*.

Postmodern, Postmodernity: Western cultural movement beginning in the late twentieth century, rejecting the possibility of universal reason, or of any common metanarrative, and so stressing the local and political nature of philosophical positions.

Premillennial: Believing that the second coming of Christ will occur before the *millennium.* Compare *amillennial; postmillennial.*

Rapture: Supposed event of the end times when Christ gathers all his people and takes them away from the earth.

Second Coming: Personal, physical, visible return of Christ, as predicted by the angels in Acts 1:11.

Theophany: Any visible appearance of God, for example in the burning bush (Ex. 3), at the oaks of Mamre (Gen. 18), etc.

Tribulation, Great: Supposed event of the *end times* when suffering beyond anything previously known on the earth will be experienced.

Universalism: Belief that all human beings will in the end be saved, and enjoy the blessings of eternal life.

Endnotes

1. Introduction

[1] http://www.timlahaye.com/about_ministry/index.php3?p=
pretrib&section=PreTrib%20Research%20Center Accessed on
15/2/07.

3. Eschatology in Isaiah

[1] Joseph Blenkinsopp, *Isaiah 56 – 66* (New York/London: Doubleday, 2002), 286.
[2] Joseph Blenkinsopp, *Isaiah 1 – 39* (New York/London: Doubleday,
2000), 451.

4. Eschatology at the Heart of New Testament Theology

[1] I.H. Marshall, 'Slippery Words I. Eschatology', *Expository Times*
89.9 (1977–78), 264–69.
[2] R.P. Carroll, 'Eschatology', in R.J. Coggins and J.L. Houlden (eds.),
A Dictionary of Biblical Interpretation (London: SCM Press, 1990),
200–203. (The article is mainly about the Old Testament and says
little about the New Testament).
[3] The phrase was coined by E. Haenchen and popularised by J.
Jeremias, *The Parables of Jesus* (London: SCM Press, 1963), 230.
[4] E.C. Hoskyns, *Cambridge Sermons*, 39, as cited by E.G. Selwyn, *The
First Epistle of Peter* (London: Macmillan, 1946), 260 n.
[5] Further reading: D.C. Allison, Jr., 'Eschatology', in J.B. Green (et
al.), *Dictionary of Jesus and the Gospels* (Downers Grove/Leicester:
InterVarsity Press, 1992), 206–209; B. Witherington III, *Jesus, Paul*

and the End of the World: A Comparative Study in New Testament Eschatology (Downers Grove: InterVarsity Press, 1992).

6. Eschatology in the Church Fathers

1. The Didache may be found in *Early Christian Fathers*, which is Volume I of *The Library of Christian Classics*, ed. C.C. Richardson (London: SCM, 1953).
2. I Clement, 23–27 (*Ante-Nicene Fathers*, vol. 1, 11f.).
3. Ignatius to the Smyrnaeans, 3 (*Ante-Nicene Fathers*, Vol. 1, 87).
4. The Epistle of Polycarp to the Philippians, 7 (*A-NF*, Vol. 1, 34), referring to 1 Jn. 4:3.
5. The Epistle of Barnabas, 15 (*A-NF*, Vol. 1, 146).
6. Dialogue, 80 (*A-NF*, Vol. 1, 239).
7. Dialogue, 81 (*A-NF*, Vol. 1, 240); a very early comment on Rev. 20:4–5.
8. Dialogue, 45 (*A-NF*, Vol. 1, 217).
9. Against Heresies, 5,2,3 (*A-NF*, Vol. 1, 528).
10. Against Heresies, 5, 35, 1 (*A-NF*, Vol. 1, 565).
11. On the Resurrection of the Flesh (*A-NF*, Vol. 3, 545–94).
12. A Treatise on the Soul, 55 (*A-NF*, Vol. 3, 231).
13. Against Marcion, 24 (*A-NF*, Vol. 3, 342f.).
14. On First Principles, 3,6,6 (*A-NF*, Vol. 4, 347): cf. J.N.D. Kelly, *Early Christian Doctrines* (London: 1968), 471.
15. On First Principles, 2,11,6 (*A-NF*, Vol. 4, 299).
16. On First Principles, 2,9,8 (*A-NF*, Vol. 4, 293).
17. On First Principles, 2,11,2 (*A-NF*, Vol. 4, 297).
18. On First Principles, 2,19,4 (*A-NF*, Vol. 4, 295): cf. Kelly, *Doctrines*, 473.
19. On First Principles, 1,6,3; 3,6,3 (*A-NF*, Vol. 4, 261, 345).
20. See Eusebius, 'Church History', 7, 24f. (*Nicene and Post-Nicene Fathers*, Second Series, Vol. 1, 308ff.).
21. On the Resurrection, Synopsis, 11–13 (*A-NF*, Vol. 6, 375).
22. On the Resurrection, 1,13 (*A-NF*, Vol. 6, 367).
23. To Pammachius against John of Jerusalem, 33 (*NP-NF*, Second Series, Vol. 6, 440f.).
24. Catechetical Lectures, 18,18 (*NP-NF*, Second Series, Vol. 7, 139).
25. Ambrose, 'On the Decease of His Brother, Satyrus', Bk.2, 'On Belief in the Resurrection' (*NP-NF*, Second Series, Vol. 10, 174–197).
26. Gregory of Nyssa, 'On the Soul and the Resurrection' (*NP-NF*, Second Series, Vol. 5, 430–468).

27 The one outstanding exception was the Christian Latin poet, Lactantius, who revived the idea of six thousand years represented by the six days of creation, the millennium then being the seventh day. He believed that the end of the six thousand years was less than two hundred years away. Cf. Lactantius, *Divine Institutes*, 7, 14–26 (*A-NF*, Vol. 7, 211–22).

28 'The City of God', 20, 7–9 (*NP-NF*, First Series, Vol. 2, 426–31).

29 J.N.D. Kelly's translation (*Early Christian Doctrines*, 480) of a passage from 'Three Homilies on the Devil', I, 8, only otherwise available in Greek (J.-P. Migne, *Patrologia Graeca*, Vol. 49, 241–76).

30 Cyril of Jerusalem, 'Catechetical Lectures', 15, 25f. (*NP-NF*, Second Series, Vol. 7, 112).

31 Hilary, Homily on Psalm 1 (*NP-NF*, Second Series, Vol. 9, 240f.)

32 The 'City of God', 20, 1 (*NP-NF*, First Series, Vol. 2, 422).

33 On the Predestination of the Saints, 24 (*NP-NF*, First Series, Vol. 5, 509).

34 Letter to the fallen Theodore, 10 (*NP-NF*, First Series, Vol. 9, 98).

35 Oration 40, On Holy Baptism, 36 (*NP-NF*, Second Series, Vol. 7, 373).

36 The Great Catechism, 26 (*NP-NF*, Second Series, Vol. 5, 496).

37 Enchiridion, 112, 113 (*NP-NF*, First Series, Vol. 3, 273).

38 Catechetical Lectures, 18, 28 (*NP-NF*, Second Series, Vol. 7, 141).

39 Oration 43, The Panegyric on Basil, 82 (*NP-NF*, Second Series, Vol. 7, 422).

40 On the Soul and the Resurrection (*NP-NF*, Second Series, Vol. 5, 467f.).

41 Augustine, On the Trinity, 8, 3 (*NP-NF*, First Series, Vol. 3, 117); and The City of God 22, 30 (*NP-NF*, First Series, Vol. 2, 509f.).

7. Eschatology in Evangelical History

1 Stephen J. Stein (ed.), *Apocalyptic Writings, The Works of Jonathan Edwards*, Vol. 5 (New Haven, CT, 1977), 411.

2 J.H. Pratt (ed.), *The Thought of the Evangelical Leaders: Notes of the Discussions of the Eclectic Society, London, during the Years 1798–1814* (Edinburgh, 1978), 256.

3 *General Baptist Magazine*, July 1854, 302–10, quoted at 302, 310.

4 Edward Irving, 'Preliminary Discourse', in Juan Josafat Ben Ezra, *The Coming of Messiah in Glory and Majesty* (London, 1827), vi.

5 I.E. Page (ed.), *John Brash: Memorials and Correspondence* (London, 1912), 68.

6 *Christian World*, 14 May 1891, 395.
7 *Advent Witness*, December 1923, 136.
8 http://www.leftbehind.com, accessed 29 November 2006.

8. Eschatology and Mission

1 Christopher J.H. Wright, *The Mission of God: Unlocking the Bible's Grand Narrative* (Leicester: Inter-Varsity Press, 2006).
2 For an example of an evangelistic course that follows the Bible story see Tim Chester and Steve Timmis, *The World We All Want* (Milton Keynes: Authentic, 2005).
3 Tony Campolo, *It's Friday, but Sunday's Comin'* (Waco: Word, 1985), 124–26.
4 Martin Luther, *Early Theological Works* (ed. James Atkinson; London: SCM, 1962), 290–92.

9. Hell

1 It is important to appreciate that the question of the *nature* of hell (ECT, HAA, or RP [see main text for the meaning of these abbreviations]) is a different question from the following questions: *Who* will be saved and *how* (the question of inclusivism, exclusivism and pluralism)? *How many* will be saved (a few? Many? Most? All?)? In fact a surprising number of combinations of answers to these questions are possible (see the grid below).

	ECT	HAA	RP	Exclusivism	Inclusivism	Pluralism
ECT				yes	yes	yes
HAA				yes	yes	yes
RP				yes	yes	yes
Few saved	yes	yes	possibly	yes	possibly	possibly
Many Saved	yes	yes	yes	yes	yes	yes
Most Saved	yes	yes	yes	yes	yes	yes
All saved (universalism)	possibly	NO	yes	yes	yes	yes

I have written 'possibly' for combinations which are logically possible but uncommon. Only the combination of some being annihilated with all being saved is impossible (and, if pushed, I can think of ways that this might be possible also).

2   We need to distinguish RP from Purgatory. In Roman Catholic the-
    ology Purgatory is the place where people who die in a state of
    grace suffer temporary afflictions for their venial sins so as to
    purge them and make them ready for heaven. It is *not* to be iden-
    tified with hell from which, in Catholic thought, there is no
    redemption. Some Universalist defenders of RP *do* see the suffer-
    ings in hell as purging (e.g. so hell is understood like a version of
    Purgatory) and others see them merely as educative, revealing the
    true nature of sin to sinners leading them to repentance.

3   Alternative strategies include admitting that the Bible teaches con-
    tradictory things and (a) that they must be held in tension and not
    made logically consistent, (b) that the different biblical visions of
    the future offer different *possible* futures but the *actual* future
    depends on human choices and is not yet fixed, (c) that one or
    both of the visions of the future is mistaken, (d) that the hell pic-
    tures present the hypothetical fate of those who reject God forev-
    er but that in the end nobody actually will.

4   (*Christian Origins and the Question of God* Vol. 1; Lon.: SPCK, 1992).

5   (Milton Keynes: Paternoster, 1995).

6   Brian McLaren's book *The Last Word and the Word After That* (San
    Francisco: Jossey-Bass, 2005) could perhaps be said to represent a
    fifth approach to hell. For MacLaren Jesus took the language of hell
    which, he says, was developed by the Pharisees to exclude 'sinners'
    and deconstructed it by turning it against them. In Jesus' rhetoric it
    is not the sinners but *those who exclude them* that are in danger of hell.
    The issue, says McLaren, is not actually about the afterlife but about
    justice now. 'The language of hell, in my view, like the language of
    biblical prophecy in general, is not intended to provide literal or
    detailed fortune-telling or prognostication about the hereafter, nor is
    it intended to satisfy intellectual curiosity, but rather it is intended to
    motivate us in the here and now to realize our ultimate accountabil-
    ity to a God of mercy and justice and in that light to rethink every-
    thing and to seek first the kingdom and justice of God' (188–89).

7   J. Moltmann, *The Coming of God: Christian Eschatology* (tr. M. Kohl;
    London: SCM, 1996), 251.

10. Heaven

1   T. Peters, *God: The World's Future* (Minneapolis: Fortress Press,
    1992), 308–309; cited in C. Braaten, and and R. Jenson (eds.), *The
    Last Things* (Grand Rapids: Eerdmans, 2002), 149.

² N.T. Wright, *The Resurrection of the Son of God* (Minneapolis: Fortress Press, 2003), 31.

³ E. Donnelly, *Heaven and Hell* (Glasgow: Banner of Truth Trust, 2001), 112. From a similar stable see E. Davies, *Heaven is a Far Better Place* (Darlington: Evangelical Press, 1999).

⁴ N.T. Wright, *New Heavens, New Earth* (Cambridge: Grove Books, 1999), 5.

⁵ J. Colwell (ed.), *Called to One Hope: Perspectives on Life to Come* (Carlisle: Paternoster, 2000), xi.

⁶ Cited in H. Schwarz, *Eschatology* (Grand Rapids: Eerdmans, 2000), 403.

⁷ Cited in C. McDannell and B. Lang, *Heaven: A History* (New Haven: Yale Note Bene, 2001), 336.

⁸ Wright, *New Heavens*, 10.

⁹ Hans Weder stresses this point in terms of a continuity-discontinuity dialectic. 'If worldly experience were not to contain any clues for eternal life, nothing can be said about it; it would remain an empty fantasy. If there were no continuity, there would be no possibility of grasping the life to come. At the same time discontinuity is essential, due to the qualitative newness of eternal life. The problem then arises of how to think together continuity and discontinuity.' See his 'Hope and Creation', in J. Polkinghorne and M. Welker (eds.), *The End of the World and the Ends of God* (Harrisburg: Trinity Press International, 2000), 193.

¹⁰ Wright, *Resurrection*, 478. C.S. Lewis presents a similar picture in both *The Last Battle* and *The Great Divorce* where heaven is presented as more real than our current experience.

¹¹ The Greek is precisely the same in 2:18, 23 and 3:12. The NIV adds the word 'false' to clarify the meaning, but it is not in the original Greek.

¹² Yet, having said this, it is also the case that the opposite problem of an over-indulgence is also a real danger. Moreover, it springs from the same well, namely living apart from Christ according to one's earthly nature (Col. 3:5ff.). Indeed, given our own consumerist culture it is arguably the case that it this over-indulgent denial of the 'new earth' that requires emphasis, rather than the ascetic denials addressed in Colosse.

¹³ It is also important to stress that the eucharist, the aperitif of the heavenly banquet, is also an aspect of our present experience that instantiates our future hope. A catholic-protestant divide is perhaps identifiable here. The second Vatican Council refers to the eucharist as a 'foretaste of the heavenly banquet'. By way of

contrast, Wesley had earlier referred to it merely as the 'pledge of heaven'. The Council is no doubt more accurate as the thing about firstfruits is that they are in fact fruits, and not merely a promise of fruit. Cf. A. McGrath, *A Brief History of Heaven* (Oxford: Blackwell, 2003), 168–71.

[14] I have presented this analysis in terms of eating and drinking. However, a similar approach would be possible in relation to other bodily manifestations such as touch and dancing. Indeed, part of this analysis would be to show how the absence of pain and suffering is also part of this paradigm. It is important to recognise that the reason there is no pain in the new earth is not because we are disembodied spirits, but rather because the Spirit-renewed bodies we have function differently.

[15] McGrath, *Heaven*, 37–38.

[16] Donnelly, *Heaven*, 120.

[17] McDannell and Lang, *Heaven*, 303–306.

[18] Augustine, *Sermons* 243:6.

[19] McGrath, *Heaven*, 181.

[20] R. Stewart, *The Resurrection of Jesus: John Dominic Crossan and N.T.Wright in Dialogue* (Minneapolis: Fortress Press, 2006), 21. See also Wright, *Resurrection*, 602–604.

[21] Cf. Wright, *Resurrection*, 296.

[22] NB the references in Revelation 7:16 to hunger, thirst and destitution may strengthen this point.

[23] Space does not permit me to address adequately the issue of rewards, but I would direct the reader to Stephen Travis' discussion of this topic. He understands them more as the 'intrinsic consequences' of our salvation, rather than as some kind of extra bonus. S. Travis, '"Your Reward is Great in Heaven": Rewards in the teaching of Jesus' in Colwell (ed.), *Called*, 3–16.

11. Eschatology and Imagination

[1] Austin Farrer, *The Glass of Vision* (Westminster: Dacre Press, 1948), 57.

[2] Romans 8:24 :' hope that is seen is no hope at all. Who hopes for what he already has?'.

[3] William Lynch, *Images of Hope: Imagination as Healer of the Hopeless* (Dublin: Helicon, 1965), 31. Original emphasis.

[4] See further on this and other aspects of the relationship between hope and imagination Richard Bauckham and Trevor Hart, *Hope*

Against Hope: Christian Eschatology at the Turn of the Millennium (Grand Rapids: Eerdmans, 1999), Chapter 3.
5   Dante Alighieri, The Inferno, Canto III.9 in Mark Musa (ed.), *The Portable Dante* (London: Penguin, 1995), 14.
6   Ernst Bloch, *The Principle of Hope* (3 volumes, Oxford: Blackwells, 1986), 451.
7   George Steiner, *After Babel* (2nd edn., Oxford: Oxford University Press, 1992), 168.
8   Frank Kermode, *The Sense of an Ending* (London: Oxford University Press, 1967).
9   Jürgen Moltmann, *Theology of Hope* (London: SCM Press, 1967), 21.

12. In God's Good Time

1   Augustine, *Confessions* (London: Penguin, 1961), 177.
2   Augustine, 'De Musica', *The Fathers of the Church* (ed. R.C. Taliaferro; New York: Ludwig Schopp, 1947).
3   J. Begbie, *Theology, Music and Time* (Cambridge: Cambridge University Press, 2000), 6.
4   J. Edwards, *The Works of Jonathan Edwards Vol. 1* (Yale University Press, New Haven, 1980), 235.

13. Eschatology and Pop Culture

1   Stanley Grenz illustrates the shift from the modernity to the late modernity by comparing *Star Trek* with *Star Trek – The Next Generation*. S.J. Grenz, 'Star Trek and the Next Generation: Postmodernism and the Future of Evangelical Theology', *Evangelical Review of Theology* 18 (1994), 322-34.
2   F. Bacon (1626).
3   A. Giddens, *Modernity and Self Identity: Self and Society in the Late-modern Age* (Oxford: Polity, 1991), 4.
4   A. Giddens, *The Consequences of Modernity* (Oxford: Polity, 1990), 53
5   Ibid., 150.
6   A. Toffler, *Future-Shock* (New York: Random House, 1970).
7   Z. Bauman, *Liquid Love: On the Frailty of Human Bonds* (Cambridge: Polity, 2003), 41.
8   http://www.creditaction.org.uk/debtstats.htm.

9   The Haunted House, *New Internationalist*, April 1997, Zygmunt Bauman.
10 J. Webster, 'Eschatology, Anthropology and Post-modernity'. *International Journal of Systematic Theology* 2.1 (2000), 17.
11 Q.J. Schulze, *Dancing in the Dark: Youth Popular Culture and the Electronic Media* (Grand Rapids: Eerdmans, 1991), 38, cited in J.G. Stackhouse, *Evangelical Landscapes: Facing Critical Issues of the Day* (Grand Rapids: Baker Academic, 2002), 14.
12 A. Robbins and A. Wilna, *Quarter-Life Crisis* (New York: Tarcher/Putnam, 2001).
13 B. Hoedemaker, 'Toward an Epistemologically Responsible Missiology', in J.A. Kirk and K.J. Vanhoozer (eds.), *To Stake a Claim: Mission and the Western Crisis of Knowledge* (New York: Orbis, 1999), 226.
14 L. Newbigin, 'The Pastor's Opportunities: VI. Evangelism in the City', *Expository Times* 98 (1987), 357.
15 J. Moltmann, *Theology of Hope : On the Ground and the Implications of a Christian Eschatology* (London : SCM Press, 1967), 16.
16 M. Greene, *Imagine*, London Institute for Contemporary Christianity and the Evangelical Alliance, see also M. Greene and T. Cotterell (eds.), *Let My People Grow: Reflections on Making Disciples Who Make a Difference in Today's World* (Milton Keynes: Authentic, 2006).

14. Eschatology and Politics

1   Oliver O'Donovan, *The Desire of the Nations: Rediscovering the Roots of Political Theory* (Cambridge: Cambridge University Press, 1996), 268.

15. Eschatology of Work

1   Miroslav Volf, *Work in the Spirit* (Oxford: Oxford University Press, 1991; repr. Eugene, OR: Wipf & Stock, 2001), 93.
2   What follows is a slight modification of material in chapter 3 of my book *The Heavenly Good of Earthly Work* (Milton Keynes: Paternoster, 2006), 68–72.
3   It is possible to translate this phrase 'to us', as in the NRSV, rather than 'in us' (so NIV). However, the context here emphasises throughout our inclusion 'in Christ' or 'in the Spirit'. Thus the theological flow of the text, tying creation's redemption into our resurrection, suggests that 'in us' is the best translation.

⁴ This section is likewise a modification of material in chapter 3 of my book *Heavenly Good*, 72–77.
⁵ For a fuller treatment of this see my book *A Theology of Work: Work and the New Creation* (Carlisle: Paternoster, 2004), 68–72, 136–51. See also Richard Bauckham, *The Theology of the Book of Revelation* (Cambridge: Cambridge University Press, 1993).
⁶ Bauckham, *Revelation*, 53.
⁷ See chapter 4 in *Heavenly Good*.

16. Living for the Future

¹ For the classic expression of this view see William Paley, *Natural Theology, or Evidences of the Existence and Attributes of the Deity Collected from the Appearances of Nature* (London: R. Faulder, 1802).
² David Hume, *An Enquiry Concerning the Principals of Morals* (1751), ed. & int. Tom L. Beauchamp (Oxford: Oxford University Press, 1998).
³ For a sustained critique of Enlightenment ethics and discussion of Christian ethics see my *Living the Christian Story: The Distinctiveness of Christian Ethics* (Edinburgh: T&T Clark, 2001).
⁴ For an extended discussion of this understanding of the sacraments of the church see my *Promise and Presence: an exploration of sacramental theology* (Milton Keynes: Paternoster, 2005).
⁵ Karl Barth, *Church Dogmatics*, IV/4, *Fragment* (Eng. trans. eds. G.W. Bromiley and T.F. Torrance; Edinburgh: T&T Clark, 1969); Karl Barth, *The Christian Life: Church Dogmatics* IV, 4 *Lecture Fragments* (trans. Geoffrey W. Bromiley; Edinburgh: T&T Clark, 1981).
⁶ Thomas Aquinas, *Summa Theologica* I–II & II–II (trans. by Fathers of the English Dominican Province; Westminster, Maryland: Christian Classics, 1981).
⁷ John Calvin, *Institutes of the Christian Religion* (ed. J.T. McNeill; trans. FL. Battles, Philadelphia: Westminster Press, 1960), III iii 9.

17. Eschatology and the Environment

¹ J. Moltmann, *Theology of Hope*, 16 (London: SCM Press, 1983).
² C. Gunton, *The Triune Creator: A Historical and Systematic Study* (Edinburgh: Edinburgh University Press, 1998), 10.

3 The Hebrew word for good, *tov*, is a strong adjective that carries more force than our general English use of the word. It is also a word that is used of God and that describes his essential nature, thus indicating the way creation points towards and reflects him.

4 Gunton, *Triune Creator*, 202.

5 R. Middleton and B. Walsh, *Truth Is Stranger Than It Used To Be: Biblical Faith in a Postmodern Age* (London: SPCK, 1995), 123.

6 My thanks go to Chris Wright for this. For more on ecology in the Old Testament see Chapter 4, 'Ecology and the Earth', in his, *Old Testament Ethics for the People of God* (Leicester: Inter-Varsity Press, 2004). Chris is careful to emphasise that this grammatical reading does not mean that humans are made only to look after God's world. Interestingly, the most recent NIV has changed its translation of this verse to read this way.

7 See Wright's chapter for this above.

8 N.T. Wright, *Jesus and the Victory of God* (Christian Origins and the Question of God Vol. 2; London: SPCK, 1995), 203. It should be noted that Wright uses the lower case for "god". An explanation for why he does this is given on page xivf. in the preface of *The New Testament and the People of God* (London: SPCK, 1995).

9 For more on this see my, *The Inspirational Jesus: Jesus, the Kingdom and Social Justice* (Chichester: CRED foundation, nd).

10 Gunton, *Triune Creator*, 202.

11 This is Wright's translation of 8:21 in *Resurrection*, 258.

12 Wright, *Resurrection*, 258.

13 There is, of course, lots of debate as to when Colossians was written and information on this can be found in all commentaries written on this letter.

14 P.T. O'Brien, *Colossians, Philemon* (Waco: Word, 1982), 61.

15 N.T. Wright, Colossians and Philemon, 71 (Leicester: Inter-Varsity Press, 1986).

16 R. Bauckham, *Jude, 2 Peter* (Waco: Word, 1983), 154. For the question of authorship and the unlikely nature of 2 Peter being written by Peter himself (whilst not precluding an acquaintance), see p. 158–162.

17 S. Bouma-Prediger, *For the Beauty of the Earth: A Christian Vision for Creation Care* (Grand Rapids: Baker, 2001), 77.

18 Bauckham, *Jude, 2 Peter*, 316–21.

19 Incidentally, another more faithful translation of v.10 says that 'the heavenly bodies will be dissolved in the heat', rather than the NIV's, 'the elements will be destroyed by fire' (Bauckham, *Jude, 2*

Peter, 315). The Greek word that the NIV translates 'destroyed' is not the same word as is used in v.6.

20 Bouma-Prediger, *For the Beauty*, 77.

21 R. Bauckham, *The Theology of the Book of Revelation* (Cambridge: Cambridge University Press, 1993), 7.

22 To look at these symbols in more depth, Bauckham's *Theology*, is an excellent introduction as, of course, is his chapter in this present book.

23 G.E. Ladd, *A Commentary on the Revelation of John* (Grand Rapids: Eerdmans, 1972), cited in R. Mounce, *The Book of Revelation* (NICNT; Grand Rapids: Eerdmans, 1977), 368.

24 R. Bauckham and T. Hart, *Hope Against Hope: Christian Eschatology in Contemporary Context* (London: Darton, Longman & Todd, 1999), 79–80.

25 Wright, *Resurrection*, 470.

26 This is Bauckham's translation in, *Jude, 2 Peter*, 324.

27 N.T. Wright, *Resurrection*, 360.

28 C. Gunton, *Christ and Creation* (Carlisle: Paternoster, 1992), 98. This is not the place to debate the merits or otherwise of vegetarianism!

29 For more on all these practical lifestyle questions, see my, *L is for Lifestyle: Christian living that doesn't cost the earth* (Leicester: Inter-Varsity Press, 2004).

30 Gunton, *Christ and Creation*, 64.

31 Although, of course, it could be questioned whether there can be truly effective social justice without corresponding ecological justice.

32 Bauckham and Hart, *Hope*, 194, 207.

33 Quoted in Gunton, *Christ and Creation*, 63.

18. We are but Shadows of our Future Selves

1 Andrew J. Kirk, *Mission Under Scrutiny* (London: Darton, Longman & Todd, 2006).

2 Eugene Peterson, *Eat This Book* (Grand Rapids: Eerdmans, 2006)

3 N.T. Wright, *New Testament and the People of God* (Christian Origins and the Question of God Vol. 1; London: SPCK, 1992), 140-41.

4 Clare Watkins in a paper to the Theology and Education Conference organized by the Stapleford Centre, January 2007.

5 Watkins, as above n. 4.

6 Tom Torrance, *Space, Time and Resurrection* (Edinburgh: T&T Clark, 1988), 17.

7   Brian Walsh, *Subversive Christianity* (Bristol: Regius, 1992), 16.
8   Lesslie Newbigin, *Truth to Tell: The Gospel as Public Truth* (London: SPCK, 1991), 64.
9   Paul Marshall and Lela Gilbert, *Heaven Is Not My Home* (Waco: Word 1998). A summary of his argument on work and creativity.
10 Raymond Fung, *The Isaiah Vision: An Ecumenical Strategy for Congregational Evangelism* (Geneva: World Council of Churches, 1992), 5, 22.
11 Marshall and Gilbert, *Heaven Is not My Home*.
12 Unknown.
13 Kirk, *Mission Under Scrutiny*.

Selected Further Reading

1. Biblical Material

Bauckham R., *Jude, 2 Peter* (Waco: Word Books, 1983).

✓Bauckham R., *The Climax of Prophecy: Studies on the Book of Revelation* (Edinburgh: T&T Clark, 1993).

✓ Bauckham R., *The Theology of the Book of Revelation* (Cambridge: CUP, 1993).

Carley, K., 'Ezekiel's Formula of Desolation: Harsh Justice for the Land/Earth.' *The Earth Story in the Psalms and the Prophets* (eds. N.C. Habel, Earth Bible 4, Sheffield: Sheffield Academic Press/ Cleveland: Pilgrim, 2001), pp. 143–57.

Carley, K., 'From Harshness to Hope: The Implications for Earth of Hierarchy in Ezekiel.' *Ezekiel's Hierarchical World: Wrestling with a Tiered Reality* (eds. S.L. Cook and C.L. Patton, Atlanta: SBL, 2004), pp. 109–125.

Fudge, E.W., *The Fire That Consumes: A Biblical and Historical Study of the Doctrine of Final Punishment* (Carlisle: Paternoster, 1994 [reprinted 2006]).

Gowan, D.E., *Eschatology in the Old Testament* (Edinburgh: T&T Clark, 1986).

Kelly, B.E., *Retribution and Eschatology in Chronicles* (JSOTSup 211, Sheffield Academic Press, Sheffield, 1996).

Mitchell, D.C., *The Message of the Psalter: An Eschatological Programme in the Book of Psalms* (JSOTSup 252, Sheffield: Sheffield Academic Press, 1997).

Mounce R.H., *The Book of Revelation* (London: Marshall, Morgan and Scott, 1977).

O'Brien P.T., *Colossians, Philemon* (Waco: Word Books, 1982).

Perriman, A., *The Coming of the Son of Man: New Testament Eschatology for an Emerging Church* (Milton Keynes: Paternoster, 2005).

Powys, D., *Hell: A Hard Look at a Hard Question: The Fate of the Unrighteous in New Testament Thought* (Carlisle: Paternoster, 1997).

Raitt, T.M., *A Theology of Exile: Judgment/Deliverance in Jeremiah and Ezekiel* (Fortress, Philadelphia, 1977), esp. pp. 206–222.

Reventlow, H.G. (ed.), *Eschatology in the Bible and in Jewish and Christian Tradition* (JSOTSup 243, Sheffield: Sheffield Academic Press, 1997).

Witherington, B. III, *Jesus, Paul and the End of the World: A Comparative Study in New Testament Eschatology* (Downers Grove: IVP, 1992).

Wright N.T., *Colossians and Philemon* (Leicester: IVP, 1986).

Wright N.T., *Jesus and the Victory of God* (London: SPCK, 1996).

Wright N.T., *New Heavens, New Earth: The Biblical Picture of Christian Hope* (Cambridge: Grove Books, 1999).

Wright N.T., *The Resurrection of the Son of God* (London: SPCK, 2003).

2. Eschatology in Evangelical History

Bebbington, D.W., *Evangelicalism in Modern Britain: A History from the 1730s to the 1980s* (London: Unwin Hyman, 1989).

Boyer, P., *When Time shall be No More: Prophecy Belief in Modern American Culture* (Cambridge, MA: Balknap Press, 1992).

Daley, B., *The Hope of the Early Church: A Handbook of Patristic Eschatology* (Peabody: Hendrickson, 2003).

Gribben, C. and Stunt, T.C.F. (eds.), *Prisoners of Hope? Aspects of Evangelical Millennialism in Britain and Ireland, 1800–1880* (Milton Keynes: Paternoster, 2004).

Moorhead, J.H., *American Apocalypse: Yankee Protestants and the Civil War, 1860–1869* (New Haven, CT: Yale University Press, 1978).

Moorhead, J.H., *World Without End: Mainstream American Protestant Visions of the Last Things, 1880–1925* (Bloomington, IN: Indiana University Press, 1999)

Murray, I.H., *The Puritan Hope: A Study in Revival and the Interpretation of Prophecy* (London: Banner of Truth, 1971).

Sandeen, E.R., *The Roots of Fundamentalism: British and American Millenarianism, 1800-1930* (Chicago: University of Chicago Press, 1970).

Weber, T.P., *Living in the Shadow of the Second Coming: American Premillennialism, 1875 to 1925* (New York: OUP, 1979).

3. Eschatology in Contemporary Contexts

Bauckham R. and Hart T., *Hope Against Hope: Christian Eschatology in Contemporary Context* (London: Darton, Longman and Todd, 1999).

Begbie, J. (ed.), *Beholding the Glory, Incarnation through the Arts* (Baker: Grand Rapids, 2000) (A collection of essays by theologians and artists).

Begbie, J. (ed.), *Sounding the Depths* (SCM: London, 2002) (A collection of essays by theologians and musicians).

Begbie, J., *Theology, Music and Time* (CUP: Cambridge, 2000).

Bouma-Prediger, S., *For the Beauty of the Earth: A Christian Vision for Creation Care* (Grand Rapids: Baker, 2001).

Bridger F., 'Ecology and Eschatology: A Neglected Dimension.' *Tyndale Bulletin* 41.2 (1990), pp. 290–301.

Carson, D.A., *The Gagging of God: Christianity Confronts Pluralism* (Grand Rapids: Zondervan, 1996).

Fudge, E.W. & Peterson, R.A., *Two Views of Hell: A Biblical and Theological Dialogue* (Downers Grove: IVP, 2000).

Gunton C.E., *The Triune Creator: A Historical and Systematic Study* (Edinburgh: EUP, 1998).

Gunton C.E., *Christ and Creation* (Carlisle: Paternoster, 1992).

Hilborn, D. (ed.), *The Nature of Hell* (Evangelical Alliance ACUTE Report) (Carlisle: Paternoster, 2000).

Lewis, C.S., *The Great Divorce* (London: Geoffrey Bles, 1946).

MacDonald, G., *The Evangelical Universalist* (Eugene, OR: Cascade Books, 2006/ London: SPCK, 2008).

Middleton R. and Walsh B., *Truth is Stranger Than it Used to be: Biblical Faith in a Postmodern Age* (London: SPCK, 1995).

Moltmann, J., *Theology of Hope* (London: SCM, 1967).

Morgan, C., *Jonathan Edwards and Hell* (Fearn: Christian Focus, 2004).

Parry, R.A. & Partridge, C.H. (eds.), *Universal Salvation? The Current Debate* (Carlisle: Paternoster, 2003).

Peterson, R., *Hell on Trial: The Case for Eternal Punishment* (Phillipsburg: Presbyterian and Reformed, 1995).

Talbott, Thomas, *The Inescapable Love of God* (n.loc: Universal Publishers, 1999).

Turner, S., *Hungry for Heaven, Rock and Roll and the Search for Redemption* (London: Hodder and Stoughton, 1988).

Valerio R., *L is for Lifestyle: Christian Living that Doesn't Cost the Earth* (Leicester: IVP, 2004).

Valerio R., *The Inspirational Jesus: Jesus, the Kingdom and Social Justice* (Chichester: Cred Papers, 2006).

Walvoord, J.F., et al., *Four Views of Hell* (Grand Rapids: Zondervan, 1996).

Re:Mission

Biblical Mission for a Post-Biblical Church

Andrew Perriman

In this innovative and radical book postmodern mission and New Testament studies collide. Andrew Perriman examines the mission of the earliest church in its historical context and argues that our context is very different and *so our mission cannot simply be a matter of doing exactly what the earliest church did.* The key question at the heart of the book is, 'How do we shape a *biblical* theology of mission for a *post-biblical* church?'

> '*Re:Mission* distinguishes Perriman as a scholar who must be reckoned with in this time of rethinking and transition. A great piece of work!' – **Brian D. McLaren**, author (brianmclaren.net)

> 'Andrew Perriman has addressed one of the most challenging facets of New Testament teaching and he does so with remarkable insight and creativity. This fascinating book makes for urgent reading.' – **Craig A. Evans**, Payzant Distinguished Professor of New Testament, Acadia Divinity College, Canada

Andrew Perriman lives in Holland and works with Christian Associates seeking to develop open, creative communities of faith for the emerging culture in Europe. He is author of *Speaking of Women* about Paul's teaching on women, *Faith, Health and Prosperity*, and, *The Coming of the Son of Man: New Testament Eschatology for an Emerging Church*.

978-1-84227-545-0

Celebrating Life

Beyond the Sacred-Secular Divide

Graham Buxton

As Christians, our engagement with the world and with culture is often impoverished as a result of unbiblical dualisms. More than we realise, the divide between sacred and secular is reinforced in our minds, contributing to an unhealthy and, at times, narrow super-spirituality. Seeking a more postmodern, holistic and, ultimately, more *Christian* approach to culture, Graham Buxton leads us on a journey towards the celebration of life in *all* its dimensions.

The first part of the book examines the roots of our dualistic thinking and its implications for culture. Part Two draws us from dualism to holism in a number of chapters that consider our engagement with literature, the creative arts, science, politics and business. Part Three draws the threads together by setting out the dimensions of a more holistic theology of the church's engagement with, and participation in, contemporary society that will lead us 'beyond the sacred-secular divide'.

'This is incarnational theology at its best!' – **Ray S. Anderson**, Senior Professor of Theology and Ministry, Fuller Theological Seminary, California.

Graham Buxton is Director of Postgraduate Studies in Ministry and Theology, Tabor College, Adelaide, Australia. He is author of Dancing in the Dark and The Trinity, Creation and Pastoral Ministry.

978-1-84227-507-1

Metavista

Bible, Church and Mission in an Age of Imagination

Colin Green and Martin Robinson

The core narrative of the Christian faith, the book that conveys it (the Bible) and the institution of the church have all been marginalised by the development of modernity and post-modernity. Strangely, post-modernity has created an opportunity for religious thinking and experience to re-enter the lives of many. Yet, despite its astonishing assault on modernity, post-modernity is not itself an adequate framework for thinking about life. There is therefore a new opportunity for Christians to imagine what comes *after* post-modernity and to prepare the church, its book and its story for a new engagement of mission with western culture. The church on the margins, through a creative missionary imagination can audaciously re-define the centre of western cultural life. This book will attempt to sketch what such an approach might look like

> 'If you have a taste for the subversive, a passion for the church, a heart for biblical engagement, and an eye on the future; this book is a must-read.'
> – **Roy Searle**, Northumbria Community, former President of the Baptist Union of Great Britain

Colin Greene is Professor of Theological and Cultural Studies at Mars Hill Graduate School in Seattle. He is author of *Christology in Cultural Perspective*.
Martin Robinson is an international speaker, a writer, and Director of 'Together in Mission'.

978-1-84227-506-1

Soaring in the Spirit

Rediscovering Mystery in the Christian Life

Charles J. Conniry, Jr.

This is a book about experiencing the presence of Jesus Christ in the moment-by-moment 'nows' of daily life. James McClendon, Jr. observed that the first task of theology is to locate our place in the story. Like finding directions at a shopping mall with the brightly coloured words, 'you are here,' the author invites us into an encounter with the 'we-are-here' place in God's Great Story. The claim of this book is that the experience of Christ's presence in the 'right-here' of our daily walk – *Christian soaring* – is the birthright of every follower of Jesus Christ. This is a thoughtful, stirring, and ground-breaking book on the neglected topic of *Christian soaring through discerning discipleship.*

> 'This book is a *tour de force* . . . and can be read with profit by believers and unbelievers, philosophers and theologians, pastors and lay people, and anyone who longs to soar in the Spirit . . . It not only blessed me but drew me to prayer.' – **Brennan Manning,** author of *The Ragamuffin Gospel.*

Charles J. Conniry, Jr. is Associate Professor of Pastoral Ministry and Director of the Doctor of Ministry Program at George Fox Evangelical Seminary, Portland.

978-1-84227-508-5

Atonement for a 'Sinless' Society
Engaging with an emerging culture

Atonement for a 'Sinless' Society

Engaging with an Emerging Culture

Alan Mann

'Sin doesn't really exist as a serious idea in modern life,' wrote the journalist Bryan Appleyard. He is not alone in his views. 'Sin' has become just as tainted, polluted and defiled in the postmodern mind as the word itself indicates.

Atonement for a 'Sinless' Society is about an encounter between two stories: the story of the postmodern, post-industrialized, post-Christian 'sinless' self and the story of atonement played out in the Passion Narrative. Alan Mann charts a way through the apparent impasse between a story that supposedly relies on sin and guilt to become meaningful, and one that fails to recognize the plight of humanity as portrayed in this way. He shows how the biblical narrative needs to be reread in the light of this emerging story so that it can speak meaningfully and sufficiently to an increasingly 'sinless' society.

'Clear, creative, deep, compelling and inspiring' – **Brian D. McLaren**, author, speaker, networker

'Alan Mann's voice is needed and welcome . . . A penetrating analysis of the world we inhabit.' – **Joel B. Green**, Asbury Theological Seminary

'An insightful, timely and creative view of the atonement for our postmodern times.' – **Steve Chalk**, Oasis Trust

978-1-84227-355-5

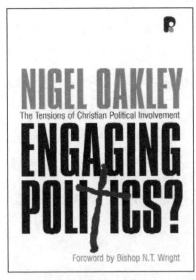

Engaging Politics?

The Tensions of Christian Political Involvement

Nigel Oakley

Nigel Oakley explores how Christians can, indeed must, engage with politics and with political debate. He shows, in chapters on Augustine, Liberation Theology, Dietrich Bonhoeffer and Stanley Hauerwas how certain tensions exist in every strand of Christian political thinking; and then he applies those tensions to case studies varying from today's highly charged debates on sexuality to the war on terrorism. This book is both an intelligent introduction to the difficult world of Christian political theology and to some of the key debates that are shaping our times.

'A constructive Christian position for the more difficult challenges facing us in our world today.' – **Stanley Hauerwas**, Professor of Theological Ethics, Duke Divinity School, North Carolina

'This book will be an important tool for individuals and churches.' – **N.T. Wright**, Bishop of Durham

'This hugely informative book will rescue Christians from simplistic or monochrome answers to the complexity of wrestling with political realities.' – **Christopher J.H. Wright**, International Director, Langham Partnership International

'A thought-provoking, stimulating and action-inducing read.' – **Steve Chalke MBE**, Founder of Oasis Global and Faithworks

978-1-84227-505-4

Public Theology in Cultural Engagement

edited by
Stephen Holmes

Public Theology in Cultural Engagement offers foundational and programmatic essays exploring helpful ways to theologise about culture with missional intent. The book opens with three chapters taking steps towards developing a general theology of culture. Part Two explores the contribution of key biblical themes to a theology of culture – creation, law, election, Christology, and redemption. The final section considers theological proposals for engagement with culture past and present with contemporary reflections on nationalism and on drug culture. Contributors include Colin Gunton, Robert Jenson, Stephen Holmes, Colin Greene, Luke Bretherton and Brian Horne.

'This book represents groundbreaking and foundational thinking.' – **David Spriggs**, The Bible Society UK

Stephen R. Holmes is a Baptist minister and Lecturer in Theology at the University of St Andrews in Scotland.

978-1-84227-542-9